Women in Early Imperial China

ASIAN VOICES
Series Editor: Mark Selden

Women in Early Imperial China

Bret Hinsch

ROWMAN & LITTLEFIELD PUBLISHERS, INC.
Lanham • Boulder • New York • Oxford

ROWMAN & LITTLEFIELD PUBLISHERS, INC.

Published in the United States of America
by Rowman & Littlefield Publishers, Inc.
4720 Boston Way, Lanham, Maryland 20706
www.rowmanlittlefield.com

12 Hid's Copse Road, Cumnor Hill, Oxford OX2 9JJ, England

British Library Cataloguing in Publication Information Available

Library of Congress Cataloging-in-Publication Data
Hinsch, Bret.
    Women in early imperial China / Bret Hinsch.
      p. cm. — (Asian voices)
    Originally published: Boston : Harvard University, 1994.
    Thesis (Ph. D.)—Harvard University, 1993.
    Includes bibliographical references and index.
    ISBN 0-7425-1871-X (alk. paper) — ISBN 0-7425-1872-8 (pbk. : alk. paper)
    1. Women—China—History. 2. Women—China—Social conditions. 3.
China—History—Qin dynasty, 221–207 B.C. 4. China—History—Han dynasty,
202 B.C.–A.D. 220 I. Title. II. Series.
HQ1767 .H55 2002
305.42′0931—dc21   2001048804

Printed in the United States of America

To Tu Wei-ming
a Confucian gentleman who practices what he preaches

Contents

Figures

Acknowledgments

Many people have read drafts of this book. Their comments, suggestions, and critiques helped me improve the manuscript and increase its accessibility. In particular I would like to thank Tu Wei-ming and Susan Weld for their invaluable guidance. I am also grateful to Wejen Chang for sharing his encyclopedic knowledge of early Chinese law. Rebecca Weiner deserves thanks for her optimism, and Mark Selden for his contagious enthusiasm. My colleagues and graduate students at National Chung Cheng University have been an endless source of intelligent discussion, often challenging my assumptions. This welcome dialogue has been an invaluable source of intellectual stimulation. Finally, Allen Yu distinguished himself as a paragon of boundless patience. Of course I take responsibility for any remaining shortcomings in the book.

I received several grants while writing this book. I would like to thank Taiwan's National Science Council, the Pacific Culture Foundation, and the Harvard Club of the Republic of China for supporting my research. In particular, my year-long fellowship at the Center for Chinese Studies in Taiwan's National Library was a welcome time of quiet reading and reflection. The ideas that matured while I was there enriched this book immensely.

Introduction

In some ways, history is akin to astronomy. The astronomer never actually sees a distant star or nebula up close. With only the faintest of traces in hand, she has to imagine staggeringly complex celestial phenomena in their entirety. Light and X rays emitted long ago are painstakingly analyzed to yield the smallest clues about distant objects. In fact, we will probably never know very much about distant bodies. The astronomer cannot possibly know the details of sunspot activity on Alpha Centauri or how many planets may be orbiting Betelgeuse. Despite firm limits to our knowledge of the universe, some understanding is still possible. The problem is how to tease maximum knowledge out of the fragmentary clues at hand.

Likewise, the historian studying early Chinese women hopes to understand a very distant world. In some ways, the historian is far luckier than the astronomer. Instead of faint glimmers of light, the historian's evidence is far more concrete. Some books and incised stones have managed to survive the ravages of centuries. Of course, this evidence about the past is very different from "the past" itself. The past is gone forever. Because we cannot directly observe what we study, we have no choice but to use the handful of clues at our disposal to imagine a vanished world of infinite complexity. As postmodern pessimists are fond of pointing out, this knowledge has distinct limits. Nevertheless, some understanding is still possible.

The sheer antiquity of the early imperial era makes it a particularly difficult time to study. The Qin and Han dynasties stand out as one of the most important eras in Chinese women's history. Of course, several other periods of Chinese history were also critical junctures in the history of women's lives. The Song dynasty perfected Neo-Confucianism, for instance, which redefined discourse about the feminine. Although historians in China universally abhor the periods when outsiders conquered China, the Northern Wei, Jin, Yuan, and other eras

1

of conquest were key periods of rapid change in Chinese society. The influence of European and American culture on late imperial society further shocked Chinese into accepting revolutionary new attitudes toward women.

The first great era of transition in the history of Chinese women occurred long before any of this and set the scene for subsequent developments. When the Qin and Han dynasties forged the first unified Chinese empire, both political institutions and daily life underwent many transformations. These changes affected women as well. In the early imperial era, China rapidly changed from a bellicose patchwork of diverse principalities caught up in unending chaos to a unified empire under a single ruler, government, and code of law. The centralized state that emerged from the morass of contending domains obviously provided a range of new female roles in government. Because Qin and Han pioneered the basic institutions of the imperial system, many of the ways early imperial theorists represented female roles in statecraft persisted to influence political discourse for the following two millennia.

Political upheaval brought changes outside the halls of power as well. Innovations in society at large accompanied these dramatic institutional changes. New law codes directed the power of a centralized state to enforce specific views of gender; for the first time books were written to educate a specifically female audience; and the goddess Xiwangmu, Queen Mother of the West, rose to become perhaps the first personified female deity to predominate as the focus of popular religious devotion. Each of these themes foreshadows numerous variations that were played out for the remainder of imperial history.

Although this survey focuses on the social roles women assumed during the Qin and Han dynasties, it might be useful to glance back in time to understand previous ideas concerning women or look forward to find traces of Qin and Han conventions preserved in later periods. Gazing across cultures can also uncover germane comparisons from other times and places and perhaps reveal universals that transcend culture-bound constructions. Nevertheless, this historical survey does not include a comparative study, which would complicate it beyond comprehensibility.

The emperors of Qin and Han ruled over the earliest unified Chinese state. Through the length of these two dynasties, abstract ideas representing women evolved considerably. The period from the Qin unification of China in 221 B.C.E. to the collapse of the Han in 220 C.E. encompasses almost four and a half centuries. The peril of ahistoricism is readily apparent. To be sure, Chinese as yet lacked a notion of change as inherently good, so modifications in technology, social organization, and cultural forms usually proceeded at a measured pace. Nevertheless, anyone approaching the early imperial era must be aware of the many transformations that took place over this long period. As will be shown, some of the basic ways of thinking about women changed considerably during this time.

The early empire, when political unification had just been completed, is also notable for its regional variation. Government edicts could unify currency, weights and measures, and even the width of axle shafts. Yet a babble of mutually incomprehensible local dialects remained. Thought and custom were often bound to particular places. Han officials had to reconcile the newly united empire's enormous diversity if they were to achieve full unity: "Every hundred *li* there were different habits; every thousand *li* there were different customs. Households had different governments; people wore distinguishing clothes."[1] Only occasionally do surviving sources give much specific information about regional diversity. But we must never forget that women's lifestyles probably differed significantly according to region and social stratum. Only rarely do the surviving sources give much evidence of this diversity.

APPROACH

Given the problems of regionalism, temporality, and individuality, studying the many places that women held in early imperial society seems more akin to a calculus equation of simultaneously moving variables than the simple addition of facts. The ideas we use to conceptualize early women must be sufficiently flexible and dynamic to embrace this complexity. Previous scholarship on early Chinese women's history has employed a variety of methods. Before deciding which theoretical tools are best for this particular inquiry, we should start by surveying the main approaches used in previous studies. This way we can benefit from the achievements of previous scholarship and be forewarned by any shortcomings.

By far the most influential model for studying early Chinese women has been the theory of ancient matriarchy. This theory developed in the nineteenth century from analysis of some of the earliest ethnographic information available to Western social theorists. However, subsequent fieldwork has thoroughly discredited this theory in the eyes of almost all Western anthropologists. In sum, there is simply no evidence that humanity ever passed through a phase of primitive matriarchy prior to patriarchy. From all accounts, it seems that male power reaches back to the dawn of humanity.

Although the theory of ancient matriarchy has had very little impact on recent Western scholarship, it remains the dominant model for conceptualizing early women's history in Asia.[2] Frederick Engels's canonization of this theory as

Marxist orthodoxy accounts for its wide influence and surprising longevity. But in recent years, this theory has begun to come under highly persuasive critical review by some open-minded Asian scholars.[3] As Asian academic communities search for satisfying post-Marxist interpretations of the distant Chinese past, the influence of matriarchy theory will doubtless continue to decline.

Among Western scholars, one important tactic for conceptualizing early Chinese women has been to simply read early history through the better-studied late imperial era to derive a static picture of Chinese women in "traditional" times.[4] Conjuring up potential problems with this method does not require much imagination. An analogous approach to the history of European women might take ideas current in Victorian England as the key to understanding ancient Roman or Celtic women's lives. Neo-Confucianism, foot binding, Buddhism, vernacular literature, a developed commercial economy, and many other novel factors all influenced the lives of late imperial women in ways utterly unimaginable to the peoples of Qin and Han. Although findings concerning women of different periods and different cultures can provide very useful standards of comparison, seeing "the Chinese woman" as an ahistorical entity falls into the trap of atemporal Hegelian Orientalism. Ideas about women held by the thinkers of Qin and Han were in many ways quite different from those prevalent in periods either before or after. Early imperial women must be understood within their unique historical context.

Another approach has been to focus on the Confucian classics as the source of primary clues for understanding early women.[5] These repositories of revered wisdom preserve an enormous range of information about the beliefs of the men who composed them. But they also have distinct limits. The classics present views of women held by very small groups of elite male scholars. Contemporary viewpoints prevalent among other social groups were often quite different from those preserved in the classics and commentaries. The privileged position of these elites gave them tremendous power to define the ideals of womanhood. Yet concepts about gender were constantly being created, revised, and contested at all levels of society, sparking continual debate and spirited resistance. The Confucian classics are very useful documents, but they are not definitive portrayals of early gender relations.

Comparing female and male identity is another promising avenue of investigation that has attracted interest in recent years. Elisabeth Croll has noted the importance of the male "other" to the construction of female identity in modern China. She theorizes that becoming a woman might be described as a form of "othering." A woman created a female identity by comparing herself with men and then either distinguishing herself from them or imitating them.[6] David Hall and Roger Ames draw different conclusions from their study of comparative gender identity in early Chinese thought. They suggest that in Chinese culture, the complete and successful person was traditionally conceived of as a having both stereotypical male and female traits. This view of gender might be symbolized by the ancient myth of brother and sister Fuxi and Nüwa, whose serpentine bodies entwined together to form a whole (fig. I.1). Although the whole person should include both male and female traits, men discouraged women from developing

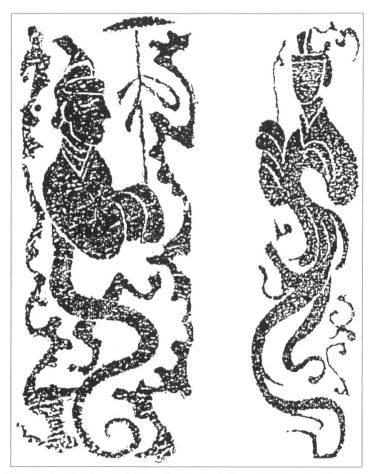

Figure I.1.   Fuxi and Nüwa. Rubbing of an incised stone. Wu Zengde, *Handai huaxiangshi* (Beijing: Wenwu, 1984), fig. 65.

masculine dispositions, thereby maintaining a hold over them. Under this system of androgynous personhood, women could never become fully human. They were always considered flawed and incomplete. "To be human, you must be male."[7]

Despite the emergence of these promising new modes of research, the search for a single "status" or "position" of women in early Chinese society has unfortunately been a far more influential method.[8] Despite the popularity of this approach, it is highly doubtful that women's lives can ever be summed up with such simplicity. Skepticism toward the utility, and even the possibility, of defining a static female social position is far from iconoclastic. A woman had many different privileges and duties. The nuances implicit in these compounded circumstances do not fit into a blunt formulation of either "high" or "low" social position. The sensitivity of anthropologists toward the diverse makeup of even tribal societies has led many to abandon the notion that all of a society's women can be subsumed within a single, unitary social position.

It is less likely that a singular "women's position" can be expressed for a huge, complex, stratified society such as early imperial China. For example, social stratum usually took precedence over gender. At the same time that an empress dowager ruled over the entire realm, contemporary slave women suffered degradation and grinding toil. And within the kinship structure, generational rank usually outweighed gender in importance. Mothers often exercised great power over their adult sons, while wives could endure suffering at the hands of their husbands' parents. Wealth could also override gender. Although a fabulously rich female mining tycoon could befriend the First Emperor of Qin, a poor woman might be reduced to begging for a place by the fire to do her spinning. Empress dowager, slave, mother, daughter-in-law, magnate, beggar—how can these diverse female identities be subsumed within a single "social position"? Gender was certainly an important factor in social relations, but women and men never interacted as a simple binary pair. Gender was always appended to particular social roles that defined the places individual women held in social hierarchies.

In recent years, the very concept of social status or position has come under vitriolic attack by many social scientists and feminists. The question most often raised by critics is, What criteria are appropriate for determining *the* status of women? Upon considering the varied customary privileges of women, the respect they received in various social contexts, their many places in the kinship structure, female roles in religious and ritual events (among a mind-numbing array of other possible factors), the concept of one female social status seems almost meaninglessly vague. It makes as much sense to derive a single status of women as to search for the "status of men." Like individual men, each woman played out a wide range of social roles that caused her status to vary considerably in different situations. With so many variables in play, dualistically classifying the status of all the women in a particular society as either "high" or "low" becomes impossible.[9]

If unitary social status is inadequate for conceptualizing early Chinese women, what approach is better? Most important, our theoretical tools must take into account the fragmentary nature of the material available for the study of early history. Unlike Song or Qing, which present a rich variety of sources, the texts surviving from the distant past are sparse as well as relatively homogeneous in perspective. As a result, we rarely know very much about the lives of individual women. But though we might not be very certain of what a particular woman did or said, we still have some important information about early women in general. Although our knowledge of actual female experience is sparse, a sophisticated and copious body of rhetoric about women remains.[10] Various thinkers discussed who women should be and how they ought to behave. Writings on morals, cosmology, government, law, and every other area of early Chinese discourse convey copious information about the ideal social roles a woman ought to assume. Great debates of theoretical and practical consequence were waged on which social roles are proper for women. And historical documents sometimes give information on the roles women actually assumed. Understanding these ideal female roles, and how individual women accepted, comprehended, and contested them, is a powerful method for interpreting the distant female past.

A study of early female roles is particularly important because of the way most early Chinese conceived of the feminine.[11] This concept was most often understood as a characteristic of various gendered social roles. To most early Chinese, "woman" was not just a static term imbedded in a fixed gender dichotomy. A woman was a person who played female roles in family and ceremonial life. Most fundamentally, womanhood was something performative, not essential. It was acted out in daily life. One was not just born a woman by having a certain biology. One became a complete and successful woman only after assuming a wide range of positive female roles. Womanhood was not a fixed or static identity. To all but the most abstract thinkers, femininity lacked the timelessness of an abstract metaphysical element. A woman was a successful social actor. She played out her gender for all to see. In acting out a range of female roles, she created herself as a complete woman.

Studying early women's lives by reconstructing the range of female social roles has many theoretical advantages. Role playing is obviously a highly flexible paradigm that can encompass social behavior in many different times and places. Grouping individual behaviors into larger social roles can also help us under-

stand general trends that might otherwise be hidden beneath the dazzling diversity of detail.

In addition, unlike many recent social theories, role playing lacks an explicit
Western philosophical bias. Some recent studies of Chinese women employ
intellectual tools that arose specifically from concerns unique to the modern
West and have nothing to do with early Chinese thought. Native Chinese
thought lacked Cartesianism, the Enlightenment, and other bugbears of current
theorists in the West. Rather than superimpose a highly alien mode of thought
(which the people we study would have found utterly incomprehensible) on our
subjects, ideally our method should take into account the ways in which the people we study understood themselves. Of course, absolute congruence between
modern and past ways of thinking is impossible. But as Max Weber pointed out,
good historical method takes account of the subjective understanding of our subjects as well as our own point of view as outsiders.

For this reason, the idea of role playing has great theoretical utility. The metaphor of life as a kind of performance is easily understood and crosses cultural
boundaries intact. Moreover, the success of this metaphor for understanding
society has already been clearly demonstrated. Sociologists have long used role
playing to create subtle models of society. For example, Erving Goffman's theory
of social dramaturgy examines the mechanics of social role playing in great
detail.[12] According to this theory, individuals in society are akin to actors in a
play. Sometimes we carry ourselves as if we were back stage, preparing for a public
performance. Other times we are on stage, in view of others, playing out chosen
social roles. As social actors, we choose the props, clothing, and makeup that
will make our performance appear most believable. In other words, we select a
role from among an assortment of standard parts, and then we assume the images
and behaviors that will make our performance seem believable to those watching
it. In real life as in the theater, the actor and audience influence each other.
Actors manipulate the audience, and the audience's reaction shapes an ongoing
performance. People manipulate their social image through role playing to elicit
a response from others, then modify their behavior in response to these reactions. To a large degree, we are the sum of the social roles we perform.

The roles available to us as social actors are the products of culture. Culture
transmits a set of social roles that embody the standards of acceptable behavior.
These roles are behavioral templates that women and men can anticipate and
copy, or else engage and oppose. In early imperial China, these standard social
roles were probably more important than they are today. Industrial societies are
extremely fragmented. People now have the opportunity to choose from among
a dizzying array of extremely different kinds of lives, so the social roles available

to each person are now tremendously diverse. But in the simpler, poorer society of early China, life was much more circumscribed by necessity. Regional diversity in customs and language was superimposed atop a substrate of economic homogeneity. Most people pursued a life determined largely by the harsh necessities of agricultural labor and the force of tradition. Few were able to choose the most important facts about their life: their occupation, home, spouse, or family. These primary social facts were usually determined for them. In this sort of society, regularities, patterns, and ideals were particularly important. For most people, success in life could not come from seeking new opportunities, but from fitting into ideal social patterns. In view of these circumstances, understanding the standard social roles available to early Chinese women should be a particularly important goal for the historian.

Given the dynamic complexity of female social roles, it is necessary to understand them in relation to the various activities and loci of experience that prevailed in early imperial society. Of course there are many possible ways to approach female roles. Some avenues of understanding, however fascinating, have not been included here for want of space. Therefore some extremely interesting subjects such as popular attitudes toward women's bodies, or the female deities of early China, must be passed over in silence. Even so, an enormous amount of ground remains to be covered. Each chapter of this book discusses an important realm of society: kinship, property and labor, law, government, learning, ritual, and cosmology. By emphasizing the different aspects of society, we can examine the roles women played from multiple perspectives.

THREE INTELLECTUAL TRENDS

No single paradigm can comprehensively sum up the social roles women played in early imperial China. Attitudes toward women were varied and often contradictory. Generally speaking, three types of thought stand out as particularly useful ways of understanding women and their proper place in the world. As these three ways of thinking interacted, their relative importance changed over time. This book charts the course of these basic intellectual shifts. To understand the roles of women in early Chinese society, it is not sufficient to just study women themselves. We must also reconstruct the intellectual context that shaped women's beliefs and actions. The content of these modes of understanding changed over time, as did their relative influence over society. Time and again, I will return to these three themes to help explain particular events and customs. In the conclusion, I will sum up the fundamental changes that these three ways of thinking underwent during the course of the early imperial period.

Pragmatism

Perhaps the most widespread and fundamental way of thinking about women was a pragmatic attitude toward gender issues. A striking contradiction that repeatedly emerges from the records of early Chinese women's history is the common disparity between elite dogma and popular practice. Time and again, elite thinkers tried to impose elaborate rituals, rules, and restrictions on women's lives. Usually they failed. For most people, daily life was ruled by the relentless exigencies of necessity rather than theoretical niceties. Prosperous intellectuals were isolated to a large degree from the material compulsions driving most people's lives. From the lofty peaks of privilege, elite thinkers strove for absolute parallelism between male and female, and between cosmos and humanity. In many cases, they seem to have been driven by the aesthetic attractions of perfectly ordered ideas instead of concern about how these systems would actually affect the lives of ordinary people. Often their ideas were impractical, cruel, and absurd.

To those tilling the unforgiving soil, the foremost goal was achieving the necessities of life and perhaps a few basic comforts. Of course they recognized customary distinctions in the ideal social roles allocated to men and women. Tradition allotted the most common roles for work, family life, and ceremony according to gender. But in most cases, the system of customary roles was informed by a keen awareness of practical considerations and tempered in application by an attitude of flexibility. Generally speaking, popular traditions often allowed women relative autonomy. This pragmatic outlook was deeply rooted in the sensibilities of ordinary people. The sheer impracticality of many elite ideas about gender evoked stubborn resistance from the massive base of the social pyramid. Only constant repetition of elite ideals, and their continual reproduction in privileged media, could gradually undermine the popular tendency toward flexible and pragmatic gender relations.

Patrilinealism

A second intellectual trend influencing ideas and discourse about women was the rise of patrilineal rhetoric during the early imperial era. Patrilinealism is something very different from patriarchy. Early Chinese patrilineal values derived from an idealized view of ancient kinship relations. According to this way of thinking, the core organization of society ought to be either large extended families of multiple generations or else lineages descended from a common male ancestor. Patrilinealists tried to reform society by reviving a set of social roles that, if followed, would have revived large-scale kinship organizations. They believed that individual interests should be sacrificed to bolster the strength of the kin group. Grandparents, parents, sons, and daughters-in-law should all live and work together. The young should obey the old. And the property of kinfolk should be held in common and managed by family elders.

Nowadays these ideas are often called "Confucian." Although these values did indeed gain most prominence through Confucianism, they long predate Confucius. Nor were these values the exclusive preserve of the Confucian tradition. They had a far broader audience. Patrilinealism was quite simply the traditional value system of the Zhou dynasty elite, whose lives were organized around kinship principles. In fact, by the time Confucius was teaching his interpretations of these ideals to his disciples, many patrilineal practices had long been in decline. Families were smaller and lineages less cohesive than before. Confucianism gave Zhou kinship values a new lease on life by putting them in an abstract moralistic and transcendental form. Confucius hoped to use patrilineal values to stabilize the chaotic society of his own day. But many others who believed in patrilineal ideals were motivated by a far less realistic sense of nostalgia, romanticism about the distant past, or utopianism.

During the early imperial period, patrilineal values gained many adherents. Confucians obviously advocated many of these ideas. But the influence of these beliefs was not confined to a specific doctrine. The systems of various thinkers showed the influence of patrilineal thinking. While daily life in Han society was often quite different from patrilineal rhetoric, these ideals nevertheless had profound influence on how many people believed their society ought to be. Social reform often began as an attempt to enforce ideal patrilineal kinship roles. As the Han progressed, the hold that patrilineal values exercised over elite minds became increasingly tight. Many influential thinkers and bureaucrats used these ideas to conceptualize ideal female roles.

The influence of patrilineal thought on women was mixed. Patrilinealism was very different from patriarchy. This value system established a series of strict hierarchies, but not all of them were based on gender. In fact, patrilineal values endowed women with some very important privileges. Mothers in particular were to be accorded profound respect and devotion. The filial son who sacrificed himself to his mother's welfare was celebrated in patrilineal art and literature. Both the more pragmatic everyday practices of Han kinship and the abstractions of patrilineal values were in constant interplay. Women could manipulate these two sets of roles to their own advantage.

Cosmology

The increasing influence of cosmology was a third intellectual trend affecting ideas about women. Theoretical cosmology became extremely detailed and systematic during the Han. By explaining how the universe works, cosmology filled the intellectual niche occupied by mythology in most other ancient cultures. This exceptional method produced significant results. The basic premise of Chinese cosmology is a metaphysical view of reality. The world cannot be adequately understood just by accumulating information about the characteristics of specific objects. We must go beyond the individual and concrete to discover fundamental universal forces. In this view, certain simple abstract patterns form a template that governs reality. Ineffable cosmic elements, strictly organized into regular patterns, coexist with the visible universe. These elements are the forces that determine the basic categories and relations governing reality. Cosmologists sought to identify these fundamental elements and then determine how they relate to one another. To this way of thinking, male and female are more than just the attributes of two kinds of people, or characteristics of the social roles they play. To the cosmologist, man and woman are also important elements in the abstract universal patterns underlying society.

The cosmological turn in elite thought had profound consequences for gender discourse. Most early Chinese discussed the relations of woman and man in terms of gendered social roles. Debates about gender relations tended to be arguments about which social roles are appropriate for each sex, and what sort of ideal behavior ought to append to each role. Pragmatists and patrilinealists differed very pointedly on the definitions of ideal female roles. But cosmologists understood gender in an entirely different light. Instead of viewing gender as interlocking sets of dynamic roles, they believed that we should see gender as a static fact. Apart from individual women and men, gender identity exists most fundamentally as an abstract metaphysical element in the systems of relations that underlie all activity in the universe. To understand what it is to be female, we should not look at the everyday world. Instead we should use our minds to penetrate the abstruse workings of the rarefied elements that order the universe as we see it. Their method was logical, not empirical. In other words, cosmologists removed gender from the mundane confines of the society of human beings around us. Instead, they transposed gender to the far loftier realm of metaphysics.

The results of this epistemological shift are clear. Traditionally, ancient Chinese had looked at the world around them and then decided what ideas about gender could help them enjoy a good life. Then cosmologists began to discuss gender in relative isolation from practical concerns. Instead of the pragmatic ambiguity of ordinary experience, ideas about gender were increasingly the product of ethereal reflections of pure mind. Empiricism gave way to a cold logic untrammeled by any reference to the lives of actual people. Not surprisingly, the essentialized woman and man of Han cosmology were often very different from their flesh and blood counterparts. Cosmologists rejected traditional gender pragmatism. Instead they advocated radical reinterpretations of gender relations, which they justified by transcendental musings about the ideal relations of universal gender elements. As a component in the idiosyncratic cosmological systems fully understood by only a small number of elite thinkers, gender became something increasingly simple, clear cut, and unequal. During the Han, cosmological gender concepts had already begun to infiltrate art, philosophy, and literature. After the dynasty's fall, the influence of this essentialized and cosmologized view of gender continued to grow. For example, much Neo-Confucian discourse about gender grew out of this early trend. In subsequent centuries, the consequences of this way of thinking about gender, which came to maturity during the Han, would be extremely far reaching.

I

The Context:
Early Imperial China

When we approach the history of people remote from us in time, anachronism looms as a constant danger. We understand history by striving to recreate images of the past in our minds. But whenever we imagine the past, we are tempted to impute our own beliefs and experiences to the people whose lives we mentally reconstruct. Unfortunately, the empathy so fundamental to historical research often distorts our vision of the past. The only way to avoid anachronistically modernizing and even Westernizing early Chinese women is to firmly ground our understanding of them in the conditions unique to their era. For that reason, any history of Qin and Han dynasty women must emphasize the characteristics of that distant age. Only then can the varied places held by women within that complex and dynamic society be properly understood.

THE ZHOU DYNASTY

Historians understand the past by noting the differences between one period and the next. To appreciate the society of early imperial China, it is necessary to understand what sort of system it replaced. A look at the eras preceding the Qin and Han periods brings to light the special characteristics of the early imperial era. And comparing the early empire with what came before it incites an appropriate sense of awe toward the monumental changes that followed China's unification under Qin.

The political system overthrown by Qin had its earliest roots in the Zhou conquest of the Shang dynasty, which probably occurred in the eleventh century B.C.E. This was not just the victory of one leader or faction over another. The Zhou were a different people from the Shang they conquered. Naturally the

15

Zhou used somewhat different methods to govern the territory they had conquered, and the culture of the Chinese heartland shifted in notable ways. This change from Shang to Zhou marked the first great revolution in Chinese history.

The early part of the Zhou dynasty is called the Western Zhou period.[1] The system of government in this era can be broadly described as feudalism. Although the details of feudalism differed in China and medieval Europe, the two systems were analogous in several important respects. The Zhou kings divided their lands into fiefs that they granted to titled nobles. In return, these nobles were expected to show fealty to their king. The rules of this system were codified as elaborate rituals. Battles were frequent, though generally small in scale. Nobles were often more concerned with intangibles such as honor and etiquette than actually killing their opponents. There was relatively little social mobility, and the economy was relatively simple.

The Zhou kings were unable to maintain control over this highly decentralized system. They decayed into irrelevance and were forced to abandon their traditional lands in the face of aggression from northern nomadic peoples. The humiliating move of the Zhou kings eastward in 770 B.C.E. marks the beginning of the Eastern Zhou period.[2] From this time onward, the Zhou monarchy continued its steep decline into obscurity. By the end of the dynasty, the Zhou kings were mere ciphers. But powerful new forces were being forged to replace them. Originally the Zhou had divided their loose-knit state into well over a hundred different polities, each presided over by a titled lord. After a long series of wars and intrigues, these fiefs gradually amalgamated into larger polities. Eventually only seven major states remained.

The rise of large-scale states required their rulers to abandon many traditional feudal customs. Education and talent increasingly replaced high birth as the prime requirement for bureaucratic office. And as government officials became highly skilled specialists, administration grew more sophisticated. Moreover, brilliant thinkers devoted themselves to theories of bureaucratic administration, providing a firm foundation for bureaucratic procedure.

In many respects the large Eastern Zhou states resembled modern European nation-states. Each had a well-functioning government, army, and code of law. Culturally, linguistically, and intellectually, each state was distinct as well. The future of China as a unified gigantic superstate with tens of millions of subjects was far from inevitable. Under other circumstances, the history of the Chinese region could very well have gone in a more European direction. The seven major states could easily have continued to develop independently as completely separate countries.

Society was also changing drastically during this period. Although evidence for the social and economic history of Chinese high antiquity is extremely thin, some important trends nevertheless stand out clearly. In the early Western Zhou era, a person's birth and relationship with the land largely determined lifelong social standing. But as the feudal system declined, Chinese society became increasingly dynamic. Currencies were introduced, and land and products were bought and sold with increasing frequency. Economic complexity gave rise to a diverse social structure. Cities grew in size and number, and some became important commercial centers. Minor nobles, together with the untitled new rich, gained prominence in government. All of these factors endowed late Eastern Zhou society, known as the Warring States period (403–221 B.C.E.), with a novel degree of social mobility. The complex large-scale society of early imperial China arose from this ferment.

Ideas had to change to keep pace with a society in rapid transition. The Warring States period stands out as the golden age of Chinese thought. Speculative thinking replaced myth, ritual, and kinship customs as the new focus of elite intellectual activity. The famed Hundred Schools of thought contended aggressively for attention and patronage. Although the contents of their theories differed enormously, Chinese thinkers of all affiliations began to deal with important problems on a far higher level of abstraction. No longer satisfied with understanding the immediate causes of important events, they tried to fathom the abstract cosmological and social forces thought to underlie daily life. Intellectual treatises became longer and better organized, allowing thinkers to delve into difficult problems. Some turned their attentions to immediately practical concerns, such as government, social organization, and ethics. Others studied ethereal cosmological forces. In every case, the result was a body of thought far more refined and accomplished than anything seen previously.

THE QIN REVOLUTION

The delicate balance of power between the seven major Zhou states began to come undone. Rulers of the various states usurped the dignities of the Zhou king and struggled to dominate their rivals. Initially they competed to be the hegemon lording over the other states in the Chinese region. But some rulers began to have loftier dreams. Eventually a man known to history by the stark title Qin Shihuangdi (The First Emperor of Qin, 259–210 B.C.E.) succeeded in vanquishing his foes and uniting China into a single vast country.[3] The Chinese quickly became accustomed to this novel state of affairs. They soon stopped thinking of their new state as an empire formed of separate countries and instead began to think of China as a legitimate country in its own right. From this time forward, the division of China into different states came to be considered anomalous and painful.

The Qin might seem unlikely candidates for creating the unified Chinese state. Originally the Qin people lay between Chinese civilization and the northern nomads, absorbing influences from each direction. Although the Qin were members of the Zhou feudal system, many people from the Chinese heartland clearly looked askance at the Qin as semibarbaric. Yet over time the Qin lords conquered a sizable state and became major players in the power politics of the Chinese region. Located astride major trade routes, they built a flourishing economy. They actively adopted administrative innovations from more sophisticated rivals and refined some of these practices to new heights. In particular, the Qin built up an elaborate bureaucracy governed by a detailed code of law, allowing the Qin rulers to centralize power. These administrative reforms gave Qin a major advantage over less organized foes. In times of crisis, the dukes of Qin could marshal their state's resources with particular vigor. Their victories were won by competent administration as much as success on the battlefield.

The structure of Qin society was also distinct. In keeping with the goal of bureaucratizing every aspect of life, Qin's rulers sought to control their populace by enrolling every man into a minutely graded social hierarchy that was modeled on the ranks of government bureaucracy. A man's official social rank could rise or fall depending on his accomplishments or crimes. Membership in higher grades carried tangible privileges. In this way, the Qin rulers tried to replace the traditional rankings of social status based on occupation, birth, age, and wealth with a system of official ranks under their own control. Never before had Chinese society been so thoroughly bureaucratized.

The First Emperor, Qin Shihuangdi, repeatedly waged unusually aggressive wars of conquest. Although today he is remembered mostly for his monumental tomb fronted by a huge army of terra-cotta warriors, he was far more remarkable in life than death. One by one, he conquered neighboring countries. Each victory was celebrated in grand style by constructing a replica of the conquered state's royal palace in his increasingly magnificent capital at Xianyang. In the end, Qin Shihuangdi conquered every rival and united the gigantic empire known as China.

Although Qin supplanted Zhou as China's new dynasty, this was far more than just a switch of ruling houses. This transition was nothing short of a revolution. The loose-knit confederation of states under the banner of the Zhou kings was a thing of the past. Henceforth China was to be ruled by an entirely different system of government. The Qin imposed their bureaucratic system across China, from the arid steppes of the north to the dense rainforests of the south, in an attempt to infuse this unstable new empire with true administrative unity. Qin Shihuangdi also instituted a radically new ideology to justify his rule. Not content with the traditional title of king, he glorified himself with the novel title emperor (*huangdi*), a neologism compounded from two terms traditionally associated with divinity. The major characteristics of the Qin dynasty were now in place: bureaucratic administration, rule by law, and a superhuman ruler with a status and scope of authority far exceeding traditional kings.

Intellectually, the Qin dynasty was an important time as well. The school of thought most commonly associated with the Qin is legalism, a body of writings concerning administration dedicated to organizing society along bureaucratic lines. But there was far more to Qin thought than just this one school. As befitted a diverse new empire, elite Qin thought was highly eclectic. Qin Shihuangdi himself displayed a sincere interest in Daoism, an eclectic array of popular religious beliefs, and even Confucianism. Qin thinkers also intensified the trend toward syncretism that had become evident in the late Warring States era. During the Han, syncretism would emerge as the dominant theme of intellectual life, as major thinkers tried to replicate the unity of their new state in the intellectual realm by bringing together elements from the various contending schools of thought. It became normal to mix together ideas from different and even contradictory sources.

Like many great empires, the Qin dynasty did not outlive its founder by very long. According to later authorities, the severity of Qin law was a major factor in the dynasty's fall. Widespread discontent toward this harsh, draconian code was said to have robbed the government of popular support. But the sheer novelty of China's unity was perhaps its greatest flaw. Powerful local elites had seen their traditional privileges eroded as states disappeared. Naturally they waited impatiently for the chance to rebel. The dynasty's charismatic founder could use fearsome personality to hold the empire together as long as he lived. But his untested son was unable to attract the same respect. Soon after Qin Shihuangdi's death, central authority collapsed and China plunged into chaos as local warlords battled for control.

In all, the Qin dynasty lasted just fifteen years. Although the Qin was one of the shortest Chinese dynasties, it may have been the most important. Prior to the Qin dynasty, the division of the Chinese region into contending states was considered the norm. Henceforth China would be thought of as a single state. Although the close association of legalism with the draconian Qin code officially disgraced that school of thought in the eyes of China's elite, bureaucracy nevertheless became the standard system of government. And subsequent rulers continued to use the audacious Qin term "emperor" as their title. From this time forward, China was seen as a unified state to be ruled over by an emperor via a bureaucracy. China's territory, dominant political ideology, and fundamental mode of government all followed basic Qin conventions for the next two millennia.

THE WESTERN HAN DYNASTY

Hindsight allows us to assess the contributions of the Qin in grand terms. However, after the death of Qin Shihuangdi it was unclear whether anyone else could reunite China and preserve this new empire, or whether the region would return to the pre-Qin system of permanent division among contending states. After a long series of wars, a rebel named Liu Bang (d. 195 B.C.E.) managed to reunite the empire. He named his new dynasty Han and is accordingly known to history by his official appellation Emperor Han Gaozu.

Qin Shihuangdi and Han Gaozu came from very different backgrounds. However much people from the Chinese heartland may have condescended to the Qin as only semi-Chinese, Qin Shihuangdi nevertheless grew up in privileged circumstances as the heir to the ruling house of a large and prosperous state. In contrast Han Gaozu, a peasant ruffian, was coarse and unsophisticated. Unable to come up with a better system of administration on his own, Gaozu more or less continued the Qin system of bureaucratic government. Yet having learned from the mistakes of the Qin, Gaozu ameliorated the system's harshness and generally reduced government interference in daily life. In addition, he supplemented the system of bureaucracy with a body of official rituals to bring order to his fractious realm. His reign was devoted to reconquering the former Qin territories and consolidating the empire into a stable state.

Because Gaozu relied heavily on the support of other warlords for his success, it was initially necessary to enfeoff them as kings and marquises ruling over semi-autonomous states. Generally speaking, Gaozu only ruled directly over the western half of China. The eastern half of his titular realm was in the hands of kings and nobles unrelated to him by blood. So the Han dynasty began largely as a confederation of princes ruled over by an emperor. Of course the kingdoms posed a severe threat to imperial authority. Over time the emperors found excuses to depose all kings unrelated to them by blood, and central authority assumed unchallenged supremacy.

While Qin Shihuangdi failed to establish a lasting dynasty, Gaozu succeeded. His son assumed the throne following his death, establishing the important precedent of heredity in imperial succession. This first succession was also especially important in the history of Chinese women. For although Gaozu's son officially assumed the throne as Emperor Hui (r. 195–188 B.C.E.), in fact his mother and Gaozu's wife, Empress Lü (d. 180 B.C.E.), controlled the government together with her kinsmen. So complete was her domination that many historians do not consider Hui to have truly reigned over China at all. This first succession in the new Han dynasty brought with it a pair of contradictory customs. The new emperor was to be chosen from among the previous emperor's sons. But the wife of the deceased ruler, now empress dowager, might in fact assume true power over the state together with her relatives. Within this new system, the symbolism and reality of power might diverge significantly. This contradiction within the Han system was a flaw that plagued the dynasty for centuries. Although this custom opened up new avenues of power for empresses dowager, conflicts between the factions supporting empress dowager and emperor repeatedly threw the government into chaos.

Empress Lü ruled through the titular reigns of Hui and two infant emperors who followed. After Empress Lü's death, Emperor Wen (r. 180–157 B.C.E.) assumed the throne. Wen is remembered favorably by history as a ruler of prudence and moderation who tried to stabilize his restless empire. During the reign of this capable monarch, the Han system sunk deep roots into Chinese society. No longer was imperial rule grounded in the fearsome personalities of its founders. The system of government crafted by Han Gaozu began to show its strengths. The dynasty had outlived the reigns of its founder and his strong-willed wife to become regularized into a stable system of bureaucratic government. Procedure increased in importance as the role of personality decreased. At many times, particularly when the emperor was a minor, the monarch was little more than a symbol.

Despite this evolution from charismatic rule to a more rational bureaucratic system, a determined ruler could still have a major impact on the state. Aside from Gaozu himself, the most ambitious emperor of the Western Han was surely Emperor Wu (r. 141–87 B.C.E.). In antiquity, a long reign generally guaranteed a degree of success. But Wu used his powers to initiate a set of policies that changed the face of Han government. Wu began to rely mainly on Confucianism as the state ideology. He initiated the earliest seeds of China's famed system of bureaucratic examinations. His armies undertook a series of campaigns in Central Asia, opening up the Silk Road to commerce with markets as distant as Parthia and Rome. But imperialism had a high price. Wu had to levy new taxes to pay for his grandiose schemes. The government also took control over mines and assumed responsibility for the production and sale of basic necessities such as iron and salt. In all, the scope of government expanded considerably during Wu's reign. But the expense of these policies could not be endured for long. After Wu's death, the scope of government decreased to more modest levels.

Following Wu's reign, the relatives of imperial consorts, known collectively as consort families, came to play an increasingly important role in government. An example will help clarify this important custom. One of the most famous instances of consort family dominance spanned the reigns of Zhao (r. 87–74 B.C.E.) and Xuan (74–49 B.C.E.). Following Wu's death, government fell under the control of a triumvirate of ministers, the most powerful of whom was Huo Guang (d. 68 B.C.E.). Emperor Zhao assumed the throne as a child, and Huo Guang linked himself to the imperial line by marrying his young granddaughter to Zhao as empress. Huo packed the upper ranks of government with his relatives and managed to dominate the government throughout Zhao's minority.

Eventually the Huo family overreached. Just as Zhao reached maturity, he died under ambiguous circumstances. The next emperor was Xuan, who mounted the throne as a teenager. The Huos poisoned Xuan's pregnant wife to make way for a Huo relative to become empress. When details of this assassination leaked out, opinion at court turned against the Huos. Following the death of family patriarch Huo Guang, his desperate family plotted to overthrow the emperor and place one of their own kin on the throne. Their plot backfired, and in 66 B.C.E. rival factions exterminated the Huo family and deposed Empress Huo.

The story of the Huo family is more than just a singularly dramatic episode in Han history. It is important as a prescient archetype that played out repeatedly for the remainder of the dynasty. Time and again, an immature or passive emperor was dominated by the relatives of his wife or mother. The conflict between male and female authority, which began with the control of Emperor Hui by Empress Lü, continued to plague imperial government for the remainder of the dynasty.

After the fall of the Huos, Emperor Xuan went on to enjoy a long and success-ful reign. But following his death, the dynasty entered a decline. In part, those at the center of government pulled back the scope of government activity. Authorities in the Han were faced with two competing models of government. Ambitious rulers such as Emperor Wu looked to the activistic centralism of Qin; others such as Emperor Wen favored the more modest example of Zhou adminis-tration. During the final decades of the Western Han, the Zhou model gained supremacy. Court expenditures were reduced, and foreign policy became diffi-dent and cautious. Concerned officials repeatedly tried to address the debilitat-ing inequalities in society by advocating reforms such as land redistribution, only to be blocked by wealthy special interests.

The quality of government declined noticeably in the final decades of the

Western Han. Emperors were weak. In several cases, consort families gained inordinate power. And sometimes favored minions of the emperor held inappropriate sway at court. All of these problems weakened the regular channels of government. The government became ineffectual and decadent, bringing long-simmering difficulties to the point of crisis. In a gesture characteristic of the age, Emperor Ai (r. 7–1 B.C.E.) toyed with the idea of abdicating and turning over the throne to his male lover. As administration decayed, popular discontent began to take form. People began to notice disturbing natural omens portending disaster. Fanatical mobs of worshippers looked to the Queen Mother of the West (Xiwangmu) for solace (fig 1.1). Specialists in esoteric wisdom began to murmur that Heaven had withdrawn its mandate from the house of Liu and a new dynasty was soon destined to rise in its place.

THE EASTERN HAN

The family of Empress Dowager Wang came to prominence in the final years of the Western Han. She had many Wang relatives ennobled or ensconced in high office. Among these was the talented and savvy Wang Mang (45 B.C.E.–23 C.E.).

Figure 1.1.   Xiwangmu, Queen Mother of the West. Rubbing of a pottery relief unearthed from Pixian tomb no. 1, near Chengdu, Sichuan. Lucy Lim, *Stories from China's Past: Han Dynasty Pictorial Tomb Reliefs and Archeological Objects from Sichuan Province, People's Republic of China* (San Francisco: Chinese Culture Foundation of San Francisco, 1987), pl. 63.

He steadily gained power until he completely dominated government during the brief reign of Ai's weak successor, the child emperor Ping (r. 1 B.C.E.–6 C.E.). Following Ping's untimely death, Wang Mang declared that a series of strange omens made it clear that the house of Liu had lost Heaven's mandate to rule over China. He announced that, in accordance with the will of Heaven, the Han dynasty had come to an end. He thereupon assumed the title of emperor and initiated a brief era that he called the Xin (new) dynasty.

Wang Mang's reign as emperor was a time of great change. An idealist, Wang undertook a series of reforms intended to establish a simpler, more virtuous society. From the modern perspective, his achievements seem mixed. Under his authority the coinage was debased, bureaucracy and administrative regions reorganized, slavery discouraged, and basic commodities placed under government monopoly. He imposed new taxes and attempted land reform. Initially it seemed as if Wang Mang's ambitious usurpation might succeed. He seems to have faced little organized opposition during the early part of his reign. Then a completely unexpected catastrophe occurred. The Yellow River shifted its course, leaving the previous northern bed for its present course to the south. The shift of the Yellow River ranks as one of the greatest natural disasters in China's long history. Huge numbers of people perished in titanic floods, and the survivors' crops were utterly destroyed. The crisis completely overwhelmed Wang Mang's government. Desperation drove roving bands of starving peasants to banditry. Some brigands painted red marks on their foreheads to distinguish themselves from government loyalists and declared outright rebellion. This uprising, apparently motivated mostly by starvation, became known as the Red Eyebrows rebellion.

The various rebel factions agreed that Wang Mang should be overthrown and the Han dynasty restored. They located a pliable member of the Liu family to serve as their puppet and set about destroying the monarch they blamed for their troubles. They soon overwhelmed the loyalist armies and decapitated Wang Mang. But the rebels were unable to bring their puppet to power. A stronger member of the Liu clan assumed the throne as Emperor Guangwu (5 B.C.E.–57 C.E.) and restored the Han dynasty. Because Guangwu established his new capital at Luoyang, east of the ruined Han capital at Changan, the second phase of the dynasty's history is known as the Eastern Han.

Guangwu proved a capable ruler. He pacified rebel bands, reunited the Han realm, and struck a skillful balance among the many factions whose support he needed. However, in the long run his administrative innovations proved the restored dynasty's greatest handicap. Guangwu shifted the focus of power away from the bureaucracy toward the person of the emperor. As long as China had a strong and capable ruler, such as himself, this dictatorial system worked efficiently. But under a weak or immature ruler, this new system enabled the relatives of high officials and imperial consorts to dominate the inner workings of government. Time and again during the Eastern Han, a strong clan of imperial in-laws ruled China in the name of a weak emperor, only to be exterminated by rivals who then ruled via another puppet. This endless cycle made Eastern Han politics particularly stormy.

For example, under Emperor Ming (r. 58–75) the scions of Empress Ma (d. 79) were ascendant. His successor, Emperor Zhang (r. 75–88), chose two sisters of the rival Dou clan as his consorts. Politics of the period were characterized by an intense struggle among the Mas and Dous for supremacy. The Mas gradually declined following the death of Empress Ma. This period was characterized by an increasing harshness in government. The next ruler, Emperor He (r. 88–106), came to the throne as a child, providing the Dous with an opportunity to declare a regency and take full control of the government. However, when He reached his majority he began to govern in his own right and ordered the Dous exterminated.

Under the following child emperors, the scholarly Empress Dowager Deng (d. 121) and her relatives dominated the state. This was another age plagued by serious natural disasters, and the empress responded by introducing more frugal customs at court. Over time the Dengs made many enemies. Following the death of Empress Dowager Deng, her family was destroyed. Next the family of Empress Yan came to dominate the court under the weak Emperor An (r. 106–125). He died without a designated heir, so Empress Dowager Yan was able to choose a child to be their puppet on the throne. But this child ruler soon died, and a new emperor had to be chosen.

This time the palace eunuchs emerged as the main rivals to the dominant consort clan, permanently changing the shape of Eastern Han politics. The eunuch candidate for the throne was proclaimed Emperor Shun (r. 125–144), and the Yans all suffered execution or exile. Shun chose an empress from the Liang family, whose members thereby achieved prominence at court. The Liangs controlled government under the next child emperor, although they fell from power and were executed following the death of Empress Dowager Liang in 159. This terrible chaos seems to have affected the quality of administration.

After the fall of the Liangs, Emperor Huan (r. 146–168) ruled in his own right. During his reign a number of important officials stepped forward to criticize the extravagance and corruption of the elite. They were correct in their belief that something had gone seriously astray in the system of government. By the reign of Huan, power had become divided among four major forces at court: emperor (if adult), empress or empress dowager and her relatives, elite landlords composing the bureaucracy, and palace eunuchs. In the final decades of the dynasty, the eunuch faction began to gain prominence. In reaction, some officials began to demand the execution of all eunuchs. Following an intense struggle, the eunuchs overcame their opposition from the consort family and officialdom. Eunuchs dominated the court during the reign of Emperor Ling (r. 168–189), persecuting leading families and packing the bureaucracy with eunuchs. To make matters even worse, many of the remaining positions in government available to noncastrated men were blatantly put up for sale to the highest bidder.

Endless intrigues, the ascendancy of eunuchs at court, and shameless simony all progressively sapped support for the Han. In 184 C.E. rumors of the dynasty's impending doom enflamed a rebellion of peasants who distinguished themselves by wrapping yellow cloth around their heads, earning them the nickname Yellow Turbans. This massive rebellion was soon crushed, but in the process security worries allowed eunuchs to gain command over important military units. Instability continued to grow. Foreign peoples invaded the declining empire, and desperation incited internal rebellions. Fury at the eunuchs for their misrule could no longer be contained. In 189 angry officials led a bloody massacre of the eunuchs. This chaos at court came as a crushing blow to imperial authority, and China descended into civil war as rival warlords fought for supremacy. At first they battled for control over the decayed Han court. But confidence in the dynasty had reached such a nadir that in 220 the strongman Cao Pi (186–220) forced the abdication of the final Han monarch. After more than four centuries, the Han dynasty had come to an end.

SOCIETY AND ECONOMY

A large and sophisticated bureaucracy including both central and regional offices governed the early Chinese empire. This system consciously repudiated the decentralized feudalistic customs of the Zhou dynasty and therefore marked a major shift in society as well as politics. In many respects, government could exert far more control over people's lives than had ever been possible under the more decentralized traditional system. And bureaucracy coupled with unity allowed China's resources to be marshaled on an unprecedented scale. Emperors constructed lengthy canals, impressive fortifications, grand irrigation works, and an admirable network of roads. However, the price for such efficiency was the alienation of most people from the workings of government. Unlike Athens or the Roman Republic, for example, where the governed had some say in their government, ordinary people in early imperial China were far removed from decision making.

One unusual characteristic of Qin and Han society was the system of ranks that functioned as an official social hierarchy. This custom began in the state of Qin and was imposed across China following unification. During the Han, the system consisted of twenty grades. Every free adult male was assigned a rank. On special occasions, such as the commencement of a new reign, the emperor would raise the ranks of every male subject by one or two grades. Because these ranks were cumulative, a man's official grade tended to increase along with age, allowing the system of official ranks to match traditional respect for seniority. These ranks constructed a carefully defined official order all the way down to the very bottom rungs of society.

In addition to government bureaucracy and official rankings, society also had a more traditional structure based on kinship. Han dynasty officials exploited the existing social fabric by employing some village elders as minor local officials. However, Qin officials considered powerful kinship groups such as extended families a threat to state authority and used taxation and the law to discourage large kinship groupings. Sometimes powerful families did indeed pose problems. Most famously, time and again the relatives of Han empresses gained control over the government. To do so, they appealed to kinship loyalties to thwart the normal processes of bureaucratic administration. Nor was this problem limited to the central government. Emperor Gaozu enthroned some powerful men as kings in quasi-independent kingdoms located within the borders of the Han state. It took decades for central authorities to reduce their autonomy. And on the local level, wealthy landlord families often dominated their locale. Members of these families used wealth, bureaucratic office, and connections to exploit the surrounding populace.

During the Eastern Han, large kinship groups began to reemerge. Extended families and clans with large landholdings transformed rural society. Large kinship groups also influenced the balance of power at the local level. For example, clans and lineage groups started several rebellions, showing them to have impressive power at the local level. However, the roles played by extended kinship groups in local society were not entirely negative. During the late second century, when the central government lost the ability to uphold public order, large clans and powerful landlord families often stepped into the vacuum. In this way, even during the chaotic years leading up to the fall of the Eastern Han, a semblance of order was maintained in many areas. In other places, strong men attracted followers unrelated by blood, creating many small power centers to rival late Eastern Han authority in the countryside.

Land could be freely bought and sold during the Han. Most peasants owned only a very small piece of land and spent their lives teetering on the edge of survival. In times of chaos, high taxation, or natural disaster, peasants often had no choice but to go into debt. The wealthy benefited from these troubles by cheaply buying up the lands of impoverished peasants. Although there was some slavery and agricultural wage labor during the Han, most large landlords preferred to rent out their fields to the landless. Of course peasants declined in social status when they became tenants. When this process was repeated innumerable times on a national scale, society became increasingly unequal. Land reform was repeatedly attempted in the late Western Han and under Wang Mang, but these efforts never succeeded. By the Eastern Han, resistance to large estates seems to have declined. The elite had probably come to accept blatant social inequality as a normal state of affairs. The rise of large landholdings certainly influenced the conduct of government during the Eastern Han. The scope of authority exercised by the emperor declined; landlord families assumed increasing power. Wealthy landlord families were often able to dominate the court as imperial consort kin. During the late Eastern Han, central authority gradually disintegrated, leading to the decentralization of authority and the reemergence of feudal-style institutions as the dynasty decayed.

Early imperial China was also noteworthy for its urbanization. The earliest Chinese cities were primarily centers of ritual and administration. But during the Qin and Han, many cities across north China had become sizeable commercial centers. The standardization of currency during the Qin no doubt stimulated long-distance trade. Each major city had officially designated markets. Local officials regulated prices, enforced contracts, and levied commercial taxes. The Western Han government actively regulated the economy, though government regulation of commerce and industry seems to have lessened during the Eastern Han.

Merchants traded in a wide variety of goods, as befitted such a large and diverse empire. Prepared foods and agricultural produce, manufactured goods such as cloth and bronze, and raw materials such as dyes and iron were all actively bought and sold. Chinese merchants conducted trade with places beyond the borders of the Han state, importing foreign exotica such as sesame seeds, rhinoceros horn, pomegranates, and glass for sale to Chinese consumers. Some merchants gained enormous wealth and invested it in land, decreasing the number of fields available to free peasants. In this way the thriving commercial economy brought inequality and poverty to the countryside. The mercantile economy seems to have thrived right up until the time of chaos preceding the collapse of the Eastern Han.

Although some merchants were wealthy, they held an ambiguous position in early imperial society. The government feared the disruptive effects of commercial wealth, and so the official social status of merchants was low. Government officials periodically harassed them. For example, merchants were sometimes singled out for military conscription or forced to colonize new lands in the malarial south. Sumptuary laws prohibited merchants from flaunting their wealth. They were subject to special taxes. And the descendents of merchants were excluded from service in the bureaucracy.

Manufacturing was conducted on a significant scale as well. The state routinely produced certain goods, such as court luxuries. In some eras the government also oversaw the production of necessities such as salt, metallic ore, and even agricultural tools. Although several Western Han administrations actively pursued manufacturing, state industry declined in importance during the Eastern Han. Aside from a few specific goods emphasized by the officialdom, most manufacturing seems to have been undertaken privately. Some products, such as brewed beverages, seem to have been extremely profitable. And textile production, a traditional female pursuit, was one of the major handicraft industries of the Han. Occasionally the scale of textile production became quite large, with hundreds of women engaged in production under the auspices of a single enterprise. This put women on the forefront of early industrial production.

In sum, increasing economic complexity caused early imperial society to become extremely diverse and increasingly unequal. The government superimposed a new system of official ranks upon traditional kinship ties and local custom. Landlords, merchants, artisans, free peasants, refugees, tenants, landless laborers, and slaves made up a diverse society. Land could be bought and sold, though of course real estate transactions did not occur in anything resembling a free market. The wealthy and powerful often abused their privileges to acquire ever increasing tracts of land. The sale of land allowed considerable social mobility, though for most people the change in status was downward in direction. Eastern Han society eventually came to be dominated by wealthy landlords living on vast estates farmed by their innumerable tenants.

THOUGHT AND RELIGION

Compared to the tremendous ferment of the preceding Warring States period, intellectually the early empire was an age of consolidation. Some editors brought together diverse articles under a single title, making a wide array of ideas available to their readers. Others strove to unify the ideas of various thinkers into a comprehensive system. For example, Huanglao thought amalgamated the classic texts of Daoism together with elements of legalism, Confucianism, ancient legend, and cosmological theory to produce a diverse and (to modern eyes) highly contradictory blend of extremely varied ideas. From the philosopher's perspective, much of the syncretistic thought of the period seems fairly specious. But these books were not written for distant posterity; they were composed to address the concerns of their day. And at the onset of the imperial era, achieving an intellectual unity to match China's new political unity was the most pressing problem of the time.

Given the diversity of Han intellectual life, it is impossible to neatly sum it up as a particular philosophy or academic school. Various thinkers pursued different problems and responded to the diversity of previous thought in different ways. Even so, we can identify several major themes that consistently inspired numerous early imperial thinkers. Perhaps the most important intellectual development was the emergence of Confucianism as the mainstream ideology at court. At the beginning of the Han no school of thought had clear-cut official sanction. Huanglao Daoism had enthusiastic supporters, legalism provided an underpinning for the conduct of government, divination texts were carefully studied, and the works of numerous other schools continued to be read.

Emperor Wu's reign marks a major turning point in Chinese intellectual history. This ruler turned to the great thinker Dong Zhongshu (c. 179–104 B.C.E.) for guidance on intellectual matters. The wide appeal of Dong's eclectic blend of Confucianism and cosmological speculation led Confucianism to be enshrined as official state ideology, a privileged position maintained until the end of imperial history. During the Han, many rancorous academic debates raged on highly technical questions of Confucian orthodoxy, such as philological criticism, textual transmission, and the correct interpretation of classic texts. Because these debates had real influence on government policy, they could become extremely acrimonious. All in all, Confucianism generally had a beneficial effect on Han thought in that it tended to turn the attentions of the educated toward questions of good government, public ethics, and sympathy for the governed.

Han thinkers were also fascinated by cosmology. For example, some scholars speculated on the precise shape of the universe. Are the heavens shaped like a dome or a sphere, or do they simply go on infinitely? Each view had its proponents and detractors. Other thinkers tried to understand the abstract forces underlying change in the natural and human worlds. They emphasized abstract concepts such as the five phases, the numerology of the *Classic of Changes* (*Yijing*), or dynamically interrelated pairs of basic elements such as heaven/earth or yin/yang. Another approach emphasized transcendental forces linking the human and natural worlds. The popularity of astrology, divination, and omens all manifested this belief. On a more theoretical level, some thinkers pondered the precise mechanism by which the various parts of the universe affect each other.

During the late Eastern Han, the quality of elite speculative thought began to decline. People increasingly turned their attentions away from secular thought toward religion, such as popular Daoism. Others abandoned rigorous inquiry for otherworldly mysticism, aestheticism, or amusing conversation. Still others sought to turn the mainstream of academic inquiry toward the study of esoteric transcendental problems, producing a genre known as apocryphal literature. Apocryphal thought was nothing new. Some Western Han thinkers such as the influential Dong Zhongshu tried to use their knowledge of cosmological forces to predict the future. But during the Eastern Han, this type of thinking became increasingly popular. Commentators on the classics propounded extravagant theories that allowed them to read their mystical ideas into authoritative texts. Apocryphal thinking turned people's attention away from the problems of government and morality at a time when Chinese society would have benefited most from this sort of discussion.

Regardless of what Han authors wrote, it is doubtful that written texts had a very widespread impact in this early era. Books were still extremely rare objects available to very few readers. The number influenced by written ideas was miniscule compared to those influenced by oral and visual media. Because books were rare, intellectuals often devoted themselves to the memorization and slavish study of a single text. Dedication to a single text sometimes became a family tradition as successive generations passed down a precious book and transmitted their accumulated insights. This sort of hermetic scholarship severely limited the impact of academic inquiry on a wider audience. Given the rarity and inaccessibility of books during the Qin and Han, it is important not to exaggerate the influence held by elite written discourse in the culture of the time.

In contrast, religion was both popular and widespread. One of the most important religious developments of the early empire was the attempt to amalgamate the confused body of mythology into coherent systems. Prior to unification, each region of China had its own unique mythological traditions, and together they shared a common body of lore. During the Han, books such as the *Classic of Mountains and Lakes* (*Shanhaijing*) and *Huainanzi* incorporated diverse strands of myth into larger systems of understanding. The historian Sima Qian (c. 145–c. 86 B.C.E.) incorporated myths about the culture heroes alleged to be China's earliest monarchs into his comprehensive account of China's history, reconciling myth with historical tradition.

Popular beliefs departed widely from the artificial intellectual systems propounded in elite written texts. Unfortunately, we know very little about popular beliefs of the period. Folk deities seem to have been numerous. Some appeared in animal form; others were associated with natural phenomena such as heavenly bodies, wind, rain, and rivers. Still others were manifestations of the dead. Deities were often affiliated with a particular place. The most famous of these popular Han deities was the Queen Mother of the West. Sacrifices were held at innumerable local shrines to appease the spirits, although skeptical members of the elite looked down on popular religion as a superstitious display of misplaced piety.

People of the early empire clearly believed in the possibility of an afterlife. In one tradition, the dead might return to earth as spirits who could assume a variety of appearances. These creatures were highly feared. Another belief held that, in addition to the physical body, each person is also composed of two nonmaterial elements called *hun* and *po*. Upon death these two souls usually separate. According to one version of the theory, the *hun* might go to an otherworldly paradise while the *po* remains with the body of the deceased. There was also a frightening possibility that a portion of the deceased might descend to the Yellow Springs, a dismal and shadowy netherworld. However, these beliefs about the afterlife were rarely elaborated or incorporated into a structured religion.

The Qin and Han also practiced an official state religion. Sanctioned rituals were regularly performed by government officials at village, county, and district altars. It seems that local people participated in these rites. In addition, the central government maintained national altars. At first the state cult emphasized worship of abstract divinities known as the five *di*. Burnt sacrifices were offered to these vague deities in the hope of obtaining their blessing. During the reign of Emperor Wu, deities of the Earth and Grand Unity were added to the official cult. Official religion changed notably in the late Western Han, when the traditional state religion was amended to focus on the deity Heaven (*Tian*), which remained the central deity of state religion for the remainder of the Han. In addition, Han emperors shouldered enormous expense to revere their ancestors. Initially shrines to deceased rulers were maintained in every administrative region, although these devotions were cut back in times of frugality. Through this variety of beliefs, the state's representatives sought the blessings of gods, imperial ancestors, and abstract transcendental forces.

2

Kinship

Kinship may be the most basic form of social organization, but the customs governing it differ widely. Such diversity is only possible because kinship is fundamentally social, not just biological. The family is an organization; kinship rules dictate its order. Because kinship is a product of human creativity rather than natural determinism, its roles and customs reflect society's most important beliefs and values. Human beings use kinship to project their ideals onto the template of basic social roles.

Nor does kinship function in isolation from other social organizations. By providing the individual with basic social roles such as "wife" or "son," kinship endows people with legitimate places in their society. Because kinship roles are so primary to human social organization, major forms of activity come to be organized around them. In early China, the roles of ritual, work, law, politics, education, and almost every other form of social activity were structured largely according to kinship.

In fact, kinship was particularly important in early Chinese society. As in other agricultural societies, the household also served as the major economic organization. Kinship stood at the very center of both society and economy. Moreover, compared to modern nation-states, the government of early China was fairly simple and its activities limited in scope. Many matters that today would be handled by large bureaucratic organizations, such as governments and corporations, were still organized around kinship. The customs regulating kin interaction were consequently the prime rules governing women's lives in early imperial society. And kinship is an inherently conservative force. Although some kinship customs gradually changed during the early imperial era, for the most part people maintained the customs and ideas about family bequeathed to them by their ancestors. As a result, many of the statements we make about Qin and Han kinship were just as true for the late Eastern Zhou.

To understand the past, we must try to reimagine the possibilities and limitations that ordinary people faced. Most people in Han China, both female and male, had few opportunities in life. A typical woman's grave was probably not far from her place of birth. There were few chances to leave home and earn an independent livelihood. Given the lack of alternatives outside the family, most women's lives were structured by relationships with their immediate kin. A woman's role within the kinship network would determine where she lived, how she spent her days, how others treated her, and even how she was mourned after she died.

This was not a world of simple gender dichotomies. Instead of an absolute patriarchy of all men dominating all women, the early Chinese kinship network enveloped women and men in a dense tangle of social roles that led them to interact in complex ways. A woman might play the roles of wife, mother, daughter-in-law, niece, younger sister, grandmother, and many other kinship identities, sometimes simultaneously.[1] Each person held multiple kinship roles. Some roles elevated a person's status in particular situations; others depressed it. A woman might be high-handed toward her son but turn meek and submissive when her father-in-law entered the room. The relationship between gender and behavior was both subtle and complicated.

These contradictory roles within the family formed the basic nexus that allowed a woman to interact with the wider world around her. These roles were not just abstract social categories. To a large extent, we *are* the social roles we play. It is difficult to say where social role-playing ends and the "real" person begins. So the kinship roles a woman assumed in relation to the people closest to her shaped both her general social identity and her overall sense of self. Defining these kinship roles is the starting point for understanding the women of early imperial China.

MARRIAGE

Although men's basic social roles were determined at birth, most women's were not. Instead, marriage was generally the most important institution shaping a woman's relations to her kin. When a woman married, she was expected to leave the familiar comforts of her natal family for the frightening unknown of a different household. There she had to assume an entirely new set of social roles. Her most important daily performance was no longer acting out the roles of sister and daughter. Instead she began to play the new parts of wife, daughter-in-law, and eventually mother. Custom, ritual, and morality all commanded a bride to be thoroughly subservient to her new senior in-laws.

Love between spouses was not discouraged. Some Han art and literature celebrated demonstrations of affection between two lovers, as with the popular romantic tale of the cowherd and weaving maid who were only allowed to meet once a year (fig. 2.1), or depictions of physical intimacy between loving couples (fig. 2.2). However, early Chinese marriage was primarily an institution based on family and property, not personal emotion. Inheritance customs were a major factor determining a bride's place within her new household. Land was the foundation of most people's wealth, and few sons inherited land outright until their parents died. This arrangement affected daughters-in-law as much as sons. A husband still economically dependent on his parents would not be in a good position to protect his bride from ill-treatment in her new home.

Placing married couples under the direct control of the husband's parents affected society at its most primary level by imbuing the older generation with considerable authority. The result was a relatively conservative society arranged around steep kinship hierarchies.[2] To succeed in life, a woman had to cope with her radical shift from the social roles into which she had been born to the new roles expected of her as she took her place among strangers. Given the primacy of the parent–child bond in Chinese social organization, being torn away from this protective relationship generally weakened a woman's position within the overall kinship structure.

Unlike adherents of the Judeo-Christian tradition, early Chinese never assumed that marriage was supernaturally mandated from the beginnings of human existence. Elite thinkers held an evolutionary view of society that was strikingly similar to modern anthropological theory. Many authors looked back to a primitive era when marriage did not yet exist. Savagery ended when the mythic sage rulers of high antiquity benevolently endowed humanity with the basic institutions and inventions central to civilization, among them marriage.[3] According to idealistic Confucians such as Mencius (fourth century B.C.E.), a golden age then ensued in which all adult women and men were able to successfully find a spouse and everyone lived in contented harmony.[4] The decay from the utopian perfection of high antiquity invoked wistful nostalgia from thinkers dissatisfied with the imperfections of their own time.

The patrilineal tradition in early Chinese thought advocated specific principles of proper marriage. These elite ideals included the primacy of kinship groups over individuals, separation of the sexes, male domination of female within the same level of a hierarchy, monogamy, ritualized relations between the sexes, procreation of sons, and moral taboos against behavior that might destabilize patrilineal kin organizations, such as incest and widow remarriage.[5] Confucian-inspired moralists in particular consistently advocated these ideals. The scope

Figure 2.1. Cowherd and Weaving Maid. Rubbing of an incised stone from Pixian tomb no. 1, Sichuan. Lim, *Stories from China's Past*, pl. 56.

Figure 2.2.   The Kiss. Rubbing of an incised stone unearthed in Rongjing County, Sichuan. Lim, *Stories from China's Past*, pl. 38.

of popular adherence to these ethical injunctions, however, varied enormously. Generally speaking, prior to the Tang dynasty, marriage practices conformed far less closely to patrilineal ideals than in subsequent eras.[6] Most fundamentally, economic imperatives often conflicted with patrilineal priorities. In the early imperial era, pragmatism still often won out over the moral dictates of patrilinealism.

Marriage in China has sometimes been pointed to as a perfect example of radical patrilineality, patrilocality, and patriarchy. Yet these stereotypes ignore the messy complexities of real life. In fact, Chinese marriage has taken on a multiplicity of forms to satisfy varied functions. Fieldwork in present-day China, for example, shows that wives often maintain a variety of ties to their natal families.[7] Although early imperial kinship was theoretically patrilineal, women of that distant era seem to have maintained similar ties to their blood kin as well.

As in contemporary China, Qin and Han women kept their natal surname after marriage. And some women's given names included the character of the father's surname, further symbolizing a lasting attachment to the natal household. For example, the illustrious Han scholar Ban Zhao was also called Ban Huiban, repeating the character of her natal surname within her given name.[8] This is an extremely potent symbolic gesture. In a society organized around kinship, individual identity was often an outgrowth of kin relations. And what could be more personal than a given name? If a married woman's name retained traces of her birth family, so did her own identity. These tight natal bonds continued even after death. The ritual canon instructed that the inscription to be placed over a woman's coffin feature her natal surname and her order of birth among her sisters rather than identification with her husband's family.[9] After a lifetime of marriage, in the end a woman was still considered to belong to the family of her birth.

These customs linking a woman to her natal family had ramifications far beyond the rarified realm of elite ritual. There were also practical reasons for maintaining and even encouraging natal ties. In a society of weak public institutions, it was extremely advantageous for a person to maintain close ties with a wide range or relatives. If a married couple could expand the scope of friendly kin who might aid and protect them, they increased their prospects in life. A husband might be eager to continue close relations with his in-laws, seeing them as a financial and human resource holding many potential benefits. Conversely, a wife's kin might expect to share in the good fortune of their in-laws. The Han emperors in particular were infamous for conferring fabulous wealth and privilege on the families of their consorts. This practice became so outrageous that it contributed in no small measure to the eventual fall of both the Western and Eastern Han. The bond between women and their natal families was so strong that it distorted the patrilineal institutions underlying early imperial government.

A wife's natal kin bonds were all the more valuable to a husband because Chinese marriage was theoretically monogamous; the relative paucity of in-laws made these relations all the more valuable. The importance of the principle of monogamy can be seen in reactions to polygamy. For example, Han moralists were greatly troubled by the disturbing precedent set by the marriage of the mythical sage Shun to two sisters. They contrived hair-splitting scholastic equivocations to bring this revered figure's actions in line with their own aversion to polygyny.[10] Even the imperial prerogative of marriage to nine carefully ranked wives had to be justified by invoking a cosmological rationale: the ruler takes nine wives to represent the union of his realm's nine regions.[11] But the Han emperors did not dare practice this hypothetically proper form of polygyny. An emperor might enjoy hundreds of consorts, but he had only one true wife.

Although monogamy was the ideal, popular customs could sometimes be more flexible. The buying and selling of concubines was an obvious exception to pure monogamy. Through the custom of concubinage, men could practice de facto polygyny while claiming monogamy for the reason that they had only one mate titled "wife." The terminology related to concubines, as well as their status, differed entirely from that of wives. Han terms for concubines incorporated diminutives and mild pejoratives such as "auxiliary" (*pang*), "little" (*xiao*), and "lesser" (*xia*) to emphasize the concubine's inferiority to the true wife.[12] Theory and practice differed on what made a woman a concubine instead of a true wife. The ritual canon traditionally defined a concubine as someone who had merely eloped (*ben*) without the consecration provided by an exchange of wedding gifts between families.[13] In practice, though, concubinage simply involved the sale of a woman by her family. She could not be resold, so she was not a slave. Nor did she have the social or legal status of a slave. But having been purchased from her family, a concubine lost any claim to the privileges accorded a wife. Wives and concubines were expected to play very different roles within the family.

During the Han, the difference between concubine and wife was considered to be of utmost importance. Authorities strove to maintain a clear distinction between the two, although men sometimes flouted the rules of kinship custom and elite ritual by raising concubines above true wives. This stress on the distinction between wives and concubines was not an arbitrary obsession. Although elite thinkers presented monogamy as a moral virtue, there were very practical reasons behind this custom. Most important, monogamy strengthened patrilinealism. Multiple wives would have fractured patrilineal kin organizations based on simple and direct bloodlines. These legal formalities grew out of the Zhou dynasty system of clan customs (*zongfa*), which sought to stabilize society by scrupulously distinguishing kinship roles. Elevating wife above concubine guaranteed that the sons of wives would inherit the lineage's property. Reducing the number of heirs minimized downward social mobility among members of the main bloodline. And by decreasing the potential for inheritance disputes, society as a whole was stabilized. Because of the demonstrated utility of monogamy, laws that developed out of clan custom preserved the ancient prohibition against setting up a concubine as a legal wife.[14] Elite intellectual systems such as ethics, ritual, and law all upheld monogamy as one of the most basic principles of civilized society.

The rigorous distinction between wives and concubines was extremely significant for its effects on women's lives. A woman's relationship with her spouse provided what was perhaps her most important social role. It was expected that all women should marry or otherwise assume a recognized relationship with a man. Marriage and concubinage systematically introduced women into clearly defined roles within the patrilineal kinship network. After a woman entered her spouse's home, her relationship with him and his family defined her new kinship identity. If a woman entered a man's family in the role of wife, she could lay claim to privileges protected by law, custom, and ritual. Concubines lacked these safeguards. The nature of a woman's relation to her spouse became a major component of her identity, and an important addition to the range of social roles she was expected to play.

DIVORCE

Although marriage was ideally a permanent condition, divorce seems to have been common in early imperial China. Many documents focus on legitimate reasons, legality, and propriety of divorce. Long before China's unification, divorce had been permissible under certain circumstances. Traditionally, divorce was regulated by elite ritual and popular custom. But in the early imperial period, the state brought divorce under the jurisdiction of the law. The Qin code contained explicit provisions allowing men to divorce their wives.[15]

Despite the encroachment of law on the regulation of marriage, custom was probably still the standard guide to divorce proceedings. The discussion over codes of propriety conducted in 79 c.e. in the White Tiger Hall touched on the criteria for ending a marriage.[16] From this discussion it is clear that ritualists still considered divorce to be under the purview of custom rather than law. Moreover, in line with the patrilineal origins of the kinship rites, ritual specialists sided entirely with the husband on the issue of divorce by stripping the divorced wife of any right to associate with her husband's family. Patrilineal principles were followed so strictly that a son was enjoined not to mourn for a deceased mother who had been divorced from his father. According to this radically patrilineal view, the bond of kinship with one's mother stems not from blood but from her marital bond with one's father.[17] This draconian injunction eloquently epitomizes the patrilineal orientation of the ritual codes.

Han dynasty records abound with examples of men who divorced their wives.[18] Theoretically a man could only divorce his wife for one of seven specific reasons: barrenness, licentiousness, failure to serve parents-in-law, loquacity, theft, jealousy, and dread disease. A wife could supposedly contest divorce on three grounds: having mourned for parents-in-law, having been married prior to a household's rise from poverty to wealth, and lacking anywhere to return. Patrilineal thinkers continued to advocate the ritual rules for divorce, particularly during the Eastern Han dynasty. In practice, however, the "seven conditions" and "three prohibitions" were often ignored. Sometimes men who divorced their wives out of blatant self-interest invoked one of the "seven conditions" as a pretext. In other instances, men divorced wives for reasons completely unrelated to these traditional conditions, such as ambition, political expediency, or financial gain.

The right of women to initiate divorce is an important measure of female freedom. In early imperial China, divorce was not just a male privilege. Women were also accorded broad leeway to leave their husbands. Female-initiated divorce has ancient roots in China. The rise of family law does not seem to have interfered with this traditional female privilege. Han records mention women divorcing husbands for a wide range of reasons, including poverty, disease, and contentious in-laws.

In a society organized so thoroughly around kinship, the consequences of a woman leaving her husband's family would have been cataclysmic. There were no clearly defined social roles for unmarried mature women, leaving the divorcée to a life of strained ambiguity. And because the patrilineal family functioned as society's main economic organization, the divorced woman found herself outside the economic mainstream. If she had not borne children prior to her divorce, there would be no one to support her if she survived into old age. The precarious future of unmarried women undoubtedly made the discontent wife think long and hard before resorting to divorce.

With few exceptions, the life of a spinster, divorcée, or widow promised to be hard. A dismal picture of unmarried women barely surviving on the edges of acceptable society haunts ancient writings. Moralists instructed rulers to pity widows, whom they grouped together with orphans, elderly, chronically ill, and other unfortunates as the weakest and most pathetic members of society.[19] Sometimes these values found concrete expression. For example, Han martial law stipulated that if a father and son were both serving in the army and one should die, the other should accompany the coffin home.[20] This provision was probably a humanitarian gesture intended to ensure that the women of a family would not be completely deprived of all menfolk due to war. A woman without a husband found herself the object of pity, outside of mainstream patrilineal society.

REMARRIAGE

Female remarriage was a controversial matter. The motivations driving women to remarry are obvious. Only marriage could allow a woman to participate fully in the patrilineal kinship system organizing virtually every aspect of society. Aside from companionship and sex, marriage allowed women clear and respectable social roles and a chance to participate in the economic and social mainstream. Given these considerable benefits, female remarriage was not uncommon. Prevalent opinion upheld the right of widowed or divorced women without children to remarry. From ancient times these women were generally allowed to marry freely, a custom that continued uninterrupted up through the Han. In fact, popular Chinese customs have generally allowed widows to remarry, even at the highpoint of Neo-Confucian influence during the Song.[21]

Despite traditional approval of female remarriage, beginning in the Eastern Zhou some moralists started to exalt the ideal of widow chastity.[22] This idea influenced certain streams of early imperial thought. For example, Qin law punished women who divorced their husbands to remarry someone else. Such a woman was to be tatooed and condemned to pound grain. Qin law mandated chastity for widows with children, although childless widows could remarry.[23] And *Records of Ritual (Liji)* prohibited all widow remarriage.[24] These documents show that proponents of strict patrilineal values tried to use both law and ritual to discourage remarriage.

As this shift in written opinion shows, some elite thinkers began using a very different perspective to view their society. They started to look at moral issues solely from the standpoint of how individual behavior affects the patrilineal family. This change explains the general trend toward codifying patrilineal values in moral and ritual codes. From this patrilineal perspective, female remarriage was indubitably very awkward. Through remarriage, a woman moved from one patrilineal family to another. In doing so, she might possibly confuse bloodlines and complicate the distribution of property. There was also a general perception that marriage was essentially a union of lineages rather than individuals. A woman married a family, not just a husband. Even a man's death did not void his wife's membership in his family. Given the rising codification of patrilineal interests into moral dictates during the late Zhou and Han, it is not surprising that some early imperial thinkers actively discouraged both female-initiated divorce and remarriage.

Although some opposition to female remarriage began in certain elite Zhou circles, this way of thinking increased markedly in popularity during the Han. As such, it exemplified the patrilineal morality of early imperial China's new elite. The powerful Han families replaced traditional Zhou feudal values with norms more appropriate to their own concerns. Because property was key to their social status, some members of this elite advocated moral systems that guarded patrilineal inheritance. Widow remarriage directly threatened the interests of this property-based elite by allowing the departing woman the opportunity to remove her dowry and possibly other property from the control of her former husband's family and handing it over to the family of her new husband. Allowing a woman to remarry risked serious economic loss to her former husband's family. Rising prohibitions against female remarriage seem to have been a useful tool for keeping property within the patrilineal family.[25] The rising popularity of dowered marriage only increased potential support for widow chastity.

The symbolic importance of women may have been another factor in rising elite opposition to remarriage. We can compare conditions in the early empire to the Song dynasty, another age that witnessed a rising emphasis on widow fidelity. Song opposition to widow remarriage occurred during a time of flourishing urban culture in which many women ceased to work and instead largely became status symbols for men.[26] Perhaps similar forces were already at work among the early imperial elite as well. Just as possession of an expensive and prestigious object, such as a bronze vessel or finely worked jade, could increase a family's status, the addition of a high-status woman to a household raised its status as well. Should she choose to divorce her husband, his family would suffer public ignominy. Were she to then remarry, the humiliation to her former husband's family would be even greater. And so the symbolic value of women as tokens of prestige exchanged among elite families seems to have led some elite thinkers to espouse moral systems opposing any opportunity for a woman to leave her husband's family.

The conflict between elite morals and popular custom regarding female prerogatives reached a crescendo during the Han. Elite writers condemned female remarriage as immoral; popular custom seems to have permitted remarriage as before. The prevailing viewpoint seems to have been that female rejection of remarriage was an expression of exemplary virtue rather than baseline decency; although admirable, it was not a requirement for respectability. This practical outlook persisted in later eras.[27] Nevertheless, polemics against female remarriage eloquently excoriated the laxity of prevailing practices.[28]

This conflict in values pushed female remarriage to the forefront of moral debate. The resulting dialogue reveals a deep disagreement over what basic social roles were most appropriate for women. Some saw a woman as inseparable from her role as wife in the patrilineal kinship network. These conservatives cast themselves as moral reformers determined to fix the evils of society by putting the interests of patrilineal kin groups first. In contrast, the pragmatic traditional view held that women ought to play a wide range of social roles. According to this vision of society, the interests and desires of individual women could sometimes override those of their husbands' families. This debate over fundamental female identity, pitting traditional flexibility against unforgiving patrilineal ideals, was framed during the Han dynasty. The controversy would continue to smolder for centuries.

Patrilineal moralists intensified this moral conflict when they began to glorify women who went to extreme lengths to resist forced remarriage. Writers and artists celebrated female paragons, such as the Zhou dynasty Lady Gui, who bemoaned remaining alive after having been forced into remarriage. The widow Liang Gaoxing was even more extreme. She cut off her own nose to repel potential suitors (fig. 2.3).[29] Patrilinealists advocated a dramatic and demanding new social role for women: the martyr to chastity.

This debate was not just theoretical. Disputes over the proper conduct of a divorced or widowed woman could tear a family asunder. The Eastern Han scholar Xun Shuang (128–190 c.e.), famed for his research into Confucianism, nevertheless adhered to old-style pragmatic behavior in urging his widowed daughter Cai to remarry. The fact that Xun Shuang would advocate the permis-

Figure 2.3. Liang Gaoxing Cuts Off Her Nose to Avoid Forced Remarriage. Reconstruction of a rubbing from the Wu Liang shrine, Shandong. Feng Yunpeng, *Jinshisuo* (Taipei: Dezhi, 1963), 3:46–47.

sive view of widow marriage is extremely significant. Xun demonstrated a deep commitment to moral behavior in public life, showing that in the late Eastern Han an upstanding moral leader did not consider female remarriage louche or unseemly. His daughter Cai, in contrast, saw the matter very differently. She accepted strict patrilineal arguments that portrayed female remarriage as wicked. Rather than sully her virtue by succumbing to her father's entreaties to remarry, she killed herself.[30]

Liu Xiang (79–78 B.C.E.) included tales of female martyrdom in his influential *Biographies of Women (Lienüzhuan)*.[31] A scion of the imperial family, Liu Xiang devoted himself to replacing Qin practices with revived Zhou dynasty morals and institutions. Liu's strong stand on female chastity is consistent with this general program to rescue society from decay by strengthening patrilineal values. His strange and moving stories of women who committed suicide to preserve their chastity became a staple of the new female didactic literature. By establishing widow chastity as one of the outstanding virtues of exemplary women and legitimizing it as part of the rising Confucian tradition, this stern belief system came to influence many of the most important thinkers of later ages.[32] Tributes to women who martyred themselves to avoid remarriage subsequently became a mainstay of female education.

Some of these stories, particularly those attributed to distant antiquity, are clearly gruesome products of the imagination. But this genre did have some links to reality. It seems that a handful of women really did kill themselves rather than submit to forced remarriage. The motivations of these self-made martyrs are not readily apparent. After all, why would a woman sacrifice herself for the sake of a value system opposed to her individual interests? And considering the precarious position of widows, why would any rational woman resist marriage?[33] Of course this is not an isolated question. All moral systems are premised on the sacrifice of individual interests for the sake of a larger group. In many cultures, women have traditionally accepted values that require them to sacrifice their personal interests in favor of their husband's family. From a woman's submission to her husband's male elders in Latin America to Hindu widow suicide, women throughout the world have espoused values that severely limit their personal freedom or cause them physical harm. But female self-sacrifice is not entirely without benefits to the individual. Many cultures reward women with high prestige when they sacrifice themselves in the name of morality. Early Chinese female martyrdom was not a cultural anomaly but simply an unusually extreme manifestation of the self-sacrificing behavior required by the moral systems of every society.

Female martyrs did not view their self-sacrifice as a purely negative act. Somewhat counterintuitively, martyrdom could also further a woman's own interests even as she sacrificed herself for others. The difficult act of self-sacrifice proved that a woman could take control over her own fate. She publicly demonstrated her own power in very dramatic terms. The martyr also gained honor by proving her willingness to adhere to strict virtue at any price. Even if a woman killed herself to preserve her chastity, at the moment the dagger pierced her breast she knew that her posthumous reputation was assured. Mutilation or suicide to protest forced remarriage was one strategy for a woman to increase her standing by acting out a difficult but respected role: the martyr to female virtue. A woman's identity was largely constructed out of the social roles she played. By choosing to play the martyr she was guaranteed honor and recognition, even if these benefits could only be achieved through suicide. A few women were willing to pay this high price to achieve respect.

FAMILY

Ever since high antiquity, the varied roles defining the relationships between a woman and her various kin shaped her identity. Shang and Western Zhou societies took kin relations as the nucleus of all social and political organization, setting the basic dynamics of Chinese society down to the present day. Although increasing social complexity diluted blood bonds, in the early imperial period society continued to use real and fictive kinship as its fundamental building blocks. Nor did these bonds function as just a series of static lines connecting individuals. A kinship role came with elaborate rules and expectations. By acting out these roles, abstract female identity took shape as an individual way of life.

Defining the most basic unit of early imperial kinship is a fundamental problem. Kinship customs in early China were far from standard. Each region displayed local variations in kin organization. For example, a post-Han text records a court case allegedly from the first century B.C.E. in the semi-sinicized northeastern region of Yan. Three men who shared the same wife brought forward a suit. After she gave birth to four children, the men began to quarrel over paternity and took the case to court. The horrified magistrate, native to a different area, awarded custody of the children to the mother and ordered the three husbands executed for their "inhuman" behavior.[34] This lawsuit reveals the diversity of early imperial kinship customs. Although this case may have been a unique ad hoc arrangement worked out privately by four people, more likely it reflects local kinship customs allowing polyandry. The willingness of the men to take the matter to court suggests that they themselves saw nothing wrong with polyandry, only with the confusion of bloodlines that had resulted. The magistrate, native to an area in which polyandry was unknown, recoiled from their *ménage* as abhorrent to basic morality. His own view of sexual morals clearly derived from the monogamous patrilineal principles codified in the customs and rituals of the Chinese heartland. This legal conflict between different views of kinship highlights the cultural confusion of the early empire. Qin and Han China was extremely large and diverse. Although China had been united politically, it was still extremely divided culturally. Kinship seems to have been more diverse than in later eras when Chinese society became gradually more homogeneous.

At first glance it might seem inappropriate to apply the English term "family" to the basic unit of Chinese kinship. A Han dynasty household that might include a man's wife, his concubines, and their assorted offspring was organized very differently from the modern Western nuclear family. However, we can rescue the convenient term "family" from the perils of anachronism by returning to the original definition of the concept. The Latin word *familia* referred very broadly to all household members subject to the authority of a *pater familias*. The Roman family might include not only relations by blood, adoption, and marriage, but even clients and slaves.[35] Resurrecting the original Latin connotations of family, which virtually equated it with the household as a whole and perhaps people living elsewhere, provides a surprisingly close analogue for the most important unit of Han kinship—the *jia*. The early Chinese *jia* could take many forms: nuclear family, groupings of distant relatives, or extended households including nonrelatives. The minimum qualification for classification as a *jia* was a group of people living together, sharing resources, and cooking together.

Han data suggest wide variation in average household size according to region, ranging from as few as two to more than forty people per household.[36] In high antiquity, large households of extended relatives were considered ideal. But from at least the mid–Warring States period onward, relatively small families seem to have been most common. The trend toward small families no doubt increased the wife's influence in the family. Instead of owing primary fealty to his brothers, a man devoted his main concern to the care of his wife and children. Although the Eastern Han witnessed the emergence of large and wealthy households among the elite, economic pressures generally discouraged such unwieldy kinship units. Even during the late Eastern Han, large extended households were probably exceptional, though of course very important politically and economically. Surviving figures from the Western and Eastern Han suggest average households contained approximately five people.[37] As an example, the records preserved by chance at Juyan describe small families of only one or two generations. Even though some households included marginal relatives such as an unmarried sister living with her married older brother, most households still consisted of only three or four people. Only one household at Juyan had as many as six members.[38]

In distant antiquity, extended families seem to have been far more common. Patrilineal ethical systems such as elite ritual guidelines and Confucianism continued to call for extended families long after they had ceased to be the dominant form of kin organization. During the Han, patrilineal interests advocated increasingly influential ethical systems based on their values. For example, moralists bemoaned the pitiful state of the childless man and reminded the son of his duty to provide for his parents.[39] Some asserted that no son (much less his wife) could own personal property as long as his parents were still alive.[40] Respecting these admonitions would encourage adult brothers and their families to continue living under the same roof. These attempts to revive ancient kinship forms struggled against decisive changes in economy and society that encouraged smaller families. Qin law forbade large families, seeing them as a challenge to state authority.[41] But though the Western Han government reversed unfilial Qin measures and even adopted a pretense of rewarding extended families in deference to Confucian ethics, social trends defied the wishful thinking of scholars looking backward to ancient large-scale kinship group.[42]

Because female identity and social roles were so closely bound up with kinship, changes in family structure and size transformed women's lives. In earliest Chinese history, women were part of large-scale kinship groups. Therefore a woman acted out many kin-based social roles simultaneously, and interaction with large numbers of distant kin defined basic aspects of her identity. But by the early empire, small kinship units had become most common. Thus a woman's interactions with her husband and his immediate family assumed prime importance. A woman's performance in the roles of wife and daughter-in-law shaped her daily life and were key factors determining how others judged her social success or failure. Although elite large-scale households of distant kin began to reemerge during the Eastern Han, relations within the immediate family continued to provide the most important female social roles.

POWER

As the importance of relations within the immediate family increased, influential thinkers began to discuss conflicts between the ideals and actual circumstances of female kin roles. Patrilineal moralists advocated a set of rules for kinship roles based on their own stringent values. Often these moral dictates differed enormously from flexible popular practices that allowed far greater individual autonomy. Increasingly important patrilineal moral systems advocated dividing authority according to social roles based on kinship and generation. Tension between these strict patrilineal ideals and pragmatic customs was nothing less than a struggle for power within the family. Female identity became one of the main battlegrounds for these debates over the privileges and duties of various kin roles.

Domestic power had already become an important topic of discussion before China's unification. Eastern Zhou thinkers advocating patrilineal values began to define the ideal female role as a submissive servitor to elder kin, particularly those of her husband's family. For example, Mencius called on women to care for their husbands' aging parents.[43] These moral dictates had practical motivations. It was clearly in the economic and social interests of a parent (father or mother) to maintain as much control over son and daughter-in-law as possible. The rhetoric of patrilineal moralists provided a high-minded rationale for the older generation to further their own interests at the expense of younger generations.

The unfortunate husband/son found himself in a no-man's-land between his wife and blood relations. Each side demanded his primary loyalty. To a large degree, distribution of domestic power was a zero-sum game. Husbands had to make stark choices between the interests of their wives and those of blood relatives. Scholars partial to patrilineal values used moral rhetoric to denigrate the wife in relation to her husband's relatives. Mencius specifically described the undutiful son as a man who cares more for his wife than his parents. Indeed, this conflict between wife and senior in-laws seems to have been a perennial weakness of the Chinese kinship system.[44] The tendency of a man to favor his wife was not easy to resist. Conventional wisdom held that "filial piety declines with (the advent of) wife and child."[45]

The tensions that Mencius alluded to continued to plague family relations during the Han. A vignette from the Eastern Han confirms that such conflicts could be extremely messy. Miao Yong lived with his three brothers. After they had all married, their wives demanded that the communal household property be divided (fig. 2.4). Miao Yong, as eldest brother, blamed himself for failing to properly instruct his sisters-in-law in family propriety and struck his own cheek in self-punishment. This act shocked his younger brothers and sisters-in-law into accepting the errors of their ways. They apologized for their temerity and the whole group supposedly lived harmoniously ever after as an extended family.[46]

This family dispute was grounded in more than just conflicting personalities.

Figure 2.4.   Brothers Establishing Separate Households. Reconstruction of a rubbing from the Wu Liang shrine, Shandong. Feng, *Jinshisuo,* **3:59–60.**

It sheds light on the conflicts between competing systems of kinship values current at the time. Miao Yong and his sisters-in-law clearly held very different views on the relative importance of various kinship roles. Miao Yong envisioned proper female roles positioned squarely within the extended patrilineal family. Not coincidentally, an extended family favored his own personal interests. As eldest male in the extended household, Miao Yong controlled a wider range of people and resources as long as his brothers stayed together. But when arguing against breaking up their extended family, Miao Yong did not mention his own interests. Instead he cloaked his pleas in the righteous rhetoric of patrilineal morals. He used dramatic self-punishment (reminiscent of female martyrdom in the name of patrilineal ideals) and Mencian-style moral rhetoric to justify his stand.

In contrast, Miao Yong's sisters-in-law had no systematic moral system to justify dividing the extended family. Their views toward kinship were motivated by self-interest and custom, not by any explicit abstract intellectual system. When confronted with Miao Yong's highly articulated moral rhetoric, they lacked recourse to an equally sophisticated ethical system that might provide a rebuttal. In this case, the force of developed patrilineal rhetoric overcame custom and female self-interest. The conflict between Miao Yong and his sisters-in-law shows the possibilities for patrilineal thought to replace pragmatic custom. Because patrilinealism developed into an elaborate moral system, it wielded considerable rhetorical power that could be brought to bear during conflicts between the interests of different kin.

Day-to-day household management was considered a female duty. Consequent authority accrued to the household's leading woman. Because household management was a vital source of female power and prestige, women vigorously competed for this duty. Sometimes mothers-in-laws and daughters-in-law struggled outright over the way the household ought to be run. The Confucian erudite Jia Yi (201–169 B.C.E.) complained about the problem of disrespectful daughters-in-law.[47] Lack of respect was a euphemism for the power struggle among women of different generations living in the same household.

The most eloquent manifestation of this conflict is embodied by the dramatic relationship between the vicious mother-in-law and her uncomplaining daughter-in-law in the moving narrative poem *The Peacock Southest Flew (Kongque dongnan fei)*.[48] The monstrous mother-in-law of the story is perpetually unsatisfied by the model conduct of her daughter-in-law, even though this gentle woman meekly accedes to her every cruel whim. Consumed by irrational hatred, the mother forces her distraught son to divorce his blameless wife. Finally the couple's torment becomes unendurable and the pair commits suicide. As in Greek tragedy, suffering brings wisdom when the old woman lives on to continually regret her malicious behavior. She realizes that her evil has brought its own punishment. Now she is alone in the world. But it is too late for her to make amends for her petty sadism.

This poem presents an implicit critique of patrilineal values, including the basic principles of Confucian social relations. Patrilinealism demands the subservience of young to old on moral grounds. The goal of this rigid hierarchy is a stable, harmonious society. But when elders obtain absolute power over the young, they are tempted to abuse it. *The Peacock Southeast Flew* does not rail against the one-sidedness of patrilinealism directly. The indictment is far more subtle. The characters in the story all fully accept the patrilineal commandments that subordinate young to old. The resulting plot resembles a social experiment. The author uses his poem to show us where patrilineal values might lead if everyone were to accept them unquestioningly. By tracing the implications of these values to their outer limits, the author shows us their destructive potential. When couched in such beautiful language and elegant style, the resulting critique is utterly devastating. While skeptics of radical patrilinealism failed to explicitly codify a competing moral system, they nevertheless used rhetorical tools such as literature to question the fundamental goodness of patrilineal ethics. Traditional customs of gender pragmatism found their most eloquent defense in the appropriately flexible and informal medium of literature.

This poem is also valuable in pointing out just how much kinship hierarchies differed from simple patriarchy. Central to the plot is the complete submission of a man to a woman; the son obeys his mother absolutely, even when her commands are mean and capricious. Their relationship shows that gender was not the only factor determining the relative status of various kinship roles. In this case, generation overrides gender in importance. In other instances, the specific social roles being enacted by two people would determine their relative power in the relationship. Instead of being imparted a singular, immutable status from her gender, a woman might play a variety of roles within the household. These roles determined not just her abstract social identity and personal sense of self, but also her relative dominance or submission in particular situations. Female gender itself was not a social role. Nor was it a social status. But specific social roles were identified with gender, influencing how society expected the people playing these roles to behave and what power they might exercise over those playing other social roles.

For example, in marriage the woman was theoretically subject to her husband's control. Superiority of husband to wife was a keystone of patrilineal rhetoric. Yet actual examples from Han life show women actively remonstrating with their husbands or openly defying them. Even the most rigid patrilinealists saw marriage as a relationship that came with duties and privileges for each spouse. Nor did the wife always move in with her husband's family; matrilocal marriage was also practiced in early imperial times. A husband marrying into his wife's family accepted a greatly restricted role. He had little if any authority over his wife and in-laws.[49]

Bloodline could also outweigh gender in apportioning relative power in marriage. Beginning in the Qin, marriage to an imperial princess was known as *shang*, meaning "to serve" or "to respect." The husband theoretically served his imperial wife due to her higher ritual status.[50] Scholars more sensitive to patrilineal ideals than the self-aggrandizement of the imperial house fervently objected to this terminology. Cosmology served as a useful rhetorical tool for criticizing the practice. According to this way of thinking, empowering the wife over husband overturned the relative positions of yin and yang, thereby bringing on chaos.[51] These protests were to no avail. The ruling family apparently believed more in the social superiority of its own members (of either gender) than in any general superiority of male social roles over those filled by women.

Not only did an imperial lady have precedence over her nonimperial spouse, but if a nonimperial woman married into the imperial line she could sometimes subsequently issue orders to her natal household. In theory, imperial marriage made her the head of the family of her birth. Of course some imperial ladies were no more than pawns in the hands of their forceful fathers and brothers. But in other cases, a woman's family would defer to her as she exercised the privileges of her exalted new role. Because she was the source of newfound wealth and power, she was certainly worthy of respect. A prime example is the Empress Ma (r. 60–79 C.E.) who ruled over the family of her birth with fearsome severity.[52] Empress Wang (71 B.C.E.–13 C.E.) forced her father to remarry his divorced former wife, the empress's mother, Lady Li.[53] The sight of a daughter giving such audacious orders to her father defied the most basic principles of patrilineal thought. But this inversion of the usual family roles would not have surprised anyone familiar with the life-and-death authority vested in the Han ruling house. When patrilinealism clashed with imperial interests, it seems that the ruling family usually won.

The power of some imperial consorts within their own families dramatically demonstrates a basic characteristic of female power and identity in early imperial China. Gender was not the only factor determining a woman's social position. The full range of social roles that she simultaneously played all influenced her prestige, abstract identity, and her power over others. Gender cannot be isolated as an abstract and independent factor in social relations; it can only be understood as one component in the many social roles that each woman simultaneously played.

MOTHERS

Motherhood was the most powerful social role available to most early imperial women. The mother's monopoly over procreation was a major source of female power, pride, and identity within the family. Ancient poetry and art extravagantly celebrated the mother (fig. 2.5). Praise of maternal kindness and compassion elevated the ideal mother to the level of sainthood. Given the terrifying dangers of childbirth, mothers did of course deserve tremendous respect for their bravery. And the horrors of infanticide show that not every mother fulfilled her maternal duties—all the more reason to praise those who did.[54]

The particular psychology cultivated by Chinese culture also influenced the bond between mother and child. Emphasis on the virtue of *bao* (reciprocity) means that one is morally obligated to love one's mother. The offspring's love and deference is not a gift freely given. This love is not simply natural or normal. It is a social obligation. One must love one's mother to repay her for all of her sacrifices. Early Chinese had no illusions about child rearing. They saw it as a difficult task. A mother's years of suffering and self-sacrifice obligated her off-

Figure 2.5.   Woman and Child. Reconstruction of a rubbing from the Wu Liang shrine, Shandong. Feng, *Jinshisuo*, 3:61.

spring to repay her with their unconditional love. The love of child for mother was therefore nothing short of a major moral obligation in the early Chinese value system.[55]

The importance of reciprocity in the bond between mother and child continues to influence Chinese morals down to the present day. Nor is it unique to China. Studies of the psychology of contemporary Japanese people find that the guilt and obligation arising from similarly intense mother–child bonds forms one of the keystones of psychological character in Japanese adults.[56] These unique social conditions form a psychology in the individual that differs significantly from that described by Freud and other classic Western psychologists. Extremely intense mother–child bonds seem to have been an ideal in early imperial China, shaping both personal psychology and group morals. When replicated in people throughout society, individual psychology took on the wider manifestation of the collective mentality underlying major social roles. A passionate devotion to the cult of motherhood has continued in China down to the present day.

Idealization of the mother gave women very practical powers within the family. Both popular custom and elite ritual upheld the authority of the mother over her children. Although some thinkers tried to bring the relationship between mother and child into the fold of patrilineal ethics by giving grown sons authority over their mothers, evidence suggests that in actual practice a grown son was more likely to defer to his mother. Historical annals relate examples of powerful mothers giving orders to obedient sons.[57] Nor was a grown son's obedience conditional on a mother's kindness or wisdom. *The Peacock Southeast Flew* depicts a cruel and foolish mother whose son nevertheless honors her with absolute obedience. The son in this fictional narrative clearly represents the moral ideal of a filial son. It is his duty to humor all of his mother's whims, regardless of whether she is right or wrong, good or evil. A Han incised stone makes the point most concretely (fig. 2.6). This work depicts an elderly woman preparing to beat her cowering grown son with a cane. Being an ideal filial son, he worries that his frail mother might injure herself as she exerts herself hitting him.

Even patrilineal thought usually favored mother over son. Although patrilineal ideals generally emphasized male prerogatives over those of women within the same generation, these thinkers stressed generation over gender when determining the relative importance of different social hierarchies. Because mothers are elder kin, their children ought to obey them. *Records of Ritual (Liji)* instructs, "When the father is dead, and the mother still alive, the eldest son should wait upon her at meals."[58] Even after her death, a son still owed his mother veneration. A particularly extreme example, doubtless more hopeful ideal than common practice, was the behavior of Ding Lan. This filial son had a wooden statue of his deceased mother made. An incised stone shows this paragon of filiality abasing himself before this wooden idol, worshipping his dead mother almost as

Figure 2.6. An Elderly Woman Beats Her Grown Son with Her Cane. Reconstruction of a rubbing from the Wu Liang shrine, Shandong. Feng, *Jinshisuo***, 3:57.**

a deity (fig. 2.7). This depiction of the ideal son shows an almost unbelievable extreme of filial love. The feelings that the perfect son felt toward his mother ought to border on idolatry.

In this respect, women of the Han seem to have faced quite different conditions than their sisters in later ages. For example, Song dynasty women were commonly seen as better off when young than old. Younger women had fathers and strong brothers to protect their interests. But an elderly widow was seen as having little authority over her sons and grandsons.[59] Female authority over sons seems to have declined markedly over time. The Han dynasty was perhaps the peak of maternal power in China.

This vision of the mother's power over her sons did not go uncontested. Advocates of patrilineal values put forward alternate interpretations of this key relationship. They often tried to portray an ideal mother/child relationship that would support their larger program of strengthening patrilineal kinship relations. For this reason, they emphasized the mother's duty to sacrifice herself for the sake of her sons rather than the son's duty to obey his mother. Many examples of this portrayal can be found in Liu Xiang's *Biographies of Women*. This work

Figure 2.7. Ding Lan Venerating a Wooden Statue of His Deceased Mother. Reconstruction of a rubbing from the Wu Liang shrine, Shandong. Feng, *Jinshisuo*, 3:24–25.

features many heart-rending encomia to mothers. Yet the mothers he singles out for praise are usually those who sacrificed themselves for the benefit of men. The most admirable paragons of maternal love are women such as Mencius's mother, who slaved away unselfishly at her loom to raise an educated, moral, successful son. This interpretation of the maternal role downplays female power over sons and emphasizes the obligation of women to sacrifice their own interests and nurture male kin. To this way of thinking, a woman is worthy of praise if she upholds male interests.

Despite the aspects of patrilineal values that might use a mother's sense of duty to depress female status, mothers could nevertheless exploit patrilineal values for their own benefit. Patrilineal thinkers usually admitted that generational seniority was more important than gender in determining a woman's relative standing in the family. The major social roles of mother and son took precedence over the more abstract categories male and female. Mothers of the Han dynasty benefited from this patrilineal hierarchy based on generational rank. The ideal of generationalism demanded that women be shown respect when they assumed the roles of mother or mother-in-law. In light of this belief, patrilineal rhetoric cannot be dismissed as merely a system for the containment and oppression of women. Early Chinese gender thought was far more subtle and complex. In many instances, patrilineal thought provided persuasive justifications for the exercise of female power.

3

Wealth and Work

A job is more than just something we do. In society's eyes, a job is also who we are. Social roles order work and earnings in standard ways. These work roles have profound implications for both individual and society. Economic roles condition thoughts and values, shape experience, and establish basic identities that society uses to view a person and the person uses to view herself. Work and wealth are two of the most fundamental building blocks of social relations. They also provided important and valuable social roles to early Chinese women.

Work is traditionally a major point of division between the sexes. In the simplest societies, most work roles are apportioned according to gender. Nor are the various economic roles usually equal. Society assigns varying degrees of prestige to different occupations. In capitalist society, prestige usually relates directly to productivity and earnings. But in a primarily agricultural society such as early imperial China, productivity and prestige sometimes diverged notably. Regardless of how work roles were related to status, differences in work and wealth invariably translated directly into fundamental social distinctions. As society became increasingly stratified, economic differences became the basis of power relations.

Economic roles had a complex impact on female identity in early China. In some cases, male monopolies on important work roles encroached on female autonomy. Forced to depend on men for many of the necessities of life, a woman would have no choice but to acquiesce to certain male demands. The custom of patrilocal marriage, in which a wife took up residence in her husband's household, exacerbated this inequality. The family was more than just a unit of kinship. It also served as the primary economic unit of early imperial society. Dependent on her new relatives for the basic means to survive, an unlucky woman might find herself at the mercy of cruel in-laws.

However, it would be distorting to equate male work roles with privilege and female roles with submission. Within the household, the sexes lived in economic

59

interdependence. Much of the work within the family was divided into male and female tasks. For the household to succeed as an economic organization, both female and male work roles had to be filled. A man supplied the family with grain, a woman with clothing. Men plowed, women carried water. Men harvested, women cooked. Men fought wars, women reared the children who would care for their aged parents. Some male roles may have been especially prestigious, but the roles of both women and men were equally necessary. Hence both were accorded due respect.

Nor were these roles easily interchangeable. Some skills such as textile production took years of expertise to master. A man would find it impossible to suddenly pick up spindle and distaff and begin making his own clothes. Men depended on women just as much as women depended on men. Neither could prosper or even survive in a degree of comfort without the other. In other words, marriage was an economic partnership. The ideal work roles of husband and wife may have differed, but both were equally necessary if either partner was to have a successful life. Under such conditions, female work roles were an important source of power and prestige for women.

WEALTH

The conflict between individual and group interests in financial matters had profound implications for women's lives. Patrilineal moralists advocated a return to the ancient multigenerational household in which distant kin pooled their wealth. Although large families were not the norm during the Qin and early Western Han, partisans of patrilineal values continued to push for a revival of the ancient ideal of communal property ownership.

It is important to remember that communality does not require equality for all members of a household. Contemporary sociology shows that people living under the same roof can have very different standards of living. In many societies with communal multigeneration households, male needs and desires end up taking precedence over those of women.[1] Similarly, patrilinealists tried to restrict women from accumulating private property. The ritual canon, a rhetorical stronghold of patrilineal thought, is clear on this point.

> If anyone give the wife an article of food or dress, or piece of cloth or silk, a handkerchief for her girdle, an iris or orchid, she should receive and offer it to her parents-in-law. . . . If they return it to her, she should decline it, and if they do not allow

her to do so, she will take it as if it were a second gift, and lay it by to wait till they may want it.[2]

This vision of a woman demurely refusing to claim even the most humble object as her own might seem to be a clear example of male dominance. But economic roles in the household were not just divided along gender lines. Generational rank was more important than sex in this regard. In the multigenerational household of the patrilineal utopia, children were completely subject to the economic control of their parents. Ritual specialists alleged that Confucius commanded, "While his parents are alive, a son should not dare to consider his wealth as his own."[3] This provision would clearly benefit elder women as well as men. Parents (including the mother) were to be caretakers for all communal household goods and property. Literal interpretation of this injunction would give widows complete control over household property. Patrilineal ideals did not simply raise male status at the expense of women. The effects were far more complex. In general, the identities and powers of senior women in the household were exalted and those of junior women depressed.

However stridently patrilinealists advocated this vision of communal property, we should not forget that these were simply the ideals of one small elite group. Actual social conditions were extremely diverse. Female control over personal and kin wealth varied greatly according to time, place, social stratum, and individual circumstance. The clearest evidence concerns the highly privileged. Many elite women seem to have exercised considerable control over their personal finances. This power may simply have been an outgrowth of their powerful social roles. For example, it seems that elite women of late imperial China had more opportunities to make decisions concerning personal and property matters than their poorer counterparts.[4] High social standing seems to have presented elite women of the early imperial era with similar opportunities.

Even before China's unification, a ruler would regularly grant his wife and mother huge tracts of land to furnish them with personal income.[5] The wealth of titled ladies increased during the imperial era as central government resources expanded under a united empire. Emperor Wu lavished fantastic amounts of money, farmland, slaves, and an opulent mansion on his beloved elder sister.[6] Other Han accounts speak of evil officials so tyrannical that they dared to seize the personal lands or goods of princesses.[7] Titled ladies clearly owned large amounts of property in their own name.

Ordinary women also had significant economic powers. Under certain circumstances a woman might control family property while her husband was still alive. A story from the Eastern Han tells of a shiftless gambler named Xu Sheng whose wife, Rong, took control of the family property so that she could support her mother-in-law.[8] This morality tale of an industrious woman demonstrates a pragmatic side to household management. In the absence of effective male leadership, a woman was expected to step in and assume control of the household. Rong was lauded for taking over the family property and assuming responsibility for household finances. Indeed, her conduct was considered exemplary. But this tale also reveals some ambivalence toward female leadership in the home. Notably, both the husband's worthlessness and the virtue of filial piety were invoked to justify a woman's usurpation of household leadership. It was clearly an unusual and awkward situation for a wife to manage household property while her husband was still alive and well. Under normal circumstances the husband took the lead in running family finances. When no competent man was available, a woman was expected to step into the breach. In other words, when no man could play stereotypical male social roles within the household, it was considered acceptable and even admirable for a woman to take on the part. The reputation of the paragon Ban Zhao, for example, was largely attributable to her admirable success in the roles of surrogate son and brother.[9]

There was a legal basis for female property ownership. According to Qin law, the wife of an official was not liable for her deceased husband's debts. This limitation of female liability implies that husband and wife were separate financial entities owning separate estates.[10] Han jurists respected this Qin precedent. One first century C.E. official feigned litigation over land with his widowed sister-in-law as an excuse for escaping the burden of unwanted government service.[11] Obviously a woman could not contest male ownership of land unless she could legally own it herself. Early imperial women clearly had legal grounds for owning and inheriting property.

The Han taxation system also treated women as economically autonomous individuals. A foundation of Han fiscal policy was the poll tax. Significantly, regardless of the prevailing rate at any given moment, the tax applied to both sexes. The tax rate for women varied according to age. As part of a government scheme to encourage the marriage of all eligible young women, unmarried women aged fifteen to thirty were liable to be taxed at six times the usual rate.[12] Perhaps to make up for the burden of sextuple taxes levied on some women, the government periodically ordered a remission of the poll tax for up to three years after the birth of a child and the grant of an additional postnatal grain allowance.[13] The taxation of women implies that they had personal property and income.

A wife's dowry was the core of her personal wealth. According to ritual texts, dowry was unnecessary. In theory only the betrothal gift or "bride price" (pin) given by the groom's family to that of the bride was necessary for a proper elite marriage ceremony.[14] Han ritual texts do not even mention dowry. Yet it seems that popular custom was at odds with ritual ideals. In common practice, dowry (*ji*) was considered more important than bride price during the Han.[15] The reasoning behind this custom can be seen in documents from later eras, when writers admitted that generously dowering a daughter had practical motivations. A daughter who received significant property from her parents was more likely to help support them in old age if their sons died young or proved incompetent. The custom of large dowries was also a compassionate custom. A wife with her own wealth would surely have higher status in her husband's family.[16] During the Han, popular marriage rites featured a gift of bride and dowry by the wife's family to the groom's family in exchange for the bride price. Whereas in later eras, such as the Song, the bride price generally exceeded dowries, during the Han the families of both bride and groom seem to have exchanged these gifts lavishly.[17] The importance of dowries during the Han is a particular characteristic of marriage and female property ownership during that era and distinguishes it from later times. The relative lavishness of Han dowries made many women independent property owners and surely raised their status in the eyes of others.

Early law and custom seem to have concurred that a wife owned her dowry. Although Qin statutes specified that the husband was manager of household property, it also held that if a wife accused her husband in court and the state subsequently confiscated his goods, she could keep items from her dowry such as slaves, clothing, and personal effects.[18] Qin law also held that a wife who committed a crime forfeited her dowry to her husband.[19] Both the ritual canon and Han law concurred that a husband divorcing his wife had to return her dowry.[20] These laws all implied that a wife owned her dowry. Moreover, in later eras it was customary for a woman to control her dowry, suggesting continuity with early imperial practices.[21]

So contrary to the patrilineal ideals of the ritual canon, women indeed owned property. A woman's ownership of private property, particularly her dowry, would have given her important powers. Personal wealth would raise a woman's status in the family. And should a woman decide that her marriage was unendurable, her dowry might allow her sufficient means to seek a divorce and begin a new life.

The mechanism of inheritance reveals more details about female property rights. Local custom traditionally determined inheritance. However, the government began to regulate inheritance as part of the general expansion of legal jurisdictions in the early empire. Under Qin law, buildings, livestock, slaves, woodlands, clothing, and personal articles could be inherited. Property was to be passed on to one's children; heirs living with the father at the time of his death were given priority as a reward for their filiality.[22] While evidence suggests that a husband was automatically his wife's heir, the incomplete surviving Qin laws fail to mention any claim of a wife to inherit her husband's possessions.[23] Under this arrangement, a widow would depend entirely on her children for support. However, it is doubtful that this official legal framework could supplant deeply rooted local inheritance customs. As for the Han, official inheritance procedures remained basically faithful to Qin precedents. Lacking the concept of primogeniture for property, the estate was to be divided equally among sons.[24]

Actual practices differed from this officially sanctioned model of inheritance. Some women inherited property from their husbands. This legacy was sometimes quite large.[25] Perhaps the most fabulously wealthy nontitled woman of the early empire was the widow Qing of Ba. She was one of a number of tycoons who took advantage of the new imperial economy's increasing complexity to amass enormous wealth. After her husband's death, Qing assumed management of the family's extensive cinnabar mines. Her shrewd business acumen allowed her to build up a fortune of legendary proportions.[26]

Archaeologists have unearthed a Han will written on strips of bamboo that is particularly informative about female property rights.[27] This remarkable document was dictated by an unnamed elderly woman from a household of modest means as her eldest son lay on his deathbed. This woman obviously wanted to draw up a will to ensure that there would be no disagreements over landownership among her numerous children after her eldest son's death. Surprisingly, the dying son did not dictate his own will. Nor did his other male siblings decide on the disposition of household property. Instead, the dying man's mother dictated his will, carefully dividing landownership and temporary rights of usage among the children she had borne by three husbands.

This old woman had clearly assumed the role of head of household. Although she may not have owned the title to her dying son's land, she controlled its bequest. As this valuable document eloquently attests, a woman could sometimes assume broad powers over family property. A woman could do more than just own property herself. If she assumed the role of household elder, she could control the disposition of many household assets, including the property of her offspring. This old woman exercised broad discretionary powers as she divided up her son's property. Apparently she loved all her children equally and gave much of her dying son's lands to his stepsiblings instead of to his siblings of the same surname, as patrilineal ideals demanded. Instead of trying to keep the dying son's property within his father's bloodline, she was concerned with ensuring that all of her children would have a decent livelihood. This case shows that the fear that women might disperse property outside the direct male line was well founded. For this reason, men throughout imperial history hesitated to give women authority over family property.[28]

HOUSEHOLD LABOR

In early China, work roles were ideally apportioned according to gender. Women were usually expected to work inside the home and men outside.[29] Men plowed and women wove. Why were so many work roles divided along gender lines? Anthropologists look to a variety of factors to explain why women take part in some of a society's basic economic activities but not others. A primary reason may be the compatibility of a given type of work with simultaneous child care: close to home, requiring less concentration (hence monotonous), less dangerous, and can be frequently interrupted without impeding progress.[30] Such an explanation would account for the basic division of early Chinese work roles between male-dominated agriculture and female textile production. Regardless of the causes, many jobs became associated with gender extremely early in Chinese history. Some elite thinkers tried to use this tendency toward division of labor by sex to impose taboos on interaction between women and men. They also tried to imbue gendered work roles with the force of moral necessity. They wanted readers to see these gendered work roles as not just customary, but as right and proper. However, economic necessity inexorably drove women and men together in the workplace.[31] Strictly confining women to a narrow range of tasks could not survive the pull toward greater economic efficiency that encouraged many wives to share their husband's profession.[32] Nor could it overcome the practical realities of life on the farm, where all family members had to pitch in to do whatever needed to be done.

The amount of time a woman had to spend working and the work she performed depended largely on her economic status. Wealthy women delegated drudgery to their servants. They could choose which work to do and limited their efforts to stereotypically feminine labor such as textile production and some housework. By strictly confining their labor to female work roles, they lived in accordance with gender ideals and claimed a measure of personal virtue. Even in many ordinary households, senior women could assign the hardest labor to low-ranking women. For most women, however, long days filled with hard work were an inescapable necessity.

The home was the center of female labor. Growing out of the wife's role as primary child care provider, she also took on most household chores. Cooking

must have consumed a good portion of a woman's day. Although men are occasionally mentioned cooking for themselves, the bulk of references in early texts
indicate that cooking was usually a female duty.[33] Since modern conveniences
were lacking, cooking the cuisine of early China was toilsome (figs. 3.1–3.3).
The cook had to slaughter animals, cut up kindling and firewood, fan up a fire
in the hearth, and carry heavy loads of water from the nearest potable source.
Complex and flavorful sauces had to be prepared to complement the proper meal.
The brewing of alcohol (a standard accompaniment to meals and also a necessity
for sacrificial ritual) was often a female preserve. Whole kernels of tough grains
such as millet could only be rendered edible through a toilsome process considered women's work. Before being cooked, grain had to be laboriously pounded,
boiled, sifted, trodden, and soaked. Considering that tough grains constituted
the staple of most people's simple diet, this drudgery was a continuous burden.[34]
Women were also ideally expected to serve and remove the food and then wash
the cooking and eating utensils.[35]

As for other housework, a wife could be expected to straighten up the bed-
dings, brush the pillows and mats, and sweep the floor.[36] Women also washed
the family's clothes. A terra-cotta Han figure from Sichuan represents a woman
carrying a pestle for pounding clothes to remove the dirt—a tedious necessary
in a time before soap.[37] In addition, according to ritual specialists a dutiful wife
or daughter ought to wait on a man during his intricate toilet, which involved
combing and binding up his proudly coiffed hair, and attending him during ritually significant bathing rites.[38] In sum, most household tasks were normally considered female duties.

**Figure 3.1.   Women Slaughtering Chickens. Painted wall brick from a Jiayuguan,
Gansu, tomb, dated to either the very late Eastern Han or Wei/Jin period. Gansu Sheng
Wenwudui, ed., *Jiayuguan bihuamu fajue baogao* (Beijing: Wenwu, 1985), pl. 68, no. 3.**

Figure 3.2.   Cooking on a Stove. Incised stone. Sun Ji, *Handai wuzhi wenhua ziliao tushuo* (Beijing: Wenwu, 1991), fig. 85.6.

AGRICULTURE: FIELD WORK AND TEXTILES

Agriculture was the basis of the early Chinese economy. Many early texts describe farming as a male occupation. Although men had primary responsibility for the crops, women helped out when necessary. On occasion women plowed, sowed, weeded, and harvested.[39] Women's agricultural roles were even acted out in ritual. Whereas elite ritual generally tried to reinforce patrilineal ideals by emphasizing clear-cut gendered work roles, other popular and court rites tacitly acknowledged female agricultural labor. For example, one Han spring festival was celebrated with the model of a clay female figurine holding a hoe.[40] And by the third century the empress and imperial consorts were a major presence in state agricultural ceremonies.[41]

Women's involvement in agriculture probably increased during the Han due to the popularization of the pit-farming method. This innovative cultivation technique, described in the first century B.C.E. agricultural treatise *Writings of Fan Shengzhi* (*Fan Shengzhi shu*), required tillers to concentrate labor and fertilizer

Figure 3.3.   Cooking in a Bronze Vessel. Incised stone. Sun, *Handai wuzhi wenhua ziliao tushuo*, fig. 85.12.

within shallow, small, square pits instead of on conventional ridges and furrows. High concentration of resources made this method especially effective in raising yields from marginal lands, thereby bringing greatest benefit to the poorest households. But because the pits were too small to use animals or large equipment, it was vital for all members of the household to participate in intensively cultivating these pits if this technique were to succeed.[42] Wherever this method of farming was employed, women's participation in agriculture became a necessity.

Many early writers paired the supposedly masculine activity of field work with the female task of textile production.[43] Because this juxtaposition was so ubiquitous, field work and textile manufacture assumed cultural meaning as more than just labor roles. These routine daily activities became ways to act out male and female identity. To early Chinese, womanhood was not just an abstract passive identity. A person became a true, complete, and successful woman by actualizing the major female roles that society expected of her. A woman weaving at her loom was doing far more than just producing valuable cloth. She was also acting

out a gendered role that contributed to her overall social identity. Spinning, sewing, weaving, and dyeing were all ways of *being* a woman.

Ancient rhetoric routinely contrasted the male field work with female cloth
making. The two were considered parallel, and came to symbolize the difference
between men and women. But as Patricia Ebrey has pointed out, we should
remember that cloth making was not yet regarded as an independent craft or
industry.[44] Generally speaking, cloth making was still considered an agricultural
activity. Hemp and silk, the raw materials for most clothing, were usually grown
on the family's lands. Making cloth was a way of processing these agricultural
products. The stereotype of male field work and female textile making engen-
dered the two major aspects of early agriculture.

Although the traditional association of field work exclusively with men was
overstated, stereotypes seem to have been fairly accurate in identifying textiles
as female labor. Women dominated all aspects of textile work in early China to
the extent that in many contexts this manufacture became synonymous with
"women's work."[45] Matter-of-fact images of women from early textual works and
archeology depict them involved with every facet of the production process: har-
vesting mulberry leaves, spinning, weaving, soaking cloth, dyeing, and sewing.[46]
Qin administrators judged the productive capacity of the average woman to be
less than that of a man with the sole exception of textile production. According
to Qin law, the work expected from one male bondservant artisan was divided
between two adult women or five girls. But for the highly skilled and traditionally
female work of embroidery, a woman's labor was considered equal to the output
of a man.[47]

A monopoly on cloth manufacture gave women a powerful role in the early
economy. In fact, from an economic perspective "women's work" was a far more
sophisticated activity than the stereotypically male work of subsistence agriculture. In most societies, industry begins with textiles. By the Eastern Zhou, China
already had a thriving cash market for textiles. These valuable products of female
labor made up approximately half the value of a household's output.[48] Quite simply, textiles were the most important manufactured product of the early Chinese
economy. Cloth was exchanged as a de facto currency and used to pay taxes.
During the Han, textiles were the focus of sophisticated commercial transactions. Surviving contracts show that clothing could be purchased on credit.[49]
These documents show the emergence of a complex sales and distribution system
around this product of female industry. The government did not fail to recognize
the economic importance of female cloth production. In 10 c.e. officials regis-
tered all female cloth makers. This close monitoring shows that the government
considered these women a prized economic force.[50]

Although the state ran some textile workshops, the bulk of the industry remained under private management.[51] On the simplest level, the women of many households produced extra cloth to trade for other goods.[52] Cloth making thereby allowed ordinary people a way to acquire manufactured goods. When practiced on a larger scale, cloth production could be a route to prosperity. Zhang Anshi (mid-first century B.C.E.) amassed part of his wealth from his wife's weaving.[53] Even as the economy changed during the Eastern Han and large estates began to emerge as the focus of production, female cloth production continued to be a staple industry of the manorial economy.[54]

Just because women produced cloth does not mean that they controlled the profits of their labor. Generally speaking, the smaller the scale of production, the greater control women had over the fruits of their output. Women had greatest personal autonomy in household production. Divorced, widowed, and some unmarried women controlled the profits they earned from spinning and weaving. Some women made cloth full time to earn a living. Biographies describe unmarried women who supported themselves by producing cloth.[55] This was one of the only opportunities for female self-sufficiency in an economy that provided most people with relatively few opportunities.

Women sometimes formed groups that would come together for communal spinning and weaving. Many women of early times seem to have worked long hours. Housework and child care, together with long hours in the fields or marketplace, must have consumed the daylight hours of most women. Accounts of women weaving together usually speak of them working after dark or in winter, the slow season for field work.

> In the winter . . . the women when dwelling in the same lanes did their spinning together at nights. Women's work for one moon was calculated at forty-five days (that is, two evening's work being counted as one day's labor). They were required to work in groups, and thereby economize on the expense of light and heat.[56]

In a society dominated by the family, a patrilineal institution, female textile production groups would have been a rare instance of a nonkin organization run by women for their own benefit. The immediate reason for forming such groups was practical. By coming together, they would save money on candles, lamp oil, and heat. In addition to these material considerations, working together would lighten their toil by giving women the chance to chat with friends and neighbors. Cloth was woven, information and opinions exchanged, and a network of supportive friendships strengthened.

Membership in this sort of group carried substantial benefits. Although intangible, the social support of an economically significant group was perhaps the most important advantage of group solidarity. Research on modern Chinese female support groups shows how membership could be considered some of the most useful "property" a person might possess. By sharing resources, the group was a source of mutual strength, protection, and security. Members in a mutual support group could pool resources then draw on them as needed. In this way, the group might function like a "support bank."[57] Founding such groups allowed Han dynasty women to improve themselves through group action.

These groups empowered members not just by solidarity but also by their exclusivity. Evening work was costly because of the need for candles and oil to provide light. By splitting costs, neighborhood associations of weaving women were so important that exclusion from the group could mean dire hardship. In one moving story told during the Han, a woman named Xuwu was too poor to contribute any candles to the weaving group. One unsympathetic group member wanted to bar her from sharing their light, but Xuwu's pleading convinced them to let her stay.[58] A similar tale relates how another poor woman worked out an arrangement whereby she would sweep the other women's rooms and look after their mats in exchange for being allowed to share the group's candlelight.[59] These stories show that by pooling resources, groups of women could come together to create a significant economic organization. Poor women struggled to gain membership in a group that could give them substantial benefits.

Confining the investigation of female cloth manufacture to economic or social factors neglects an important aspect to this activity. Because textile making was regularly paired with field work as the two major economic roles that allowed participants to act out gender differences, cloth production was elevated into a profoundly moral activity. Making cloth was not just a necessity. The woman who made cloth was praised as a good person because she fulfilled the social role expected of her gender. Classical philosophers such as Mencius praised female sericulture as a moral imperative, noting that only if women tend silkworms can the aged be respectfully cared for by providing them with silk.[60] By making textiles, a woman not only helped provide for her family but also assumed a normative social role that confirmed her own femininity—both of which were highly virtuous acts. As a result of this reasoning, textile making was usually portrayed as a highly moral female activity. The good woman spun and wove even when not compelled by economic necessity.

For example, ancient palace ladies were ideally expected to make cloth and sew court robes. The utopian royal bureaucracy advocated by the *Rites of Zhou* (*Zhouli*), a text probably redacted in the Western Han, included officials to oversee the manufacture of silk and hemp cloth, embroidery, dyeing, and tailoring by palace ladies. The quality and quantity of the production of each concubine and female servant in the palace were to be carefully checked, with the finished goods presented to the king and queen and subsequently stored for later use.[61] This text describes an ideal court. In this perfect world, royal ladies produce cloth even though they do not have to work. Their motivation is moral, not practical. Cloth making was yet another female role, and a particularly admirable one. By assuming this role, the palace lady publicly proved her virtue. In a utopia of early Chinese imagining, even the highest-ranking women worked at making textiles. The meaning of this work was social and moral rather than economic. They labored at this task not for the economic value of their output, but simply to be good women.

In many instances, the ideals of elite thinkers seem to have had little impact on society. But the moralization of textile manufacture gained many important believers. For example the Empress Ma, famed for her virtue, often enjoyed visiting the palace "weaving house" to watch women industriously raising silkworms and weaving.[62] It was not enough for Empress Ma to just passively *be* a woman. She wanted to actively assume the role of a woman. By purposely acting as the good woman was expected to act and devoting herself to the stereotypical female activity of sericulture, she garnered praise. Empress Ma employed the labor roles associated with her gender to gain prestige. The Han annals praise her as a moral exemplar. Manipulating the social role of virtuous weaver was a useful strategy that could help even an empress to achieve social success. Art of the period reflects these ideals. A stone carving of a woman working at her loom shows her sporting a broad smile (fig. 3.4). She enjoys her labor because she is happy to be doing something so good.

TRADE

Women of early times had ample opportunities to exercise their business acumen. And the rewards for both women and men in trade could be enormous. As one Han proverb enviously put it, "To prick embroidery does not pay as much as leaning upon a market-door."[63] It seems that women were a common sight in the marketplace. They were involved in selling everything from basic foodstuffs to luxuries such as silks and pearls.[64]

A Han legal document sheds some light on female roles in commerce. This text records a suit brought by a military commander and part-time merchant named Li Fa against his employee Kou En. Li hired Kou to transport a load of fish to a different area and sell them. Li then had his wife, named Ye, travel a

Figure 3.4. Smiling Weaver. Rubbing of an incised stone unearthed near Chengdu, Sichuan. Lim, *Stories from China's Past*, pl. 12.

considerable distance by cart to pick up the money Kou was expected to earn from the sale. However, upon her arrival Ye found that Kou had been unable to sell the fish for the promised price. Kou loaded items of his own property onto the cart as partial payment of his obligation and returned home with Ye to settle the dispute with Li Fa.[65]

This document matter-of-factly describes a woman responsible for an important business transaction. She exercised significant discretionary power in trying to solve an unexpected problem. Originally Ye merely intended to pick up a large amount of cash and take it back home safely. But when Kou failed to obtain the expected price for the fish, she had to deal with the unexpected setback. She managed to return home with the debtor Kou and some of his property to help repay his debt. Ye showed herself to be an important, trusted, and competent partner in family business dealings.

Moralists of the time viewed the merchant as a parasite who cheats the inno-
cent consumer by increasing the prices of goods without adding any value to
them. Resentment against both female merchants and their male counterparts
boiled over in verse. "Male and female vendors, selling cheap, / . . . The sons and
daughters of these merchants / Were more beautifully garbed than the [wealthy
consort families] Xu or Shi." "Shopgirls were dressed more lavishly than [the
noble] ladies Ji or Jiang."[66] Envious landlords used moralistic language to criticize
wealthy female mercantile upstarts who flaunted their prosperity with parvenu
gaudiness. Yet criticisms of female merchants did not emphasize their gender,
only their economic role. The female merchant was a moral counterpoint to the
weaver woman. Producing textiles confirmed a woman as a normative female,
hence virtuous. In contrast, a woman in commerce failed to enact the normative
social roles associated with her gender identity. Virtuous labor roles were closely
associated with both gender and agriculture. But work as a merchant lay completely outside the traditional scope of both gender and labor. By departing from
gendered work norms, both female and male merchants became equally disrepu-
table in the eyes of the landed elite.

SERVICES

The service economy provided women with some additional economic opportunities. Of course the early Chinese economy was still fairly simple. Most people
struggled to produce the bare necessities of life. Accordingly, the vital economic
roles most tied to gender identity involved the production of goods, not services.

In a time of primitive transportation technology, human muscle power was
still an important way for moving people and goods. Some women transported
people by pulling hand carriages or poling ferries.[67] As for goods, women drove
carts, carried things in baskets perched on the head (fig. 3.5), and moved things
by clutching them under the arm.[68] This toil was very important work. In an age
of slow and laborious transport, carrying goods in baskets and jars from place to
place performed an invaluable service. Simply by transporting basic goods,
women played a vital part in the flow of necessities, wealth, and information
throughout the empire.

Women were usually exempt from mandatory government corvée labor, one
of the most unpleasant duties shouldered by men. However, extraordinary circumstances could force the government to draft women into corvée service. For
example, in 192 B.C.E. 146,000 men and women served for thirty days building
the city wall of the new Han capital.[69] But those were unusual times when an

Figure 3.5. Carrying a Jar on the Head. Female figurine unearthed at Jinqueshan, Shandong. Sun, *Handai wuzhi wenhua ziliao tushuo*, fig. 30.12.

unstable new dynasty required an unusually large pool of labor to rapidly complete its basic infrastructure. Under normal circumstances, only women condemned as bondservants worked for the state in capacities such as transporting grain, raising domestic animals in imperial parks, and working in various government offices.[70]

Other service jobs performed by women required considerable training. Shamanistic magic was a respected yet feared skill practiced by some women.[71] The shamans (*wu*) of antiquity seem to have been local sorcerers, diviners, and healers who served as the informal clergy of an ecstatic folk religion. Many *wu* were women. Popular religion provided opportunities to women that the state and ancestral cults lacked. Formal religion and ritual absorbed a great deal of patriarchal rhetoric, limiting female participation. But popular cults seem to have maintained a high degree of primitive sexual egalitarianism.

One of the principal duties of the *wu* was healing, a power shared with shamans in many other societies such as the peoples of central and north Asia.[72] Early Chinese believed that some diseases were caused by demonic possession. The healer had to use magic to expel malevolent demons and return the patient

Figure 3.6. Acupuncture. Painted stone from Liangchengshan, Weishan, Shandong. Sun, *Handai wuzhi wenhua ziliao tushuo*, fig. 75.13.

Figure 3.7. Acrobat. Incised stone unearthed in Peng County, Sichuan. Sun, *Handai wuzhi wenhua ziliao tushuo*, fig. 98.10.

Figure 3.8.   Bronze Lamp in the Shape of a Female Servant. Unearthed at Mancheng tomb no. 2. Sun, *Handai wuzhi wenhua ziliao tushuo*, fig. 89.5.

to health. Han records cite examples of *wu* curing disease through incantation.[73] One Han medical text includes a medical incantation invoking the awesome name of the "shamaness mistress" (*wufu*) to scare away the demon possessing a sick child.[74] This wording suggests that women shamans were commonly involved in the ritual exorcism of disease.

A more reliable tradition of herbal medicine and acupuncture existed side by side with shamanistic healing practices (fig. 3.6). Many of the nonshaman healers named in early sources were female as well. It is not surprising that some of China's earliest physicians were women. Most prescriptions consisted of herbs and foods. The timeless role of women as gatherers of wild plants would have made them the obvious repositories of folk medical lore.[75] Some women who specialized in medical knowledge were highly sought-after as physicians.[76] For instance, Qin legal records mention a female bondservant who specialized in gynecology, while Han records speak of female physicians to the empresses.[77]

According to herbal wisdom, food has medical value. Unlike the division in Western science between food and medicine, the Chinese have long seen proper diet as a way of preventing and treating illness. Even today, when most Chinese people become sick they immediately alter their diet. Early medical theory held that each of the five flavors of food has a particular therapeutic value. Proper combinations of these flavors could benefit the sick. *Rites of Zhou* describes a "culinary medicine" office in royal government in charge of harmonizing the royal diet for medical purposes.[78] This link between food and medicine would have lent women added respect as healers, considering their daily experience with meal preparation.

Besides healing, women served in a variety of other minor service occupations. Some entertainers such as musicians and acrobats were women (fig. 3.7). Other women displayed skill in the murky art of physiognomy. They claimed to be able to foretell a person's fate by reading the placement of physical features.[79] A lactating woman might earn her keep as a wet nurse for the rich.[80] Still other women worked as domestic servants or household slaves. The estates of the wealthy required a huge staff that invariably included many female servants (fig. 3.8).[81] And most slave women seem to have worked in service occupations, primarily as domestic servants and entertainers.[82] Finally, circumstances compelled some women to earn their livelihood through prostitution.[83]

4
Law

Law and administrative regulations became increasingly important with the advent of centralized imperial government. Before China's unification under the Qin, people of the Zhou states lived with a chaotic patchwork of local custom and law. A mature legal system emerged during the Qin dynasty and continued with modifications through the Han. These collections of statutes and precedents were no overnight creation. The legal edifice of the early empire was constructed atop values and procedures first articulated by the rulers of ancient states. Gradually this system evolved into a comprehensive and well-organized legal apparatus. Although only a small portion of this legal code survives, documents unearthed from Han tombs provide a glimpse of this sophisticated legal system. Ongoing archaeological work promises future revelations that might significantly alter our view of women under early Chinese law.

The social function of law is largely a matter of interpretation. And the interpretation of society is often ideological, not empirical. There are two main views of how law functions in society. Conservatives stress the positive contributions of law. They see law as a highly rational institution that smoothes cooperation among individuals and fosters social stability. Predictable rewards and punishments benefit everyone. According to this optimistic point of view, the regularity and stability of a systematic legal code is synonymous with justice. In contrast, progressive theorists emphasize the law's restrictive nature. Law is a tool that allows a small political elite to control large numbers of people. And social controls bring the most benefits to the elite who legislates and enforces them. To this way of thinking, the law reinforces social inequality in the name of justice.

Neither of these views is exclusively correct, nor are they necessarily mutually exclusive. Both the positive and restrictive social functions of law affected women of early imperial China. On the positive side, laws against sexual violence and the enslavement of free women benefited female interests. And the prosecution of robbery and murder brought advantages to everyone, regardless of gender. However, in other respects the law limited the social roles of women by enforcing patriarchal ethics in the name of justice. More abstractly, law became a way for the social elite to coerce others to accept their own ideals of womanhood. Many early laws contain explicit interpretations of what a woman is and how she should act. Law was therefore an important means for defining and enforcing ideal female roles. It also provided a way to punish people who held alternate views of which social roles women ought to play.

Debate over abstract concepts such as the law's social functions should not obscure the conscious intent of jurists who framed the laws. Fear of chaos was the major motivation for those who wrote and enforced the law. Whereas modern Western law was often written in reaction to authoritarianism, early Chinese law was more often a reaction against anarchy. Early Chinese administrators strove to create a system of law that would encourage social stability. By outlawing violent crime and theft, enforcing wills and contracts, and taking steps to shore up certain kinship values, Qin and Han officials used judicial tools to expedite social, economic, and moral order.

Qin and Han jurists, unlike those of later times, avoided thorough Confucianization of the legal code. However, Confucian-inspired ideas sometimes coincided with the state's pragmatic goal of encouraging social stability. In such cases, the law might take on a moralistic tone. For example, a Han legal dictum held that the penalty for beating one's older sister should be harsher than that for beating a younger sister.[1] In this instance, the law upheld the principle of seniority within the family central to patrilineal morals. This law shows how patrilineal values could be used as a carefully defined template of roles and ethics dedicated to maintaining social order.

The most heinous crimes were classified under moralistic rubrics that heaped ethical outrage on top of anger at the violation of state interests. Prior to the Han, exceptionally terrible crimes such as matricide were often classed as "impious" (*budao*), literally meaning "not [in accord with the] Way." By the Han, terminology had changed somewhat. Though moralistic description of matricide remained, *budao* had been replaced by the moralistic vilification "great refractoriness" (*dani*).[2] So law and moralized kinship ideals were sometimes overtly conjoined in the legal code of the early empire.

WOMEN UNDER EARLY LAW

Early jurists believed that all human beings share an innate humanity regardless of gender, and women deserve fair treatment as much as men do. Of course, fairness did not necessarily denote equality in the minds of those raised in an unapologetically hierarchic society. Nevertheless, legal due process theoretically extended to women as well as to men. One measure of the detail and care taken in suits involving women can be seen from the records of the case against a woman being tried circa 100 B.C.E., which was recorded in copious detail on strips of wood.[3] This meticulousness shows that women could be afforded due process before the law. Women also enjoyed protections against false accusation. When a governor falsely accused the wife of Wei Xiang (chancellor, 67–58 B.C.E.) of murdering a female slave, the accuser was sentenced to be cut in half at the waist for perjury.[4] When the system worked as it should have, justice was neither summary nor arbitrary. These safeguards could benefit women as well as men.

As part of this effort to treat all people fairly (if not equally), early legal codes show some concern for the protection of particularly vulnerable women such as widows and slaves. These provisions seem to have been an outgrowth of the voluminous tradition of ancient moralistic literature exhorting rulers to defend the weak. A text on statecraft from the third century B.C.E. singles out widows as a defenseless group whom the good ruler protects against arbitrary judicial proceedings.[5] Early imperial law tried to prevent unscrupulous officials from using their power to exploit powerless widows. And Han legal safeguards for weak women extended a degree of protection to female slaves. Murder was illegal, even the murder of a slave. The wife of a powerful Han eunuch suffered arrest and execution for murdering a female slave and throwing the corpse down a well.[6] Of course the wealthy and powerful could probably have circumvented these basic legal safeguards intended to protect weak women. But at least the state showed some concern over the harshest threats facing the powerless.

Special rules governed the imprisonment of women being held as witnesses. Aside from the exceptional case of imperial consorts, Qin and Han law generally lacked provisions for permanently imprisoning convicts as a form of punishment. But the accused awaiting trial and convicts awaiting execution were temporarily imprisoned alongside witnesses who were detained to ensure their attendance at trial. Conditions in these institutions could be nightmarish. In the two prisons of Eastern Han Loyang, for example, no separation was made between the sexes.[7] Even rank could not guarantee protection. When Emperor He dismissed Empress Yan for allegedly practicing black magic, all her relatives (including the empress's elderly maternal grandmother) were thrown in prison and beaten to death.[8]

Some Han jurists believed that women should not be interned under such cruel conditions. Edicts of 4 C.E. and 27 C.E. forbade officials from imprisoning women as witnesses.[9] Furthermore, out of deference to rank, an order of 174

B.C.E. protected mothers and wives of marquises from unauthorized summons or arrest.[10] This edict partly insulated noblewomen from becoming victims of the deadly intrigues poisoning the upper levels of government during the period. But this rule was more than just special protection for the social elite. Specifically protecting female nobles while leaving their menfolk to face the regular workings of the judicial apparatus shows a clear differentiation of the sexes. Some Han officials believed that women are fundamentally different from men and hence deserve gentler treatment.

The law reached into the confines of the family to try to protect wives from physical abuse. Women had not always enjoyed this sort of legal protection. According to legend, when a Zhou dynasty man named Zhu Fu found out about his wife's affair with a neighbor he beat her to death. Readers apparently accepted the idea that a man should be able to murder an adulterous wife with impunity.[11] But under the Qin code, a man beating his wife could be punished, albeit relatively lightly.[12] For example, if a husband beat his wife for being too talkative, thereby resulting in a torn ear, broken limb or finger, or a dislocated joint, he was to suffer the humiliating and ritually mutilating punishment of having his beard shorn.[13] And during the Han the possibility of female-initiated divorce gave abusive husbands additional pause. As the perceptive Ban Zhao noted, a husband should not beat his wife for the simple reason that she might divorce him.[14]

The law also took a clear stand concerning rape and some forms of involuntary sexual servitude. In contrast to "consensual fornication" (*hejian*), rape was classified as "forced fornication" (*qiangjian*).[15] This emphasis on force shows that rape was seen primarily as a form of violent assault. Han records overflow with rape cases, inevitably numerous in such an unequal society.[16] The frequent recourse of rape victims to the courts demonstrates an expectation that rapists could and should be punished.

Under early imperial law many women had liberal recourse to accuse those who had wronged them, a vital legal safeguard. To appreciate the importance of this privilege, we should note that this legal protection did not extend to everyone. Qin law sought to reinforce hierarchical social roles. Thus children could not denounce their parents, nor slaves their masters.[17] But women could accuse men of wrongdoing. The ability to accuse men in court, leading to incarceration, trial, and punishment, reflects well on attitudes toward women. Early imperial jurists believed that women could tell the truth, and they were allowed to accuse others of crimes. And in a system that generally forbade social inferiors from accusing superiors of a crime, it is very noteworthy that a woman could accuse a man. From this judicial standpoint, women and men were theoretically equal.

One of the most vexing problems facing Chinese jurisprudence has always been balancing the interests of the family with those of individuals and society as a whole. Early imperial law did not take a clear-cut approach to this conflict. For example, the Qin legal system bolstered the interests of individual women by allowing women to denounce their husbands. However, as if to discourage wives from doing so, the law stated that if a wife's accusation led to her husband's banishment she was to share his punishment. This provision deviated from the standard treatment of a woman whose husband suffered banishment for (as an example) official corruption, in which case the wife did not share his exile.[18] This contradictory regulation epitomizes the conflict between individual and group interests. While recognizing that women could accuse men of wrongdoing, it simultaneously adhered to the principle that a wife would share her husband's guilt. A woman was both an individual and a family member. Sometimes the different interests of these two roles clashed. When forced to choose, Qin law usually upheld the sanctity of the patrilineal kinship structure over the interests of individuals and society as a whole.

KINSHIP

First and foremost, early law sought to stabilize society. Therefore the law usually strengthened existing institutions and values. However suspicious government officials may have been toward strong families, which posed a threat to government authority, they realized that the family was also a useful tool for promoting the social stability that early Chinese called "harmony." Yet strengthening the family often decreased the power of the state at the grassroots level. Early jurisprudence sometimes reveals a tension between conflicting loyalty to state and kin. Confucius raised a basic problem when he argued that the father who conceals the misconduct of his son and the son who conceals the crimes of his father both deserve praise.[19] Confucius lauded them for following traditional patrilineal kinship values. But this reasoning provided a convenient moralistic justification for hiding criminal activity, making it an extremely dangerous doctrine.

This conflict between loyalty to state and loyalty to kin attracted the attention of ethical theorists. Han Ying, writing in the second century B.C.E., distinguished pragmatic justice (strengthening the state) from moral ideals (strengthening kinship). He also broadened the problem's scope from a son's relationship with his father to that with both his parents: "In the case of the son who conceals the misconduct of his parents, justice is not being strictly observed. . . . But though [it] . . . impair justice, still the right way of acting lies therein."[20]

Eventually Han jurists came to a compromise between conflicting duties to state and to family by enforcing the social roles constituting the patrilineal kinship hierarchy.

> Henceforth, if a child conceals a parent, a wife conceals a husband, or a grandchild conceals a grandparent, this is not to be brought to trial. But if a parent conceals a child, a husband conceals a wife, or a grandparent conceals a grandchild, this crime is to be punished by execution.[21]

A grandson could hide an accused grandmother with legal impunity because patrilineal values demand that inferior serve superior within the family. But a husband had no such obligation to protect his wife, who was inferior to him within the patrilineal hierarchy. Under this compromise, gender relations therefore receded in importance relative to the particular kinship roles each person played. Gender identities like woman or man were unimportant in this regard; only family roles such as mother or son really mattered. The righteous son should hide his mother from authorities if she is suspected of a crime, but a father should not conceal an accused daughter.

Early legal practice attempted to define and strengthen major kinship roles. For instance, a grandson was legally obligated to treat his grandmother well. In line with patrilineal values, seniority within the family outweighed gender in determining the relative legal status of these two individuals. Nor was this an empty injunction. In the second century B.C.E. the king and queen of Liang were punished for behaving badly toward the king's grandmother. They had allegedly threatened her, refused to visit her when she was ill, and in the end failed to attend her funeral. As punishment, the king had his territory diminished by five prefectures. His wife, however, suffered execution.[22]

Although this prosecution probably had its roots in political intrigue, the legal reasoning involved is important nonetheless. At first glance these respective punishments seem reversed in magnitude. As a blood relation, surely a grandson should be punished more harshly than a granddaughter-in-law for unfiliality toward his grandmother. But this reasoning seems based on patrilineal values that demanded greater filial duty from a woman toward her husband's family than was expected of her husband himself.

This case is also useful in understanding how gender concepts influenced legal reasoning. The legal positions of neither grandmother nor granddaughter-in-law were determined simply by their gender. Officials viewed each woman according to her relative social position within the patrilineal kinship system. The law simply enforced the ideal behavior expected of two ideal kinship roles. Infiltration of patrilineal values into the legal code influenced the legal identity of women by enforcing the ideal gender relations of patrilineal morals. This accused was judged not as a woman but as a granddaughter-in-law. Her failure to play out this important social role properly brought on a draconian punishment. Under early imperial law, specific kinship roles took precedence over gender.

MARRIAGE

Early lawmakers faced delicate problems in ordering the vital relationship between wife and husband. Because marriage was so important, some wanted to bring the institution under legal jurisdiction. Before the Qin, some preimperial law had already tried to regulate marriage.[23] However, ancient attempts by the state to control marriage seem to have reached a dead end. Most people preferred to follow entrenched local customs that already organized marital matters. In the Han, popular custom won out over law as the main body of rules regulating marriage. The lack of Han marriage law seems to indicate not the loss of these codes, but simply that marriage regulations never existed in highly structured written form.[24] Early imperial officials preferred to let local custom regulate most aspects of marriage.

The Northern Qi dynasty (550–577) was the first dynasty to systematically codify marriage law. Prior to that time, officials seem to have settled marital disputes on an ad hoc basis. Although there was no comprehensive code of marriage law in the early empire, individual decision and piecemeal regulations nevertheless gradually extended some state influence over the institution. For instance, the erudite official Dong Zhongshu (c. 179–104 B.C.E.) often turned to the *Spring and Autumn Annals (Chunqiu)* for inspiration in solving marital disputes, as indicated by the few remaining fragments of his *Deciding Cases (Jueyu)*.[25] It seems that some jurists compiled collections of legal decisions regarding marriage, as in a lost work by the first-century official Bao Yu. Yet collections of verdicts on marital cases were likely intended as useful suggestions for magistrates rather than as binding precedents.[26]

A few statutes and cases show some official attempts to provide a basic legal framework for relations between husband and wife. For example, prior to the Qin dynasty the statutes of the state of Wei punished polygyny (in the form of having two chief wives) with execution. This precedent was followed into the Han.[27] Moreover, the law carefully distinguished between wives and concubines; any man reducing his wife to concubine status would be liable for punishment.[28] Notably, however, these statutes merely enforced traditional principles such as monogamy. Rarely did the law dare to contradict customary conceptions of marriage.

Where early law took a stand on the nature of marriage, it often treated wife and husband as a single legal unit. Qin law tried to create a series of concentric circles of mutual responsibility radiating throughout society. Neighbor was held responsible for neighbor, brother for brother, and spouse for spouse. In one very specific rule, if a husband committed suicide and his wife did not report his death to the authorities, she would be punished.[29] This law highlights the mutual responsibility of husband and wife in the eyes of Qin authorities. Such a mentality further welded the married couple together as a single entity, strengthening the importance of this bond in society as a whole. State intervention in marriage seems to have been limited mostly to attempts to minimize the possibility of blood feuds that might result from vague or contested marriage ties. The state generally intervened in marriage only to the extent that such laws could further social harmony.

DIVORCE

While most aspects of marriage remained outside legal jurisdiction, the Qin state regulated the dissolution of marriage. A large body of vocal opinion demanded the regulation of divorce by law or explicit ritual rules. Patrilineal values found expression in ritual works that discouraged divorce by imposing strict conditions. This school of thought envisioned the family as the centerpiece of all social relations. Therefore they were not keen to see families broken up. They did not sanction female-initiated divorce. And they even tried to impose strict conditions on male-initiated divorce.

In contrast with attempts by patrilineal thinkers to limit divorce, local customs were apparently fairly relaxed on the matter. In popular practice, both men and women seem to have been able to initiate divorce with relative freedom. Interestingly, Qin divorce law drew from both custom and patrilineal ideals. Male-initiated divorce was relatively unrestricted, in accord with popular custom. But female-initiated divorce was viewed less favorably, in line with patrilineal thought. Male-initiated divorce under the Qin seems to have been a fairly simple matter. Administrators were concerned only that appropriate local authorities record all divorces. In this respect, Qin law differed from legal practices such as Islamic *talāq* under which a man simply verbally renounces his wife to divorce her without any bureaucratic process.[30] Although a Qin man could divorce his wife seemingly without constraint, the husband was required to report the divorce to the authorities in writing for it to become official. Punishment for failing to report a divorce consisted of a fine levied on both estranged spouses.[31] Other than this procedural technicality, Qin dynasty men seemed able to divorce their wives freely and without having to cite due cause.

In contrast to the liberal divorce rights enjoyed by men, the admittedly ambiguous evidence suggests that Qin law did not officially permit women to divorce their husbands. Although the Qin is often stereotyped as a "legalist" *(fajia)* government, this hostility to female-initiated divorce highlights the influence of the patrilineal kinship ideals most closely associated with Confucianism. Patrilinealism viewed women in terms of their specific roles within the kinship hierarchy. According to this way of thinking, women may not have been inferior to men in any general sense, but a wife was inferior to her husband. Following this patrilineal ideal, Qin law specified that any woman who "abandoned" her husband and married another could be punished.[32] Another statute specified the circumstances under which a runaway wife could be punished, but unfortunately these conditions have been lost due to textual corruption.[33]

As Qin law regulated divorce, it seems consistent that Qin authorities also sought to control the remarriage of widows. This prohibition was also in line with the general patrilinealization of Qin family law. Under Qin law, childless widows could freely remarry. Widows with children, however, were forever bound to their first husband's family and therefore could not remarry. According to this patrilineal reasoning, her children tied her irrevocably to her husband's bloodline.[34] However, an inscription on one of the stelae erected by the First Emperor not only prohibited widows with children from remarrying but also placed a parallel obligation of fidelity on men. Husbands were prohibited from any sort of extramarital sexual liaisons. Qin law followed patrilineal thought in trying to lock husbands and wives into monogamous fidelity. Qin administrators probably adopted this patrilineal viewpoint for practical reasons. Limiting sexual activity to marriage and concubinage would decrease social tension.

Han officialdom deregulated divorce, falling back from the Qin goal of gaining control over family life. In doing so, they allowed lenient local customs to prevail. This laissez-faire attitude removed all sense of legal process from divorce. The effects on women were mixed. Husbands could simply cast off their wives at will, making a wife's status less secure. But deregulation also benefited women by allowing them to divorce their husbands. Han women frequently exercised this privilege.[35] Nevertheless, male prejudice against female-initiated divorce remained. Occasionally local officials judged cases in which a woman left her husband to marry another, after which the abandoned husband requested that his ex-wife be punished. Officials decided these cases on an ad hoc basis or according to local custom. Local agents of the Han government often assumed the traditional role of village headman and enforced local custom as well as the code of law.[36]

Prohibitions on widow remarriage were also swept away along with the short-lived Qin.[37] Han statutes seem to have contained no prohibition against widows remarrying. Of course widow remarriage still had its opponents. The Eastern Han thinker Wang Fu (c. 90–c. 165 c.e.) advocated a Qin-style law against female remarriage. He suggested that remarried women and their second husbands be punished by having their heads shaved and being banished to the frontier.[38] Another moralist opined that women who marry three times should be sentenced to pound grain.[39] Yet these moralistic suggestions never seem to have been heeded by the central authorities. Han officials were far less interested in controlling kinship roles than their Qin predecessors. Although patrilineal rhetoric intensified, its effects on government policy toward the family remained negligible.

INFANTICIDE

Pregnant woman were sometimes accorded special treatment under the law, presumably out of respect for their fetus and their own temporarily vulnerable condition. In particular, pregnant women were to receive special care and consideration while in confinement. Under this so-called lenient detention, pregnant women were supposed to receive gentler treatment during interrogation and perhaps some amelioration of the harsh prison environment as well.[40]

Protection also extended to the unborn. A Qin case in which two women fought, causing one to miscarry, resulted in the apprehension of the woman held responsible for the miscarriage.[41] This same desire to protect the fetus from harm led to at least one instance in which a pregnant woman condemned to death was granted a temporary stay of execution until after the delivery of her child.[42] These cases suggest that authorities considered the unborn child a human being who deserved basic legal protections.

Newborns also obtained special legal safeguards in light of their helplessness. Authorities periodically tried to deter infanticide, which was probably common during periods of hardship. Popular custom seems to have generally accepted infanticide as an unavoidable evil. In deference to accepted practice, pre-Qin legal systems seem to have had weak prohibitions against infanticide or none at all.[43] The Qin distinguished between deformed and healthy infants, sanctioning the killing of the former but heavily punishing infanticide of the latter.[44] Raising a disabled child would have been a heavy burden for ordinary people. Qin authorities acquiesced to the common view that such children were better off dead.

Legal penalties for infanticide seem to have initially weakened after the fall of the Qin. New Han laws saw to it that killing a child was considered as serious as killing an adult—at least in theory.[45] But the frequency of references to infanticide in Han records shows that this humane legal vision was fulfilled only haphazardly. During the Eastern Han, local officials repeatedly issued warnings against the practice.[46] The frequency of these exhortations suggests that infanticide was still common. Punishment for infanticide seems to have varied depending on the moral outlook of powerful officials. Penalties ranged from forced labor (as in subsequent legal codes) to death.[47] However, because popular custom sanctioned infanticide, in all likelihood the murder of newborns probably went unpunished in most cases.

WITCHCRAFT

Witchcraft was perhaps the most serious and feared crime under Han law. It was also an offense closely associated with women. Although men were sometimes accused of sorcery, the Han elite assumed that women had special access to dark magical forces. The witch was a powerful but terrifying female social role. Legal terminology usually described black magic as "invoking curses" (*zhuzu*) or "magical poison" (*gu*).[48] Witch hunts seem to have been a relatively new preoccupation for the Han elite. Although Qin legal fragments mention a woman accused of intending to poison others, generally speaking, prior to the Han dynasty the Chinese elite paid little attention to the dangers of magical poison.[49] But at the Han court, fear of supernatural imprecations and poisons reached the point of outright hysteria. Several bloody witch hunts decimated the court, reaching up into the ranks of the imperial family.[50]

Manipulation of the supernatural was one of the most potent sources of female power. Witchcraft terrified potential male victims. In respect to black magic, men saw themselves as inferior to women. Men used the law to redress this imbalance by punishing this unsettling female power with dreadful severity. Witchcraft was classified as a type of "great refractoriness" (*dani*), a category that included the most heinous crimes deserving the harshest punishments. Women were also accused of the even more terrible "shamanistic poisoning" (*wugu*) that combined magical poisons with the mysterious powers of ecstatic shamanism.[51]

Not only did Han law punish witchcraft with the severest punishments, but the entire family of the condemned was often executed as well.[52]

Witch hysteria often had political implications. Several Han reigns saw major witchcraft trials that implicated the highest echelons at court. Two witch hunts swept the court of Emperor Wu during times of crisis. Empress Chen (r. 141–130 B.C.E.), Wu's first consort, found her position weakened by her inability to produce a male heir. Jealous rivals availed themselves of this chance to destroy their foe. They accused Chen's daughter of witchcraft as an excuse to unseat her mother. Once this witch hunt began, it rapidly spread in scope to implicate large numbers in the alleged conspiracy. Three hundred people eventually lost their lives in the ensuing madness. The life of Empress Chen was spared but she lost her title and endured the humiliation of demotion to a minor consort.

Her successor was Empress Wei (empress, 129–91 B.C.E.). As with many Han empresses, the Wei clan parlayed their connections with the throne into great power and wealth. Although the formidable Empress Wei managed to stay aloft amid internecine court intrigue for three decades, she was finally laid low by the machinations of a rival consort's relatives. History repeated itself when the many enemies of the Wei leveled allegations of witchcraft to justify their annihilation. The Weis were exterminated and prominent members of the government were executed as well for practicing witchcraft.

Comparing the similarities between the dramatic falls of the Chens and Weis reveals a clear pattern.[53] In many eras, the families of imperial consort struggled with one another for control of the government. As the fall of both these families shows, witchcraft was an extremely convenient grounds for legitimizing a palace coup. Any empress who appeared weak or vulnerable risked having opportunistic foes accuse those around her of black magic. As a tool of court warfare, witch hunts were as potent a weapon as they were dangerous. Once started, it could not be predicted who would eventually be implicated in the ensuing hysteria. Of course, this emphasis on the function witch hunts played in politics does not mean that the persecution of witches was purely opportunistic. Although cynical officials and palace ladies may have consciously manipulated the destructive course of witch hunts, only a sincere belief in black magic could have incited such destructive hysteria. Those who denounced sorcery for political gain recognized that the strong association of women with witchcraft made witch hunts an ideal weapon for toppling a powerful empress and her kin.

Execution for witchcraft was carried out in public as a warning to other witches. Although imperial relations were usually shielded from humiliation in front of the mob, some relatives of the emperors were publicly executed for sorcery.[54] A woman shaman of nomad origin was roasted alive as punishment for black magic, reviving the ancient custom of shamaness sacrifice.[55] Those convicted of magical *gu* poisoning continued to be punished after death. Under the Han ritual system, empresses were to be buried jointly with their husbands in the same tumulus. But women considered guilty of particularly serious crimes such as *gu* poisoning were buried separately.[56] As this custom shows, the terrifying role of witch canceled out a woman's normative role as wife. Accusations of witchcraft placed a woman beyond the pale of regular social and kinship relations.

5

Government

Sometimes social history intersects with politics. Defining the subjects of this book as "early imperial women," makes the political system of the time a key component of their identity. But most of these women lacked political power in the conventional sense. Political organization and elite ideology had little impact on them specifically as women. Government generally affected them in much the same ways it affected their husbands and sons—as members of a particular family, region, or class rather than through gender.

The lives of some women, however, were not usual. A tiny minority were members of China's ruling elite. For these privileged women, happenings in government directly influenced their daily lives. The early imperial system of government allowed a few women to play very powerful roles. Certain female roles in government carried prestige, wealth, and power over others. These roles obviously underwent significant changes as China's patchwork of contentious states unified into a monolithic empire led by a powerful man—or woman. No social roles for women were more powerful than those in government. And none underwent more dramatic changes. The expanding power of government during the early empire opened up remarkable new opportunities for women at court.

Political power in China was traditionally hereditary. Power in each Zhou dynasty state was concentrated in the hands of a lineage whose members were regarded as legitimate rulers. This custom united politics with kinship, an institution that already offered the influential roles of wife and mother to women. In China rulership was a family business, and women exercised significant power within the family. Extending kinship to politics meant that traditional female roles in the family became imbued with fantastic new potential. The wives and mothers of emperors became important players in court politics as they extended their powers from the imperial family to the empire as a whole. Some empresses dowager dominated weak or young emperors outright. For much of the Han dynasty, these mighty women, or their fathers and brothers, became the true rulers of China. Many weak or youthful Han emperors were no more than figure-heads; some were mere infants. In such cases, real authority rested with the empress dowager and her natal kin. Although patrilineal values often restricted female autonomy, these ideals also presented social roles sanctioning certain types of female control over men. The imperial clan's kinship customs allowed wives to sway their husbands, and mothers influenced or completely controlled their sons.[1]

Some men opposed female participation in government. It is not hard to fathom this resistance. More power for the mothers and wives of rulers meant less power for men at court. Women increased their power at the expense of the regular bureaucracy. Of course the officialdom regularly struck back. These attacks against female influence at court mark the most important beginnings of antifemale ideology in elite Chinese thought.

Why did women want to plunge themselves into the murky and often fatal world of court intrigue? The perennial attraction of power for its own sake was doubtless an important motivation. And power brought real benefits to those who exercised it. But beyond the allure of command there was the fear of becoming a passive victim of the mistakes of others. Ancient custom held that everyone in a family or even a clan was held responsible for the crimes of one of its members. Some women probably entered the arena of politics to ensure their own survival. Miscalculations by less adept male relatives might cost a high-ranking lady her life. In a memorable case, when the warlord Xiang Yu (d. 203 B.C.E.) struggled desperately with Liu Bang (the future first emperor of Han) for supremacy, he captured the mother of Liu's prime minister Wang Ling. After Wang Ling's mother committed suicide, depriving her son's sworn enemy of a useful hostage, the enraged Xiang Yu boiled her corpse in retribution.[2] This violent precedent set the stage for the murderous intrigues of the Han. Court ladies knew from a long string of bloody examples that their personal stakes in the endless rounds of power struggles were very high. When a faction lost a major struggle, all of their relatives might be ruthlessly exterminated. With their very survival at stake, many court ladies took a keen interest in the affairs of state swirling around them.

It would be a grave mistake to view women in early Chinese government as a monolithic faction acting toward a well-defined, unified female goal. The views of women on the pressing issues of state were as varied as those of male counterparts. However, the means for women to achieve power differed from those available to men. Blocked from serving in the external bureaucracy, ambitious women often only had duplicitous methods left at their disposal. The palace became a virtual battleground of women competing with each other for favor and power. Rival concubines used a variety of weapons. Slander, elaborate plots, and magic rounded out their arsenals. The lady who possessed good connections, high aspirations, and little moral sensibility could sometimes become a powerful éminence grise by the indelicate (but highly effective) tactic of slaughtering all potential rivals.

Most important, palace ladies fought one another for the attentions of the emperor. More than anything else, this recognition would give them the most power. Court ladies of early history feared nothing more than the entry of beautiful and accomplished rivals into the seraglio.[3] Overcoming and even exterminating potential female rivals within the palace was the necessary first step for any lady hoping to seize control of the government.

TITLES

Patents of nobility conferred elite women with high social standing and prestige that could often be converted into political power. Moreover, noble titles often came with land grants that gave the holder a large regular income.[4] Shang and Zhou rulers regularly granted land to titled ladies.[5] During the Zhou, male and female nobles often received lands called "bathing benefices" (*tangmuyi*). These land grants generated revenue to pay for the costly and elaborate bathing rituals required by custom. Gradually these lands came to provide a noblewoman's general expenses, though the ancient name "bathing benefice" was retained into the Han.[6] By the dawn of imperial history, custom had long allowed noble ladies independent titles and lands.

Noble titles became highly standardized during the imperial period. Under the Qin, only men could hold one of the coveted twenty ranks constituting the basic official social hierarchy.[7] However, the First Emperor presented his mother with a lavish land grant to provide her an independent income.[8] Not only did Han emperors follow the Qin precedent of granting lands to the mothers of emperors, but they also gave land and title to other close female relatives as well.[9] Han imperial consorts received an aristocratic title equivalent to a male rank in addition to a grade in the government bureaucracy. Although the Western Han title of baronet (*jun*) was granted to both sexes, it was most regularly given to imperial princesses and the emperor's maternal grandmother. The title baronet carried with it a "bathing benefice" or "food benefice" (*shiyi*), usually consisting of an estate near the capital.[10] In the Eastern Han this title was also routinely granted to the emperor's wet nurse and occasionally his sisters-in-law or other female relatives.[11]

The titles and land grants held by elite ladies contradicted the patrilineal assertion by the authors of ritual works that a woman could only hold her husband's rank.[12] This was merely wishful thinking on their part. Women did in fact hold grants and noble titles independent of their husbands. This custom uncoupled some elite female roles from those held by immediate male kin. The system of ranks at the apex of Han society was still androcentric. But a woman's aristocratic status was not determined via her husband, but instead by the degree of her relation to the emperor.

MILITARY POWER

Mao's dictum that power grows from the barrel of a gun applies to ancient China. The imperial system emerged from chaotic warfare in the wake of the Zhou dynasty's collapse. Because imperial authority originated on the battlefield, military power had much closer links to politics than it did in late imperial history, when civil authority triumphed over martial might. The exclusion of women from military power stands out as a major obstacle facing the ambitious court lady in early imperial times. Although imperial consorts regularly obtained important generalships for their fathers and brothers, they themselves were kept far from the battlefield.

Writers of various persuasions, realizing the destabilizing influence of female military power on male-dominated institutions, concocted reasons to discredit women's involvement in war. Some rationales were relatively mild. Scholars who convened at the White Tiger Hall in 79 C.E. saw women's role in war as more annoyance than threat. They complained that female resentment over long separation from their menfolk complicated long-term military expeditions.[13]

Other views were more critical. An intriguing piece of archaeological evidence seems to clarify the relation of women to warfare. Alexander Soper's interpretation of a problematic battle scene at the intricate Han dynasty Wu Liang shrine sees this artwork depicting a battle between King Wu Ding of Shang (allegedly a remote ancestor of the lineage who built the shrine) and the Gui Fang barbarians (fig. 5.1). Interestingly, the figures' headgear suggests that half of the non-Chinese troops are female. If this interpretation of the scene (backed up by persuasive inscriptional evidence) is indeed correct, the iconography seems to be equating female participation in warfare with barbarism. The Han dynasty artist used this scene to contrast Chinese with foreign and civilized with barbaric. Amazon warriors symbolized the absence of normative gender roles basic to civilized life.[14] The enemies are clearly barbarians because they have female

Figure 5.1. Battle Scene. Rubbing of an incised stone from the Wu Liang shrine, Shandong. Édouard Chavannes, *Mission archéologique dans la Chine septentrionale* (Paris: E. Leroux, 1913–1915), vol. 2, pl. 53, no. 109.

soldiers. Normative social roles have always been an important element in the Chinese definition of civilization. As this artwork suggests, during the Han the exclusion of women from warfare was seen as a basic component of civilized behavior.

Dating back to antiquity, the traditional female role in warfare seems to have been logistical support. For example, in one encounter between the armies of Lu and invaders from Jin the women of Lu "toiled and brought up supplies without resting."[15] Qin urban defense utilized all sectors of the population: able-bodied men fought, women carried provisions and built fortifications, and the elderly guarded the cattle and horses and also gathered wild plants for food.[16] Battle was not an everyday occurrence. But war presented women and men with a set of social roles that differed from the everyday activities of farmer and weaver. Even so, in times of war the basic ideal work roles continued to be based on gender.

During the Han the site of most warfare gradually shifted. Most Zhou dynasty wars were fought in the Chinese heartland among rival states. But after unification, only civil wars or popular uprisings were fought out in China's interior. Most battles now took place as campaigns on distant, sparsely populated frontiers. This change in the locale of conflicts meant that armies could no longer rely on informal logistical support from local female civilians. The Han military had no choice but to develop a standing logistical network. The change in the location of most warfare removed women even farther from war.

Under these new circumstances, rebellions furnished the most likely occasion for female participation in warfare.[17] The early empire was a time of social ferment exacerbated by lingering regional tensions and perennial administrative problems. A series of violent popular uprisings flared. One of the most important was known as the Red Eyebrows rebellion. This uprising, which began in 22 C.E., was named for the red war paint that the rebels daubed on their foreheads. A woman known as Mother Lü led one of the most important branches of this bloody uprising. The rebellion began when Mother Lü led a vendetta against a local official responsible for her son's execution. Mother Lü raised several thousand supporters from the sympathetic populace, stormed the county capital, and beheaded the hated administrator. She died soon afterward, but the uprising Mother Lü helped initiate continued to gather momentum and soon merged with other local rebellions. The cataclysmic revolt of the Red Eyebrows ultimately precipitated the fall of the usurper Wang Mang and restoration of the Han imperial house.[18]

A remarkably similar rebellion has come to symbolize Vietnamese nationalism. Chinese control of northern Vietnam lasted more than a millennium, from 111 B.C.E until 939 C.E. In 40 C.E. two daughters of a local general (surnamed

Tru'ng in Vietnamese and Zheng in Chinese) led a rebellion against a local official who had arrested one sister's husband. Tru'ng Trac raised an army and
attacked government forces. Although the insurrection began as a vendetta, as
Tru'ng Trac captured territory she ruled it as a queen. Standard Chinese historical accounts (always questionable sources regarding controversial actions by
women) record that when the Han emperor sent an army to crush this rebellion,
many of her troops thought that a woman lacked sufficient stature to face such
formidable opposition and deserted their queen's banner. In 43 c.e. the remnants
of the rebel force suffered decisive defeat at Chinese hands. According to Vietnamese tradition, which portrays this war as a nationalistic uprising, the Tru'ng
sisters thereupon heroically drowned themselves; Chinese chronicles record that
they were ignominiously captured and executed.[19]

Similarities between the uprisings led by Mother Lü and Tru'ng Trac point to
the roots of this unexpected female power to initiate rebellion. Neither rebellion
started over abstract differences with the central government in regard to ideology or policy. These women's motivations were far more concrete and personal.
The two women raised the banner of rebellion in reaction to terrible wrongs
perpetrated on a key man in their family: a son or a husband. At the most fundamental level, these female-led rebellions began as local vendettas by the families
of executed men against local officials who ordered the deaths.

Why were so many men willing to follow women into war against powerful
government forces to pursue a family vendetta? Their legitimacy as leaders of
rebellion derived from their kinship roles as mother or wife, not from their individual merits. When a family lost its pater familias, a woman could step in to
head the kin group in its struggle for revenge. A woman acting on her own would
be unlikely to convince others to follow her into rebellion. But when a woman
invoked her role as dutiful family head, kinsmen and neighbors might follow
her down a path leading inexorably to the battlefield. She attracted support by
appealing to ancient kinship values demanding revenge. After a female-led
rebellion accomplished its immediate goal of reprisal against a particular enemy
in the government bureaucracy, unleashed passions began to find new avenues
of expression. Having defied the state, the rebellion now had to be fought out to
its ultimate conclusion. New goals and an ideology began to emerge. The Red
Eyebrows dedicated themselves to the overthrow of the usurper Wang Mang (r.
9–23 c.e.); supporters of the Tru'ngs attempted to break away from their distant
Chinese masters and found an independent kingdom.

These incidents show that in local politics, female power in popular rebellions
mirrored female authority in the central government. In both cases, the political
power of women derived not from individual merit or abstract female identity

but through a woman's specific kinship roles. The mother of an emperor might gain power at court. The mother of an executed grandee might gain power on the local level. In both cases, women translated authoritative female roles within the kinship structure into power outside the home. Patrilineal kinship rules may have restrained the women who occupied depressed social roles, such as daughters-in-law. But the same set of customs also accorded mothers and wives privileged social roles that could sometimes justify seizing political power.

OFFICE

During the Han, women began to manage many of the myriad daily activities of the inner palace. Palace ladies were organized into carefully delineated formal ranks with specific duties corresponding in structure, if not importance, to the external male bureaucracy.[20] Ironically, the increasing formalization of female power in the palace coincided with a marked exclusion of women from official bureaucratic process in the government as a whole. The male bureaucracy fought hard to exclude palace women from most of the vital functions of government. Ambitious ladies could extend their power beyond the court only by undermining the male bureaucracy's authority. Otherwise, consorts and female relatives of the emperor were officially limited to trivial court offices overseeing the complex yet relatively mundane business of running the enormous imperial palace.[21]

Female participation in palace offices evolved gradually along with the rise of bureaucratic administration in general. In the Qin and Han, genealogy and connections were often more respected than formal civil service rank. Moreover, imperial consorts used court intrigues to wield power outside the inner palace and did not have to limit themselves to the grand titles but minimal powers of palace bureaucracy. Nevertheless, the general trend toward increasing bureaucratization in early government began to constrict women's roles in politics. A history of the inner palace in early imperial times is a story of the rise of a female palace bureaucracy.

The basic structure of the early imperial palace bureaucracy came together during the Qin; Han successors kept most of this organization, extemporizing minor changes as the need arose. As a general principle, Qin and Han rulers sought to institute specific bureaucratic offices to manage each duty of government administration. Parallel with the accelerated bureaucratization of government, the Han also provided equivalent bureaucratic and noble ranks for each grade of imperial consort. The utopian *Rites of Zhou* provided the theory behind this new practice. This work advocated an idealized system in which the ruler's many palace ladies were to be distinguished as one of the nine consorts (jiupin), dynastic ladies (shifu), or female attendants (nüyu). Although not correlated to specific bureaucratic offices, these women were to be assigned official duties within the palace depending on their rank. The nine consorts oversaw education of lower-ranking concubines; dynastic ladies dedicated themselves to ritual observances; and female attendants kept track of the order of precedence in the king's bed.[22]

The Han implemented the general concept of equating rank with official duties as advocated in Rites of Zhou, but took the idea one step further by formalizing imperial consorts into a bureaucratic hierarchy. At first the Han simply continued the Qin system of dividing imperial consorts into eight ranks.[23] But a female population explosion in the palace required better organization. Early Western Han emperors had roughly a dozen consorts each. But by the reign of Emperor Wu the inner palace had several thousand inhabitants. In response, the number of ranks for consorts expanded from eight to fourteen.[24] Each of the highest thirteen ranks was equated with an office in the external male bureaucracy. For example, the highest-ranking concubine, known as the Zhaoyi concubine, had a "bureaucratic" grade equivalent to that of the imperial chancellor.[25]

These ranks were not just empty honors. Managing an establishment as enormous as the imperial palace required a large and highly efficient organization. Complex bureaucratic organs evolved to manage the innumerable details of palace life.[26] For example, one palace office managed the households of empress dowager and heir apparent. Specific offices were devoted to matters such as ritual sacrifices, food preparation, textile production, music, living quarters, and marshalling the palace's multitude of servants and eunuchs. Still other palace offices managed matters from maintaining palace buildings to dealing with myriad imperial relatives.[27] In 18 b.c.e. the various palace departments were finally centralized under the jurisdiction of a single office.

In light of the size and complexity of the apparatus running the emperor's household, organizing the palace ladies into a bureaucratic hierarchy seems to have been a rational move.[28] Although some palace ladies were able to handle complex bureaucratic functions, many probably lacked the education, training, and inclination necessary to run such a large organization efficiently. As a result, although women theoretically led the palace household bureaucracy, men dominated many offices and functions. Some male palace officials were eunuchs, but others were uncastrated high-ranked nobles and men of talent. Not only did convention exclude women from participating in the outer bureaucracy, but even within the palace men regulated many aspects of official routine.

EMPRESSES

Although palace ladies held lofty titles and palace offices, real female power in government derived from kinship roles. The early Chinese state was ruled not by an isolated individual but by the Liu family. Thus when an emperor died, both the government and the ruling lineage suddenly lacked a male head. Custom dictated that the choice of ruler was an internal matter for the imperial family to decide, not a government affair. This temporary void in the kinship hierarchy allowed the ruling line's senior woman to assume the role of kin group head. She could then use this authority to choose and legitimate a new male ruler.[29]

Powerful men might interfere with the process, and imperial concubines might resort to assassination or other forms of intrigue to upset the usual order and have a son declared ruler. Nevertheless, in theory only the empress dowager had final formal approval over imperial succession. The most telling instance of this process from the Han was the controversial dismissal of Liu He in 74 B.C.E. after a twenty-seven-day reign as emperor. He was deposed and replaced by Emperor Xuan on the authority of the empress dowager.[30]

Changes in the Han dynasty's basic institutions also gave empresses dowager more leverage over government. The stabilization of Han rule gradually made the abstract institution of emperorship more important than the person who actually held that rank; the throne became more important than the man who sat on it. Elaborate rituals and moral teachings upheld the imperial dignity, evolving into a sophisticated ideology centered on the symbolism of the emperor. As the idea of emperorship became detached from any individual ruler, empresses dowager and their relatives could easily manipulate it for their own benefit. When an emperor was weak due to youth, illness, or incompetence, others could seize real control of the emperorship. The sudden and unexpected death of a ruler could also work to an empress dowager's advantage.[31] In such cases, an empress dowager could use her privileged kinship role to dominate not just the imperial family but the government of all China.

Han institutions often followed Qin imperial precedents, modifying but generally accepting basic Qin administrative practices. The role of women in Han government, however, lacked Qin imperial antecedents. To the contrary, the strong-willed Qin Shihuangdi refused to be dominated by his mother and ordered her to leave his palace to prevent her from meddling in important matters.[32] The relative powers of emperor and empress dowager reversed with the change of dynasties. Soon after the founding of the Han, an emperor's charisma became far less important than the majesty of imperial institutions. As emperors devolved into symbols, ambitious empresses dowager could usurp their powers.

The tradition of powerful empresses dowager began soon after the founding of the Han. Empress Lü acted immediately after the death of her husband, Emperor Gaozu in 195 B.C.E. to seize power over government by acting as regent of the youthful Emperor Hui. As regent, she ruled practically as an emperor by issuing decrees *(zhi)* in her own name. Ideally empresses could only issue edicts *(zhao)*. Issuing a decree usurped the emperor's most basic prerogative.[33] So complete was Lü's control of government from 195 to 180 B.C.E. that the historian Sima Qian, author of the classic account of the era, did not recognize Hui as having reigned because all the decrees issued during his so-called reign were issued in his mother's name.[34]

Archeology confirms Sima Qian's assertions. A peasant working in fields near the Wei River during the Cultural Revolution discovered a square seal of the finest translucent jade topped with dragon and tiger. The seal's inscription reads "Seal of the Empress Dowager." Considering the location of its discovery near the site of the Western Han capital, the seal was probably one of Lü's six seals of state. It was lost in this field during the chaotic looting of her tomb, only to be unearthed during a very different time of chaos.[35] A dowager's seal made of this precious material and with iconography featuring these particular creatures would have been a clear usurpation of imperial authority. Custom usually limited jade seals of state to the ruler.[36]

Empress Lü and her Han successors did not bother with the more subtle Tang dynasty charade of hiding a ruling empress dowager behind a screen when the emperor pretended to hold court audiences himself. Han dowager regents received officials in full public view at the opposite end of the throne hall from the titular ruler and received a copy of every memorial presented to the emperor. This behavior earned the animosity of those who believed that an adult emperor ought to rule in his own right. The founder of the Eastern Han dynasty, Emperor Guangwu (r. 25–57 C.E.), so detested Empress Lü's shamelessly blatant usurpation of imperial power that he ordered her ancestral tablet removed from her husband's shrine in retribution.[37] But if Guangwu hoped to keep imperial consorts from gaining power, he failed. During the Eastern Han, empresses dowager became more involved in court politics than ever. Despite Guangwu's deliberate desecration of Empress Lü's memory, that powerful woman had nevertheless set a precedent for female domination that was played out repeatedly during the reigns of weak emperors throughout the remainder of the dynasty. Even under powerful emperors, copies of memorials went to both the emperor and empress dowager. The empress dowager's kinship role as the emperor's mother entitled her to a say in affairs of state.

CONSORT KIN

As the imperial system developed, the relatives of empresses progressively gained political power. During the Eastern Han, the height of power for empresses dowager, nine out of thirteen emperors were mere puppets.[38] True authority was vested in imperial women and their kin. Some Han empresses dowager used weak emperors as pawns to legitimize their own authority. More often, however, both emperor and empress dowager were manipulated by the empress dowager's male relatives. Some experts on ritual declared that the parents of a ruler's spouse were not considered his subjects, elevating imperial in-laws to a uniquely privileged status.[39]

Wang Mang temporarily deposed the house of Liu from China's throne by using a Wang empress. But the case of Wang Mang was obviously extreme. Consort relatives gained their power from the prevailing dynastic system and usually preferred to work within it rather than overthrow it. By exploiting their kinship connections with the reigning Lius, imperial in-laws repeatedly rose to supreme power, only to be annihilated by rivals and replaced by yet another consort family. An unusual and destabilizing characteristic of Han government was the cycle of domination by successive families of imperial in-laws. The importance of the mother's role within the kinship system made this remarkable political system possible.

In the early Western Han the humble social origins of most consorts checked their power. Perhaps out of genealogical insecurity, the first Han emperors selected consorts of humble backgrounds.[40] Liu Fu (fl. late first century B.C.E.) attacked the practice of taking consorts from low social origins with the caustic assertion, "Rotten wood should not become a pillar; base people should not become masters."[41] Elitist critics blamed the presence of "base people" in the imperial harem for natural disasters wrought by heaven as punishment for this grotesque distortion of the acceptable social order. Gradually Han rulers revived the Zhou custom of marrying women from prominent lines. The social origins of Han imperial consorts grew steadily more exalted as the Liu emperors became unquestionably legitimate.[42]

Weak rulers sometimes had their empress foisted upon them. In other cases the emperor selected his own empress from among his many consorts. Many reasons are cited for the elevation of women to the supreme rank of empress, including marriage to the emperor while he held a humble position, a woman's family connections, birth of a son, outstanding virtue, and even love. Western Han rulers generally tended to select empresses from the daughters of close relatives while Eastern Han empresses mostly came from the great families of the realm.[43] These prestigious backgrounds only added to consort family power later in the dynasty.

Sometimes two empresses dowager were alive at the same time, as with the coexistence of the Dowagers Wang (wife of the deceased Emperor Yuan) and Zhao (wife of Yuan's deceased son). In such a situation the patrilineal rules of kinship hierarchy came to bear. Power was apportioned according to generational hierarchy. Belonging to an older generation, Empress Dowager Wang held precedence over her son's wife.[44] In another case, after the death of Emperor Wu, control of the government went to a woman who had never been empress. Both parents of Wu's successor, the eight-year-old Emperor Zhao, were already dead. Consequently, Zhao's older sister Princess Eyi seized the seals of state.[45]

The power of consort kin was not entirely pathological. Some of these consort relations proved extremely useful to the state. Particularly in the early Western Han, many imperial in-laws proved worthy of honor, power, and wealth by performing extraordinary services. Empress Lü's relatives in particular played an important part in helping Liu Bang capture the throne and found the dynasty.

During the Eastern Han, however, the power of consort kin clearly threatened the quality of government. The key role that the landed elite played in overthrowing the usurper Wang Mang and reestablishing the house of Liu gave them a decisive voice in shaping Eastern Han institutions. They monopolized government, using intermarriage with the Liu emperors as a justification for their dominance. As the importance of kinship in administration increased, some regulations exploited the tensions among competing great families to retain a semblance of institutional checks and balances. For example, families with matrimonial ties were forbidden from supervising each other in office to discourage collusion. But minor administrative regulations could not restrain the growth of kinship as a political force. Marriage alliances among the great families or between these families and the house of Liu became the focus of factional politics.[46]

The various consort clans may have reached dizzying heights of authority and grandeur, but their predominance was inevitably ephemeral. Marriage or blood ties to a particular ruler were no basis for permanent power. The death of an emperor could suddenly and catastrophically alter the fortunes of his in-laws. Even while the ruler was still alive, his wandering eye might raise or lower the status of any one of the multitude of ladies occupying the palace. Poetry noted the fickleness of an emperor's attentions.

> Fourteen ranks in the harem,
> Each one plied her charms in search of favor.
> "Prosperity and decline" followed no constant rule;
> They merely depended on personal whim.
> Empress Wei rose to prominence by virtue of her ebon hair;
> Flying Swallow was favored for her light body.[47]

A family's continued power depended on repeatedly marrying its women to emperors. Yet during the Western Han, no single consort family was ever able to marry its relatives into the imperial line for more than three generations; the most women one family ever married to Han emperors was five.[48] When kinship ties to the ruling Lius became too weak, a consort family's fortunes collapsed.

Empresses themselves sometimes met an unhappy fate, including dismissal and forced suicide. After the death of a key supporter, rivals usually exterminated the entire consort clan.[49] The aftermath of Empress Lü's reign serves as both precedent and example. After this feared lady died, jealous members of the Liu clan and her enemies in the officialdom immediately began to challenge the Lüs. Once Lü control of the military had been carefully neutralized, the Lius and their allies banded together to utterly annihilate them.[50]

During the witchcraft hysteria of 91 B.C.E. the suicide of Empress Wei paved the way for her natal family's complete destruction. The sole survivor of the massacre was the boy who eventually grew up to become Emperor Xuan.[51] A similar scenario played out during Xuan's own reign when the death of his powerful in-law Huo Guang in 68 B.C.E. allowed the rival Xus to exterminate the Huos.[52] Names changed, but the basic scenario remained the same: diminishing links to the Liu line or death of a key kinsman spelled doom for the rest of the family.

Bureaucrats were the perennial enemies of consort kin. The concentration of enormous landed estates in the hands of consort families evoked both jealousy and fear in officialdom. Empress Lü initiated the open warfare between empresses dowager and recalcitrant officials by high-handedly executing her critics in the bureaucracy. This outrageous tyranny inflamed in government officials a permanent hatred toward subsequent empresses dowager and their kin. Throughout the dynasty, officials organized informal factions to oppose the consort clan of the moment. The motivation for this perennial conflict is not hard to fathom. Reducing the powers of consort relatives increased those of the bureaucracy. Regular officials and imperial in-laws were born enemies.

The power of consort relatives led to the rise of the other great enemy of officialdom: the eunuchs. Being the only nonrelatives regularly allowed near the empress, eunuchs inevitably shared influence with the women they served. Eunuchs also formed a pool of ambitious, well-placed men outside the external bureaucracy who hungered for power and wealth. Some eunuch factions banded together with consort relatives. Others allied themselves with emperors who wanted a counterweight to consort kin ambitions in the palace. During the late Eastern Han the eunuchs seized control of the government, much to the detriment of the state.

When Emperor Huan wanted to seize power from his Liang in-laws and rule in his own right, the only power capable of overthrowing the Liangs was the eunuch faction. Huan managed to destroy the Liangs in 159 C.E., but this only handed real power to his eunuch allies. Eunuch power reached such extremes that the mothers of senior eunuchs imitated empresses dowager and began to interfere directly in government affairs, further reaffirming the privileged position of motherhood in early society.[53] After Emperor Huan's death in 167 C.E., tensions between eunuchs and officials broke into open hostilities. Historians usually cite a loss of support for the eunuch-dominated house of Liu as a prime cause for the fall of the Han dynasty.[54]

Massive rerouting of authority away from the emperors, initially undertaken by the empresses and their kin, undermined the institutional strengths of the Han dynasty and hastened its fall. For women to gain power within a system of government based on patrilineal principles, they had to undermine its fundamental institutions. The struggle of the mothers and wives of the emperors to gain power within a government in which legitimate authority belonged to men brought chaos upon China. The ultimate outcome was dynastic collapse.

ANTIFEMALE RHETORIC

The continual struggle for power between consort kin and officialdom inspired the enemies of imperial ladies to create rhetoric that justified excluding women from government. This rising tide of antifemale discourse systematized, popularized, and intensified earlier ideas opposed to female autonomy and power. Female political power rested on the prestige of key kinship roles, particularly mother and wife. Critics of female power tried to weaken this advantage by emphasizing a woman's innate femininity over her particular social roles. In other words, they argued that a woman is female first and a mother second. This shift in priorities allowed them to denigrate powerful consorts by arguing that women are intrinsically evil and untrustworthy.

Rising rationales for excluding women from the most important functions of government mark a key turning point in the history of Chinese women. Because so much early imperial discourse about the feminine arose as resistance to the abuses of influential ladies at court, it took on an extremely negative hue. The new imperial system produced a misogynistic ideology that became permanently embedded in elite thought. These antifemale concepts influenced elite rhetoric about women for the remainder of imperial history.

Some criticisms of influential women were very general. Officials interpreted strange occurrences and natural disasters as omens foretelling doom on account of the large numbers of palace ladies and the influence of their relatives.[55] This view depicted these women as the physical embodiments of abstract elements imbued with the feminine. Women were believed to represent the female-associated elements in various cosmological systems such as yin, Earth, and *kun*. Thinkers opposed to female political power repeatedly warned that an excess of feminine-associated elements in the cosmologically sensitive space of the court could unbalance the entire cosmos. Weird natural events proved that gendered elements in the palace needed readjustment, inevitably to the detriment of the women residing there.

Confucian morality could also undermine female privileges at court. Some critics of female power used the Confucian moral dictum that enjoined rulers to live frugally to condemn palace ladies as wasteful and extravagant.[56] This view portrayed the empress dowager not as a venerable mother but as an evil luxury. Since ancient times, some moral works had reduced women to their sensual attributes. In the eyes of many ancient thinkers, women were a corrupting sensual pleasure comparable to drunkenness and wasteful extravagance. Female beauty itself became proof of evil.[57] A woman could be simultaneously praised for her beauty and blamed for the immoral sensuality it represented. By reifying woman as an embodiment of sensuality, this strain of ancient political ethics barred the virtuous ruler from allowing court ladies any involvement in public matters.

Han officials revived this ancient antifemale rhetoric to criticize the involvement of imperial consorts in affairs of state. Bureaucrats and their sympathizers might not always have had full control over government, but as the educated elite they monopolized interpretation of the past. They could always vent their rage toward empresses and their relations by excoriating female participation in the government of prior ages. Through the course of the Han, women gained an increasingly bad reputation for undermining good government. Historians began to blame a particular woman for the fall of each dynasty.

Early historians looked upon a dynasty's fall as a profoundly troubling event. A change in dynasty overthrew the social, ritual, and cosmic hierarchies ordering the world. Therefore scholars took great trouble to explain the causes of these terrible upheavals so that future generations might avoid the mistakes of the past. According to a tradition of historical scholarship that culminated during the Han, Zhou conquered Shang because of their virtue. The Shang had begun as a righteous dynasty but had gradually grown dissolute. The final king of Shang allegedly lived a life of debauchery and cruelty. Thus the Zhou conquest of Shang was not only justified and inevitable, but could be considered a highly moral act.[58]

As historiography became more systematized under the Han, historians portrayed the final ruler of each dynasty as a cartoon of wickedness. They proved the legitimacy of each new ruling house by describing how depraved the old dynasty had become in its final years. Historians paired each evil last ruler with an even more reprehensible consort. Blaming the fall of a dynasty on a ruler's wife would have made sense to an audience accustomed to thinking of kinship as an important factor in politics. To be fair, under this new view of politics female influence was not entirely negative. Political rhetoric claimed that good women could have a beneficent influence on the state, and compared the virtuous and loyal official with a good wife.[59] But an emphasis on the negative influence of women on government became increasingly widespread.

Liu Xiang's *Biographies of Women* carried this interpretation of history to an extreme. His work implied that a good woman is the cause for the successful beginning of a dynasty and an evil woman is the primary cause for its fall.

> From ancient times, the virtuous kings certainly had an upright wife as a mate. If their consorts were upright, then they flourished; if they were not upright, then there was chaos. The success of Xia was by Tu Shan and its ruin by Mo Xi. The success of Yin was by You Shen and its ruin by Da Ji. The success of Zhou was by Tai Si and its ruin by Bao Si.[60]

As time passed, the reported extravagances and atrocities of the evil women of mythologized history became increasingly flamboyant. Eventually these monstrous viragos reached the proportions of one-dimensional caricature. They became simplistic symbols of depravity rather than depictions of real people. For example, Mo Xi, the beautiful but wicked consort of Jie (last ruler of the Xia dynasty), supposedly led the dynasty to ruin through her extravagance. Jie built her apartments of carnelian and ivory and presented her with a bed made of gems. As the common people starved, the debauched royal couple had dried meat hung in the trees as wasteful decorations and rowed around a pond of beer in a pleasure boat. She advised her husband on matters of state and wore a sword.[61]

Likewise the last ruler of the Shang followed the advice of his evil consort, Da Ji. She loved erotic music and dance, wasted the state's wealth on extravagances, encouraged drunkenness, allowed naked men and women to gambol about the palace, and tortured her enemies to death in ingeniously cruel fashions. When the conqueror King Wu of Zhou arrived at the Shang capital, she dressed in her finest robes to seduce him. As proof of his virtue, however, the upright Wu ordered her executed before she had a chance to throw herself on his mercy.[62]

The last queen of the Western Zhou, Bao Si, was just as evil. The unnatural spawn of a sinister black snake that impregnated her seven-year-old virginal mother, she also seduced her husband, King You, into extravagance and irresponsibility. For fun, she had the king light the signal fires that warned of an enemy attack and laughed at the hasty arrival of the troops responding to her frivolous prank. However, when a real attack finally came, troops failed to respond to the king's signal fires, leading to the demise of the Western Zhou.[63]

These exaggerated mythic images of an evil woman leading a dynasty to ruin became popular just as the power of Han empresses and their relatives threatened both the house of Liu and the careers of the scholar officials who wrote history. They contested female power in government with an increasingly virulent antifemale ideology. By combining antisensual ethics with a colorful reading of the murky events of remote antiquity, officials found a powerful weapon for fighting female influence at court. It was too late to remove women from Han government; institutions and customs had already evolved that made them an integral part of the imperial edifice. The best that their rivals could do was to popularize a negative image of powerful women. They undermined female political prestige by manipulating views of womanhood to their own advantage. The influence of this antifemale rhetoric was significant. Long after the particular political circumstances that produced this misogynistic rhetoric had passed, stereotypes of the evil woman in government remained as fossilized conventions in elite thought.[64]

6

Learning

Learning comes in many guises. People in a rapidly changing and highly technological society often see sagacity as the ability to manipulate large amounts of new information and adapt it to use in highly dynamic situations. In a primarily rural world bound more by respect for tradition than an urge to change, erudition had a very different definition. The educated person might hope to master the customs organizing social interaction, entertaining folklore that transmitted a common cultural identity, or religious practices explaining and even harnessing the supernatural. The literate minority would memorize and discuss a small number of revered texts.

When the women of early imperial China accumulated and displayed literate wisdom, it affected the social roles available to them. Proper female roles in culture did not go uncontested. Debate on the nature of female wisdom was a contentious topic. During this key era of intellectual systematization, Han dynasty thinkers strove to clearly delineate the relationship between women and knowledge. Many believed that women could be wise and good. But female education was also a useful vehicle for furthering patrilineal ideals. Some types of female education sought to confine women to restrictive social roles. In this era, thinkers of all orientations pioneered many new conceptions of ideal social roles for women. By embedding these ideals into a full-blown literature of female education, many Han conceptions of female identity became mainstream thinking and persisted to influence subsequent periods.

IGNORANCE AND CULTIVATION

Not every man thought women wise. Many ancient texts portrayed women as innately stupid and unteachable. Female ignorance gradually became conventionalized into literary tropes. A universal idea was said to be known by "even

111

women and babes"; a simple idea was said to be so obvious that a woman could grasp it.[1] The formulaic language of *Etiquette and Ritual (Yili)* would have a bride's father deprecate her as "dull and unteachable" to the matchmaker as a proper show of polite humility.[2] A man who believed what a woman said was criticized as a fool.[3] The Han dynasty intellectual world inherited this ancient body of thought and language portraying women as unintelligent.

An opposite trend in early thought saw women as capable of cultivation and able to reach the heights of wisdom. By early imperial times, commentators on the earliest stratum of the *Classic of Changes* were arguing that the essence of femininity is responsiveness (*kun*). This reflexive quality implied that cultivation and improvement were possible for women.[4] However wayward a woman might be, she could always better herself. Moreover, the Confucian vision of the Way (*dao*) also allowed female cultivation. Confucians believed that men and women improved themselves by cultivating the Way as the path to moral perfection. Mencius declared to his (presumably) male reader, "If you do not practice the Way yourself, you cannot expect it to be practiced even by your own wife and children."[5]

This view of the Way saw the possibility of moral improvement as so fundamental to human nature that it transcends gender, an optimistic and broadly inclusive vision of human nature covering women as well as men. To this way of thinking, femininity was secondary to a fundamental human essence shared by everyone. Humanist universalism, which undermined gender distinctions, permeated Confucian discourse. For example, *Doctrine of the Mean (Zhongyong)* declared that the most basic forms of moral behavior were found in the correct interaction of husband and wife. The author stated outright that both sexes could practice these moral virtues.[6] The universal humanism of Confucianism recognized the possibility of female virtue, allowing women to overcome negative ancient stereotypes of female ignorance and immorality. And if women could be good, a few might become morally great. Han rhetoric flirted with the possibility of comparing a particularly virtuous woman to a sage (*sheng*), the pinnacle of wisdom.[7]

Female wisdom gained so much respect that even men wary of female literate learning saw a role for women in the education of their sons. Yet many thinkers believed that the wisdom a mother imparted to a son was likely to be moral rather than intellectual. Even authorities who downplayed female intellectual capacities sometimes admitted that women are morally perfectible, allowing them respected roles as exemplars of virtue and teachers of ethics. This link between virtue and wisdom elevated female prestige. Illiterate women could hold highly sophisticated ethical views. This emphasis on morality as a respected form of wisdom meant that mothers could play an important role in educating their children.

A woman's moral education of her child could begin in the womb; people believed that beneficent influences on a pregnant woman were transmitted to the fetus.[8] Immediately after giving birth, a mother became moral guide and teacher—a role that might continue after her children were fully grown.[9] It was her duty to discipline her offspring to bring out the essential good inherent in their underlying nature. A mother's guidance of her children's moral development lasted into school days. After literate education had begun, the mother was still responsible for guiding her children by word and example.

The tale of Mencius's mother, popular among Han readers, sums up the ideal maternal role in literate education. One day the young Mencius failed to apply himself to his studies. When his mother heard about his sloth, she shocked the young sage by cutting a thread on her loom, thereby ruining a day's work (fig. 6.1). Through this dramatic demonstration she impressed on her son the danger

Figure 6.1. Mencius's Mother Cutting the Thread on Her Loom. Late imperial woodblock print. Liu Xiang, *Gulienüzhuan* (Shanghai: Shangwu, 1936), p. 21 (1:11).

that one wasted day poses to developing proper character.[10] Moral education was a full-time pursuit requiring iron discipline.

Readers enthusiastically embraced this moving story. Mencius's mother manipulated two respected social roles to lend force to her point: mother and weaver. Both roles commanded high moral authority. The devoted mother slaving tirelessly at her loom to provide for her son was itself a moving image of the good woman. And a woman's skill at the loom was analogous to literate learning among the male elite—both were sources of livelihood, prestige, and financial security.[11] Mencius's mother used her respected role as industrious and self-sacrificing mother to demand improvements in her son's behavior. And her sacrifices obviously worked. Mencius's success as moral paragon was largely due to his mother's careful guidance.

The possibility of a cultivated woman teaching and advising wayward men seems to have disconcerted patrilinealists, who had to reconcile female submission to men in higher kinship roles with the potential for superior female moral accomplishment.[12] The problem was straightforward: If women can be good and men bad, should a good woman use her virtue as an excuse to upset kinship hierarchies dominated by bad men? For example, if a bad husband tries to commit evil but his good wife knows better, what should she do? Individual moral accomplishment had to be reconciled with a patrilineal system that, while seen as basically good, might be manipulated by bad people.

The careful phrasing of Han Ying's compromise betrays these tensions. "The wife, being pliant and submissive, is obedient. If her husband acts (in a manner) not in accordance with the proper way, though frightened, she herself urges him (to be good)."[13] Han Ying maintains female submission to male superiors and allows a good woman only the possibility of meekly remonstrating with bad men above her. In the end, though, Han Ying seems to believe that the good wife ought to obey her bad husband, even if he forces her to embark on an evil course.

SCHOLARSHIP

Some women went beyond moral accomplishments to embrace literate learning as well. A few well-placed women gained fame for their patronage of scholarship and literature. For example, Empress Dowager Liang (d. 150 c.e.) supported those who studied and commented on the classics, becoming a great patron of the imperial academy. To encourage serious scholarship among the officialdom, she ordered that the sons of all high officials attend the academy twice a year.[14] Other powerful women took a more partisan role in actively promoting a particular school of thought. Officials might be dismissed from court for espousing academic views contrary to those of the current empress dowager.[15]

Empress Dou (d. 135 B.C.E.) was the most enthusiastic female patron of scholarship in the early empire. She used every means at her disposal to propagate Huanglao thought, an amalgam of various ideas based largely on Daoism. Her partisanship came at a sensitive time. Confucianism was not yet entrenched as the official ideology of the new imperial system. Empress Dou wanted to make Huanglao the official doctrine of government. She forced Emperors Wen and Jing, as well as all members of the Dou family, to study the writings attributed to the mythical Huang Di and Laozi and to practice their teachings.[16] Under her enthusiastic support, Huanglao reached its height of popularity. The various Laozi and Huanglao manuscripts unearthed at Mawangdui attest to the success of her proselytizing.[17] Empress Dou was so insistent in advocating Huanglao that she blocked the careers of important officials who made no secret of their preference for the rival doctrines of Confucianism. Only after Dou's death could Emperor Wu, who was highly sympathetic to many Confucian ideas, radically alter imperial ideology by appointing a vigorous advocate of Confucianism to head the government.[18]

The popularity of both syncretistic Huanglao and orthodox Daoism among palace ladies deserves explanation. Daoism has often been described as a "feminine" ideal for the way in which it advocates stereotypically feminine behavior (such as quietude and submission) to compensate for the overly "masculine" tendencies among many in its intended audience.[19] Because Daoism seeks to unify all opposites, it should not be seen as either completely "feminine" or "masculine" in outlook. But because Daoism lacked the patrilineal elements implicit in Confucianism and ritual thought, women might find it particularly amenable. Considering the strong feminine associations with Daoism, it is no wonder that this way of thought attracted vocal and assiduous female advocates during the Han.[20]

Elite women did more than just patronize literature and philosophy written by men. Some ladies from high-ranking families and the imperial line were themselves fully literate. A few distinguished themselves with outstanding literary accomplishments. Literacy seems to have been related as closely to social background as to gender. Ordinary women who spent their lives caring for babies and carrying pots of water on their head would have had little use for literate learning. But women born into the educated families who supplied the empire with its officials had different opportunities in life. They had access to books and grew up around men imbued with a profound respect for learning. Some fathers among the elite actively educated their daughters, believing that this would allow them access to profound moral wisdom locked away in the written word.[21]

The erudite Ban Zhao (45–120 c.e.) advocated female education with enormous subtlety. Her carefully phrased arguments suggest a fear among some men that literacy might undermine female loyalty to husbands and fathers. Ban Zhao portrayed female education as a way of strengthening patrilineal values, but from the form of her arguments it is clear that many people suspected otherwise. She defended education for women by pointing out that *Records of Ritual* states that children should be taught to read at age eight. Presumably this statement included girls as well as boys. Her choice of rhetoric in this matter was ingenious. By referring to the sort of ritual text the patrilinealist opponents of female education revered, she used their own ideas against them. She also defended female education on utilitarian grounds, again appealing to the values most likely to resonate with her critics. She argued that if women can read, they will have access to the historical and ritual texts that will teach them patrilineal values, such as obedience to their husbands.[22] According to this view, a female mind enlightened by immersion in morally upright texts would inevitably tend to favor female subservience to the patrilineal hierarchy, a premise supported by Ban Zhao's own personal example.

Although Ban Zhao believed that women should receive literate education, she clearly considered nonwritten wisdom far more important for female students. She followed earlier works such as *Rites of Zhou (Zhouli)* in stressing ethics, proper speech and comportment, and handiwork as the most basic topics of female education.[23] Generally speaking, Confucian-oriented education consisted of two main fields: morals and literature. Men were always expected to master both. But Ban Zhao thought that women should concentrate mainly on the former. A full literary education was of course an admirable ornament to a woman's learning. But her basic goal should be moral cultivation.[24] Skeptical observers have read this stress on female virtue as a rhetorical tool for depressing women's cultural status.[25]

Ban Zhao's emphasis on moral learning was the start of a long tradition of specialized moral learning for women that lasted through the Tang dynasty. Afterward, although female education continued to place particular stress on moral development, the curriculum for women increasingly resembled that for male students.[26] Ironically, the example of Ban Zhao herself was used in late imperial times to undermine Ban's explicit message that nonliterate ethical accomplishment should take primacy over literate learning in female education. The writings of Ban Zhao, universally praised as model texts that exhorted women to devote themselves mainly to the nonliterate study of virtue, ironically proved that a woman could excel in book learning. Late imperial advocates of literate female education used the fact that Ban Zhao's mastery of the written medium undermined her advocacy of oral education. Efforts by late imperial women to establish a female literary tradition almost always began with Ban Zhao.[27]

Although some men had reservations about literate female education, many elite women were clearly literate. Some even excelled in reading and writing. *Biographies of Women* mentions two women particularly skilled in letters: one deciphered a coded message sent by her son that none of the male courtiers could read, while another wrote such an eloquent elegy for her husband's funeral that his disciples "were unable to correct even one character."[28] One official's wife was so skilled at calligraphy and composing essays that she often wrote letters on behalf of her less talented husband.[29] And most famously, in 167 B.C.E. a woman named Tiying personally wrote a memorial to the throne requesting mercy for her father, a provincial official who had been found guilty of a serious crime (fig. 6.2).[30] The ability to draft this formal petition shows a familiarity with the difficult stylized language of court documents.

Some women went beyond letters and minor essays to undertake a serious study of the classics. At this level, female scholars aspired to reach the heights of sophistication occupied by the most learned men. Han dynasty women made lasting contributions to scholarship on works as important as the *Book of Documents (Shangshu)*, *Classic of Changes (Yijing)*, *and Records of Ritual (Liji)*.[31]

Some female scholars were particularly interested in history. There was a good reason for this predilection. During the Han, the essence of history was thought to consist of previous moralistic examples to be emulated and disastrous errors to be avoided. As such, it formed a major practical component of any future ruler's education. With the ascendancy of empresses dowager at court, it was desirable that these powerful ladies should be well versed in history. For example, because Empress Dowager Huo held titular control of government at the beginning of Emperor Xuan's reign in the first century B.C.E., her grandfather (the powerful kingmaker Huo Guang) saw to it that an accomplished scholar tutor her in the *Book of Documents* to prepare her for her weighty duties.[32]

Han women certainly did not limit themselves to the hoary *Book of Documents* in their studies of the past. Three famed scholars, all surnamed Liu, were so enthusiastic about the *Zuo Commentary (Zuozhuan)* that they taught it to all of their family members, including their women. The Lius's schooling of women-folk in this classic earned them the scorn of the scholar Huan Tan (43 B.C.E.–28 C.E.), who categorically criticized literate female education.[33] Some women showed strong loyalty to this important text. The disagreements between the

Figure 6.2. Tiying Presents a Memorial Requesting Mercy for Her Father. Late imperial woodblock print. Lü Kun, *Lü Xinwu xiansheng guifan tushuo sijuan*. In *Siku quanshu cunmu congshu* (Tainan: Zhuangyan Wenhua, 1995), vol. 3:129, p. 515 (2:8a).

famed scholar Liu Xiang (79–8 B.C.E.) and his wife illustrate this tendency. Although Liu Xiang mocked the *Zuo Commentary* and studied the rival *Gu Liang Commentary*, his wife continued to recite the *Zuo*.[34] At the time, the choice of *Zuo* versus *Gu* was considered a major intellectual statement. For a wife to defy her husband's preference in this matter, especially a husband so accomplished and renowned, showed considerable self-confidence.

And of course there are the contributions to historical scholarship by the accomplished Ban Zhao. She was instrumental in compiling and editing *Records of the Han (Hanshu)*, the standard history of the Western Han dynasty. It is unfortunate that her contributions to this exhaustive compendium rarely receive the credit they deserve. Although the *Records* were begun by her father and mostly written by her brother Ban Gu, the composition of several sections and final editing were left to Ban Zhao after her brother's untimely death.[35]

Nor did women limit their interests to history alone; other fields of learning also sparked the curiosity of literate women. Some female scholars were especially noted for their breadth of erudition. The Empress Dowager Ma (d. 79 C.E.), wife of Emperor Ming, "chanted the *Classic of Changes*, memorized the *Classic of Songs (Shijing)*, and discussed the main principles of the *Spring and Autumn Annals*."[36] She disliked the *Elegies of Chu (Chuci)*, dismissing them as overly florid. Her own more severe tastes inclined toward the writings of the philosopher Dong Zhongshu and the historical annals of Emperor Guangwu. She composed occasional belles lettres and annotated her husband's biography.[37]

Not content to study the works of others, some talented and creative women inevitably tried their hand at scholarship and essays. The incomparable Ban Zhao was a polymath who wrote in a range of genres, including didactic literature, history, poetry, and memorials. Some of her work has been preserved. Unfortunately, Ban Zhao's case is exceptional; the vicissitudes of time have been at least as unkind to the writings of women as to those of men. Many female authors are now known only by their reputation. As a case in point, a Han woman named Xu Xiaoji authored a *Biography of Laozi (Laozizhuan)* as well as a book in six sections entitled *Discussions of the Classics (Shuojing)*, presumably referring to the Daoist canon. Both works have been lost.[38] The intellectual accomplishments of elite women of the early empire were clearly both considerable and varied.

LITERATURE

The most numerous literary works written by Han dynasty women that happen to survive are poems.[39] Perhaps as with the court ladies of Heian Japan, women of early China may have found it more socially acceptable to engage in the creative fancies of poetry than in the more serious business of philosophy and scholarship. And the poet assumed a respectable public role that nevertheless allowed her to express intimate thoughts and emotions normally kept hidden from view. Poetic conventions presented women with a way to escape from ordinary social conventions that denied them freedom of expression. As such, poetic composition was a rare form of individualism in a society that valued the group, and liberty in a culture that taught conformity. Nor were female poets yet smothered by an enormous and oppressive tradition of male-authored poetry written from the female perspective, as was the case in later periods.

In an age when literature and music were still closely linked, many Han dynasty professional musicians were women (fig. 6.3). Higher up on the social scale, elite ladies also wrote verse. Some women produced a sufficient body of poetry to be collected into an individual anthology. As with most early poetry, however, these collections have been lost. Xu Shu (fl. mid-second century c.e.) and Cai Yan (fl. late second century c.e.) each had their collected verses edited and distributed. However, only a few miscellaneous poems of extremely high quality happen to survive.[40] The considerable oeuvre of Lady Ban (late first century b.c.e.), a favored consort of Emperor Cheng, now survives in a few frag-

Figure 6.3.   Musician. Female tomb figurine unearthed at Yuzhuang, Henan. Sun, *Handai wuzhi wenhua ziliao tushuo,* **fig. 97.8.**

ments. But these remnants earned the admiration of no less than the immortal poets Li Bo and Wang Wei, whose taste in fine poetry can surely be trusted.[41] Lady Ban particularly enjoyed poems with upright moral content. She actively sought out good moral and literary influences from great women of the past, suggesting at the beginning of a distinctly female tradition in literature. As Lady Ban wrote, "I arranged before me pictures of women as models; / Regarding the women scholars and considering their poetry."[42]

Most of the remaining fragments of poems by Han women have survived only because they happen to have been quoted in historical works. Early historians, gifted with a sharp literary sense, would often quote a poignant poem for dramatic effect. For example, Xijun (fl. early second century B.C.E.), the daughter of a Han king, provided the historian with a poem conveying the despair of a lady forced into a detested marriage of state with the elderly ruler of the Wusun nomads.

> A yurt for a home, felt for walls,
> Eating meat, drinking milk.
> I often dream of home, my heart aching,
> I wish I were a goose, flying back to my old roost.[43]

This lachrymose woman mourns the vanished delights of her past life. These sad lyrics could just as easily have been written about the extinct body of accomplished women's poetry, whose few surviving fragments tantalize us with the certainty that greater glories have been lost forever.

DIDACTIC TEXTS

Books dedicated to female education paralleled the methods and goals of male-oriented Confucian rhetoric. Confucianism teaches conformity with the behavioral roles believed to constitute a good and orderly society. This ethical system attempts to transform people by convincing them to fit into ideal social roles. In this way, they become good and content. And when key people in society adhere to their proper roles, society itself improves, much to everyone's benefit. But classic Confucian works had a major shortcoming: they were usually directed to a specifically male audience. The Confucian canon rarely addressed the unique roles and problems facing women. Consequently, during the Han dynasty, when Confucianism became the main state ideology and patrilineal values were on the rise, some thinkers tried to remedy the gender bias of Confucian discourse by composing didactic moral works specifically for women.

These books presented idealized visions of female social roles with eloquence and considerable detail. The basic message of this genre was similar to that previously directed at men. Women should restrain their behavior by conforming to carefully defined patrilineal social roles. Committing ideal behaviors to heart and using these guidelines to direct daily conduct, women could achieve goodness, respect, and success. But female didactic texts differed from male-oriented counterparts in stressing gender distinctions. If gender was to be understood, differences between the sexes had to be articulated. And to the early Chinese mind, social differences usually took the form of hierarchies. Therefore moralists set forth ideal gendered social roles unambiguously distinguished as superior and inferior to guide ethical female behavior.

Why would women accept these stern limits on their personal autonomy? These ideals were certainly not easy to follow. By modern standards, they seem unfair and draconian. But it seems that many women of early imperial China accepted them. Their primary motivation seems to have been a sincere desire to be seen as good. The woman who adhered to ideal female social roles was rewarded with a reputation for virtue. If she sacrificed her own interests to abide by gendered patrilineal roles, those around her would invariably praise her as a good daughter, wife, or mother.

.More abstractly, submitting to the patrilineal hierarchy held psychological benefits. A woman who accepted these carefully defined social roles would have had many stable points of reference in her life. She knew what she ought to do and why she was doing it. This certainty could give her a secure sense of self. In other words, these texts presented not just an ideal lifestyle based on patrilineal thought but also a detailed blueprint for how to be a woman. Abiding by standard social roles not only allowed a woman to be praised as virtuous but also gave her a clear and consistent sense of herself as a complete and successful woman.

Ban Zhao's *Admonitions for Women (Nüjie)* was written by a woman for a female readership. She explains in her introduction that she wrote this book for her daughters to study in preparation for marriage.[44] However, her daughters seem to have already been grown and probably married at the time, so this statement seems to have been a rhetorical convention. The book was really intended for an audience far beyond Ban's immediate family. *Admonitions for Women* persuasively proselytized patrilineal concepts such as female chastity and obedience to kinship hierarchy. It served as a model for later didactic literature aimed at women, and was widely read from the Eastern Han onward.[45]

Admonitions for Women has elicited strong reactions from both admirers and detractors. In tribute to Ban Zhao's persuasive arguments in support of female submission to male superiors, the traditional male intellectual mainstream has canonized her as China's greatest female scholar. From a Marxist or feminist viewpoint, however, Ban Zhao appears to be the alienated tool of misogynistic reactionaries. A more dispassionate reading of this subtle work must transcend such black and white extremes. To put the matter in present-day terms, Ban Zhao tried to reconcile a "conservative" advocacy of chastity and submission to kinship hierarchies with a "progressive" advocacy of female literacy and cultivation.[46] Given these considerable contradictions, this text defies simple translation into modern ideologies. It is more useful to try to understand how readers of the time would have understood these complex ideas.

A conventional reading of *Admonitions for Women* sees it as an orthodox statement of how Confucian principles can be applied to women's lives. The contrast between Ban Zhao's own stringent morals and more relaxed popular customs makes her part of the gradual shift toward Confucianism through the course of the dynasty.[47] Ban Zhao emphasized concepts that fit with key patrilineal values embedded in the strict moral rhetoric of the New Text School of Confucianism. From this perspective it seems that Ban Zhao participated in the ongoing movement of patrilinealizing all aspects of social relations. Confucians and ritualists had already actively pursued this project. In using patrilineal values to advise women on correct behavior, Ban Zhao was simply applying an increasingly important mode of discourse to a new area of concern.

We should not forget that to increasing numbers of educated people in early imperial China, the moral dictates of patrilineal values were synonymous with the standards for a successful life. When they wanted to judge their own accomplishments or those of others, they would use this set of unusually strict values. A woman who lived in accordance with the values put forth in Ban Zhao's primer of good female behavior would undoubtedly have earned the admiration of influential people around her. In a society founded on patrilineal kinship relations, this work gave women a concise and easily understood guide to living a life that those around them would have celebrated as successful and praiseworthy.[48]

However, Ban Zhao's goal may not have been so simple. Yu-shih Chen has recently put forward an exciting alternative reading of *Admonitions for Women*.[49] Although Ban Zhao employed the Confucianized rhetoric of patrilineal values in her writings, she was a broadly learned woman who did not confine her studies to one school of thought. In fact, close analysis of this work's language has revealed remarkable similarities with texts on Huanglao and military strategy that were also in vogue during the Han. Instead of simplistically advocating the self-sacrificing morality of patrilinealism, these ways of thought advised women to follow a doctrine of self-preservation by tactically modifying their behavior to survive under the particular conditions of the moment.

This philosophy of personal survival developed in response to centuries of dangerous chaos that had threatened China's elite with an endless series of plots and intrigues. The murder and demotion of many palace ladies shows that these dangers threatened women as much as men. *Admonitions for Women* can be interpreted as a very pragmatic handbook teaching elite women how to survive the life-threatening intrigues at court and in the household. Assuming an outward appearance of meekness and obedience would have made a woman seem less threatening to those around her, thereby increasing her chances of surviving violent plots. If she did not seem dangerous, others would be less likely to scheme against her. From this perspective, *Admonitions for Women* seems like extremely sophisticated strategy teaching women how to survive in a dangerous age. The savvy woman could adopt the self-effacing rhetoric of patrilinealism as a kind of ideological camouflage that would render her innocuous in the eyes of her enemies. Instead of condemning Ban Zhao's thought as a heavy-handed tool for oppressing women, we might alternatively interpret it as an inspired guide for survival and success in the dangerous world of Han dynasty intrigue. The domination of government by Ban Zhao's disciple Empress Deng (d. 121 C.E.) proves that elite women could indeed use patrilineal rhetoric to their own advantage.

Admonitions for Women was not the first or only piece of didactic literature aimed at a female readership. It was merely the most famous exemplar of a copious genre, most of which has been lost.[50] Prior to Ban Zhao there was a book called *Pattern for Women (Nüxian)*. Although the full text no longer exists, two brief quotations in Ban Zhao's work show that this ancient book also advocated patrilineal values. A daughter-in-law should obey her husband's parents, and a wife should respect her husband's opinions. This ancient work suggests that Ban Zhao was building on an existing genre of a female didactic literature that advocated patrilineal values.[51] Other Eastern Han and Wei works explored similar themes.[52] Ban Zhao did not originate the genre, nor did it end with her. She composed her work within much larger intellectual and literary traditions.

Similar to abstract didactic works in intent if not form, the genre of exemplary female biography also matured during the Han. These different genres had overlapping goals, as seen in Ban Zhao's literary output. She not only wrote the famed *Admonitions for Women* but also annotated *Biographies of Women* and produced an independent work, apparently a treatise on female biography, entitled *Admonitions from the History of Women (Nüshizhen)*.[53] Though echoing shared themes, the paired traditions of female-oriented admonitory works and exemplary female biography followed established genres. Early Chinese often studied ethics and biography in tandem. Ethics provided moral theory. But life was always more complicated than the philosopher's absolutes could encompass. Therefore biographies of historical personages were used to demonstrate virtue and vice in action. To use modern terminology, *Admonitions for Women* was theory; *Biographies of Women* was practice.

Female biography also took inspiration from Sima Qian's innovative brand of history. Sima Qian made the past seem more immediate and dramatic by emphasizing the importance of key individuals in shaping momentous events. Though highly confusing from a chronological point of view, Sima Qian's *Records of the Historian (Shiji)* revolutionized historical writing by focusing on individuals who personified specific moral traits and then classifying these representative personages according to type. While Sima Qian abandoned the chronological format supposedly favored by Confucius, he nevertheless advanced the Confucian project of moralizing the past. Sima Qian's style of history allowed the historian to render more precise moral classifications of individual personalities for the reader's edification.

Sima's technique solved a major problem endemic to biography. The biographer must somehow choose selected events from a person's life and form these incidents into a coherent and meaningful narrative. In effect, a person's life must be turned into a story that adheres to current literary conventions so that readers will find it entertaining or edifying. Sima Qian believed that the meaning of a person's life is primarily moral. Superimposing an ethical template onto biographical history gave people's lives a larger meaning, allowing them to be made into compelling stories. Following Sima Qian's insight, female biography adopted a similar approach. Biographies of women written during the Han usually sought to highlight virtuous or evil behavior. Female readers could use these unambiguous examples as practical guides for their own behavior.

The greatest work of early female biography was *Biographies of Women (Lienüzhuan)*.[54] The tireless editor and scholar Liu Xiang collected material on women's lives and arranged their biographies according to the moral traits exemplified by these famous women. Liu brought together female archetypes such as outstanding mothers, female sages, and women deemed unusually wicked.[55] These were not just amusing stories about prominent women. He wrote the work with a very specific goal in mind. He intended the book as a warning to Emperor Cheng against the evil machinations of his favorite Zhao Feiyan and her sister, who were rumored to have murdered two imperial heirs and persecuted their female enemies. Not coincidentally, the female victims of the Zhaos were relatively educated. The particular political circumstances behind the composition of *Biographies of Women* explains why Liu praised virtuous, wise, and educated women, and warned that evil consorts inevitably have catastrophic effects on the state.[56] He was using biographies of past women as a veiled critique of the current political situation.

Although Liu Xiang seems to have written *Biographies of Women* for an express purpose, subsequent audiences forgot the details behind its creation and read it more generally as a practical moral primer on ideal female behavior. Although both women and men have important roles to play in society, traditional historical biography had slighted female lives, leaving a vacuum in female education. According to this broader reading, Liu Xiang remedied this problem by supplying female counterparts to Sima Qian's good and evil men of the past. These exemplary women provided memorable, three-dimensional embodiments of positive female social roles.

The success of Liu Xiang's work can be seen in the inevitable imitators. The Eastern Han author Liu Xi wrote a different *Biographies of Women* that has failed to survive.[57] Moreover, Liu Xiang's ideas seem to have influenced local values.[58] During the Eastern Han, communities began rewarding a chaste woman or righteous wife by erecting an honorific tablet at her door.[59] For example, neighbors in one village recognized the virtuous self-sacrifice of a local widow who cut off

Figure 6.4.   Chaste Jiang Drowned Rather Than Leave Her Home without Her Husband's Permission. Feng, *Jinshisuo,* **3:4.**

her ear to avoid forced remarriage. They inscribed the village gate "Righteously Behaving Widow Huan" and presented her with a share of the sacrificial meats.[60] Other women who epitomized patrilineal values also had posthumous tablets and portraits commissioned in their honor by admiring communities.[61]

Even pictorial art imitated the female moral biography of Liu Xiang's text. At about the same time that Liu brought together his biographical collection, pictures illustrating virtuous women also seem to have been gaining popularity.[62] Like the paintings on medieval European rood screens or the narrative elements of Hindu temple architecture, early Chinese pictures of virtuous women supplemented a complicated textual tradition. Visual art was a useful tool for popularizing elite ideals. Didactic visual media extended female moral biography to a nonliterate audience while supplementing appreciation of patrilineal ideals among the literate. Even Liu Xiang's own original text reputedly had accompanying illustrations, now unfortunately lost.[63]

A few examples of this artistic tradition have escaped destruction. An exquisitely painted Eastern Han tomb lintel and pediment, now in the Museum of Fine Arts, Boston, juxtaposes upright officials on one side of the stone with virtuous women on the other.[64] The figures on both sides represented exemplary

Figure 6.5. The Virtuous Aunt of Liang Burned to Death Rather Than Immodestly Expose Herself to Public View. Reconstruction of a rubbing from the Wu Liang shrine, Shandong. Feng, *Jinshisuo,* **3:32–33.**

people admired for adhering to strict ethics. Positioning men and women on opposite sides of the composition emphasized that each sex had different yet parallel social roles regulated by similar moral values. Patrilineal morality united the sexes within a common system of values while simultaneously differentiating them by confining each sex to separate roles. In this way, women and men were both united and distinguished within an all-encompassing worldview.

More famous than the Boston stone is the depiction of chaste and virtuous women at the incomparable Wu Liang shrine in present-day Shandong. The complex pictorial scheme of this extended series of incised stones follows Sima Qian's concept of general history; the lives of exemplary individuals embody the spirit of the past.[65] The inclusion of stories about notable women from Liu Xiang's *Biographies of Women* transposed gender ideals from an elite textual form to a pictorial medium comprehensible even to the illiterate. Who could fail to be moved by images of the Virtuous Aunt of Liang who perished in a burning building rather than immodestly expose herself to public view, or Chaste Jiang who drowned in a flood rather than leave her home without her husband's permission (figs. 6.4, 6.5). Visual art made female biography concrete and dramatic. Through visual media, elite ideals could reach people at all levels of society. Subsequent literature and art followed Han examples in repeatedly replicating ideal roles for women taken from patrilineal rhetoric and then thoroughly disseminating these views throughout society.

7

Ritual

Ritual has almost as many interpretations as there are interpreters. Even a ceremony as simple as a handshake can convey many profound meanings.[1] By functioning simultaneously on so many different levels of significance, ritual evokes enormous resonance in both participant and observer. Thought is abstract idea; ritual is concrete action. Early Chinese used ritual to express important social and cultural patterns.

Jack Goody provides one widely quoted definition of ritual: "a category of standardized behavior (custom) in which the relationship between the means and the end is not 'intrinsic.' "[2] Unfortunately, this definition is problematic. A definition of ritual as an action whose means and ends are not clearly connected (from the anthropologist's point of view) resides with the observer rather than the performer. To a shaman, dancing to summon rain might seem to be obvious cause and effect. But when the anthropologist interprets this belief according to the alien cognitive criteria of social science, it is declared nonrational and hence ritualistic. Different observers may give conflicting interpretations of a ritual's meaning, but these disagreements only emphasize the fundamental richness of ritual as a means of ordering and explaining our world.[3] Ritual evokes many diverse interpretations and responses because it is so profound.

In early imperial China, ritual placed the individual within larger social, religious, and cosmological conceptual systems. Through ritual performance, the individual assumed appropriate roles within the community. In particular, ritual integrated a person into the kinship network at the heart of society. Ritual performance was therefore an important tool for defining the ideal behavior of each social role and defining the principles of orderly social interaction. Ritual accomplished this by publicly categorizing people not as unique individuals but as performers of general roles. By defining each person's place in the world, ritual helped create, justify, teach, and maintain personal identity as well. Through ritual, the individual renounced the sense of unique individual self only to have the self reemerge with greater force as a fully integrated member of the kinship network and social community.[4]

Ritual was fundamental to constructing a sense of self among the women of early imperial China. The performance roles of ritual, rite, and etiquette told a woman who she was and what she should do. These formalized practices taught a woman the meaning of her femininity while providing acceptable roles for expressing her female identity within the all-important patrilineal kinship network. In performing these acts, women distinguished themselves from men and assumed specifically female roles within comprehensive social and cosmological systems. Ritual was therefore one of the most important means to become a complete and successful woman.

It is tempting to cynically interpret ritual as a system created to control women's behavior. Adhering to these restrictive codes of conduct certainly reduced individual autonomy. But rituals clarified the major roles that constituted society (e.g., woman, mother, wife, daughter-in-law, and empress) and socialized individuals to accept these roles. This accumulation of richly layered social roles lent a person subjective identity. Ritualized roles did not just demarcate social differences; they also defined the self and established orderly modes of social interaction for members of both sexes.

Moreover, as an all-inclusive hierarchical code of social relations, ritual controlled men as well as women. A man also had to subordinate himself to his superior in a given social hierarchy. Sometimes this meant obeying a woman of superior age, generation, or social stratum. To judge the effect of ritual in constraining female behavior, it would not be accurate to simply point to a few rules and automatically conclude that all early Chinese ritual denigrated women. Rules limiting female behavior must be compared to those that restrained men. A rule-based society grounded in ritual roles reduced everyone's autonomy, but in return it provided order, meaning, and a sense that the world is a good place.

DEVELOPMENT

A large and sophisticated body of ritual writings came together during the Eastern Zhou and Han periods.[5] The distinction between elite ritual (li) and popular custom (su) was vague. Ritual often began as popular custom that had become progressively formalized and stylized. Conversely, sometimes officials urged ordinary people to follow elite ritual in an effort to raise popular moral standards. Therefore the social scope of ritual enlarged enormously during the Han.[6]

Because ritual was so important, Zhou philosophers analyzed it in detail. Xunzi (third century B.C.E.) put forth a particularly influential definition of ritual as a natural extension of human feelings.[7] By linking ritual with Confucian moral philosophy, Xunzi and others began to use ritual as a tool for codifying patrilineal social roles.

Xunzi's student Li Si (d. 208 B.C.E.), infamous to later eras for his ruthless realpolitik, influenced the First Emperor of Qin in a surprising way. Li reiterated his teacher's ideas about the importance of ritual, convincing his ruler to make it a cornerstone of the new imperial system. The first Han dynasty ruler followed this precedent. Emperor Gaozu also relied on ritual to regulate society and legitimize government. Rulers and ruled could each refer to the rites to determine what was expected of them, allowing the realm to become stable and good. The Han elite found ritual a valuable technique for managing their subjects.

Most information on early Chinese ritual comes from three sources, all of which seem to bear the mark of Western Han editors: *Rites of Zhou (Zhouli)*, *Etiquette and Ritual (Yili)*, and *Records of Ritual (Liji)*.[8] Most of the ceremonies described in these three works probably represent only ideals of how some ritual experts thought that stylized performances should be conducted. In many cases they probably do not portray rituals as they were ever actually performed. Yet all three texts were extremely influential. Each was widely distributed and reverently studied. They summed up the ideals of an increasingly influential school of thought and had profound influence on both the Han and later eras. In fact, these rules were more revered in some later periods than in the society that produced them.[9] Nevertheless, during the early imperial era, political ritual had already become an important source of legitimacy and majesty for the Han emperors; in cosmology, the rites came to be seen as the force maintaining the delicate balance between heaven, earth, and human beings; and in social relations, ceremony and etiquette regulated the interactions of individuals to promote harmony and preserve social distinctions.[10] In short, ritual permeated and organized the most vital aspects of the human and supernatural worlds.

Intimate familiarity with ritual was in many cases the legacy of high birth. The Zhou dynasty *shi* elite used ritual practices to distinguish themselves from the untutored masses in much the same way that members of the Western middle class use "good" table manners as a sign of class identity (fig. 7.1).[11] This tendency to identify ritual knowledge with exalted birth continued into the Han. In his *Biographies of Women*, Liu Xiang judged the consorts of rulers according to the dual standards of virtue (defined as adherence to ritual standards) and birth.[12] And during the Eastern Han, when genealogy was more highly valued, the great families stressed ritual to distinguish themselves as superior and aloof.

Figure 7.1.   Serving Food. Incised stone unearthed at Baiji, Xuzhou, Jiangsu. Sun,
Handai wuzhi wenhua ziliao tushuo, **fig. 81.11.**

Ban Zhao's repeated calls for her privileged female readers to strictly observe the
rites seems to be a strategy to strengthen elite group identity through common
ritual.[13] This was also a way for women to raise their individual status in society.
The familiarity with ritual displayed by elite ladies shows that the rites were far
more closely associated with status than gender. In fact, women sometimes had
an advantage over men in this regard. Shusun Tong initiated the Western Han
system of court ritual by first teaching it to court ladies who then demonstrated
it to the court as a whole.[14] He apparently considered women more amenable to
ritual learning than the crude soldiers who made up Gaozu's court.

The systematization of ritual during the early empire created coherent standards for good female behavior. More than just a set of formalized rules for
acceptable conduct, ritual constructed a wide array of ideal social roles. Many of
these roles enacted gender distinctions. Rituals therefore embodied specific
views of model female behavior. Even when these roles were no more than utopian ideals, they nonetheless presented women of the Qin and Han with authoritative guides for female behavior that demanded serious contemplation.[15]

MARRIAGE

Of all the ceremonies a woman could experience in her life, none altered her
existence as decisively as marriage. Through this liminal event the bride shifted

her primary allegiance from one group of kin and ancestors to another. This momentous transformation affected a woman's basic essence; she was to be referred to as a *nü* before the marriage rite and a *fu* afterward.[16] This nomenclature shows that the marriage rite was believed to fundamentally transform women. The role of wife brought with it new social roles that made her a different kind of person.

The ritual canons contained copious regulations on the proper conduct of marriage.[17] However, marriage generally remained the domain of local custom. Despite calls by for marriage to be reformed and systematized along the lines of elite ritual, marriage customs received only haphazard influence from ritualists.[18] Early discussions of marriage by ritual experts usually had more to do with how an author believed the ceremony should be conducted than with actual practices.

Prior to the marriage ceremony came the important task of choosing a mate. A few Zhou and Han records mention marriages arranged directly by the couple themselves.[19] An affectionate strain in early Chinese art and literature suggests that love may have been the motive behind some unions (see, e.g., fig. 2.2). Han Ying held carefully considered views of marriages arranged by a couple themselves. He points out that whereas a couple usually did not arrange their own marriage, this sort of marriage was permissible as long as their motives were pure.[20] However, most surviving records show that marriages were usually arranged by the couple's parents, elders, relatives, or social superiors.[21]

Matchmakers played an essential role in the arranged marriage.[22] But dealings with a matchmaker could be frustrating. Comic portrayal of matchmakers in ancient literature lampooned the overly eager go-between more intent on making a match than telling the truth. "She praises both parties equally: to the groom's family she says, 'The girl is fair,' and to the bride's, 'the boy is wealthy.' "[23] Despite these timeless problems, matchmakers continued to expedite marriages for very practical reasons. Most obviously, the matchmaker kept in contact with a large number of families with children of marriageable age, expanding the range of choices. Moreover, using a matchmaker allowed a young woman to avoid the potentially humiliating stares of critical suitors.[24] This custom also kept young people away from each other until marriage, decreasing opportunities for premarital sex.[25] Ritual theorists paid tribute to the importance of matchmakers by institutionalizing matchmaking as a government office in the utopian *Rites of Zhou*.[26]

Sources disagree on the proper age of marriage. Ritual texts specify thirty as the ideal age of grooms and twenty for brides.[27] But the highly critical scholar Wang Chong (27–c. 100 c.e.) dismissed these figures as erroneous and claimed that they had never been valid, even in ancient times.²⁸ Qin dynasty law presents another ideal, specifying the heights that a prospective bride and groom must have reached before being allowed to marry—obviously a highly variable measure.²⁹ Han records mention a few cases of child marriage. Because such marriages usually involved imperial unions of great political significance, they had little to do with regular customs.³⁰

In actual practice, marriage ages seem to have been much lower than those specified by ritual ideals. One imperial decree ordered unmarried women to pay five times the normal poll tax beginning at age fifteen, showing official encouragement of a much younger marriage age than the ritual ideal.³¹ Surviving records seem to indicate that many women married between the ages of thirteen and nineteen.³² Men were usually slightly older than their wives at the time of marriage. Although contemporary Westerners might be struck by the youthfulness of these nuptials, studies comparing immediately preindustrial Western European society to those in other parts of the globe show the "traditional" European marriage age of about twenty-three for women and twenty-six for men to have been unusually high compared with the human population as a whole.³³ Most nonindustrial societies maintain average marriage ages closer to those of Han China than to Europe.

The marriage customs followed by most people in early imperial times seem to have been far less formulaic and detailed than the complex formulae advocated by ritual specialists. In theory the marriage ceremony included fixing a date, exchanging gifts, officially requesting the bride's name, presenting an auspicious divination, and transporting the bride to the groom's home.³⁴ However, those actually arranging weddings seem to have placed greatest importance on the exchange of gifts between families and a grand wedding dinner, a celebration not mentioned in any ritual text.³⁵ By making the bride's journey between families the wedding's focal point, the ritualist's model wedding emphasized the distance between the in-laws. In contrast, popular practices built ritual unity between the two families by emphasizing the exchange of gifts and sharing special foods.³⁶

The marriage ceremony also affected individual identity. Bride and groom assumed the roles of wife and husband, adding an important new dimension to their gender identities. Various sections of *Records of Ritual* interpret the wedding as illustrating "the separation that should be maintained between males and females" and establishing "the righteousness to be maintained between husband and wife."³⁷ Without the marriage ceremony, "husband and wife would be embittered, and there would be many offenses of licentiousness and depravity."³⁸ According to this reasoning, spouses were united as husband and wife, but these new social roles nevertheless maintained "the separate character of the intimate relations between male and female."[39] Marriage may have united the sexes, but it did so by distinguishing relative differences. Through marriage, both spouses assumed new social roles defined by both gender (man/woman) and kinship (husband/wife).

SACRIFICES

Ritual regulated the numerous sacrifices at the heart of both state and popular cults. According to Durkheim, religious rites establish and maintain the conceptual categories by which members of a culture organize their perceptions of the world.[40] The epistemological dimension of ritual empowered different groups in early Chinese society. Although many rites favored the interests of the powerful by supporting the status quo, the weak and disenfranchised could use religious practices to control, order, and comprehend their world.[41] Female participation in the sacrifices of early China gave women important roles within the religious and cosmological schemes used to envision and organize the world. Religious sacrifices were performed through gendered roles that located female identity within a broader context and gave meaning to a woman's sense of self.

Records of Ritual argued that one of the prime reasons a man must marry is that a wife must participate in many sacrifices if they are to succeed. When the ruler of an ancient state wanted to wed, he was to entreat the father of his prospective bride, saying, "I beg you, O ruler, to give me your elegant daughter, to share this small state with my poor self, to do service in the ancestral temple, and at the alters to (the spirits of) the land and grain."[42] *Rites of Zhou* divided ancient ritual into two types, depending on whether or not the queen participated. This work classified ritual according to the increasingly popular binary yin/yang cosmology. Rituals involving the queen were defined as "yin rituals" (*yinli*). These included seasonal ceremonies, funerals, and proper service of state guests, as well as the grand sacrifices.[43] Although female participation was mandatory for many important ancient rites, in most cases the consort's role was inferior to that of the ruler. For example, *Rites of Zhou* instructed that whereas a king was to have six different types of sacrificial garments, the queen was limited to only three kinds.[44] Women were necessary actors in ritual, but they often participated in ways that marked their inferior status within social and political hierarchies.

During the Han, ritual became more organized and standardized to match the order implicit in imperial political unity. Han ceremonial consisted of five gen-

eral types: sacrificial, exorcistic/purifying, fertilistic, cosmological, and ceremonial.[45] Imperial ladies had a role in observing all five kinds, although they were
barred from playing specific roles in the rituals of each class.[46] As in the Zhou,
their participation was necessary but limited, an apt reflection of female status
in the patrilineal family.

The most important female-dominated state rites were the sacrifice to the First
Sericulturalist (Xiancan) and the empress's subsequent stylized gathering of mulberry leaves.[47] Han Ying praised the ceremonies in which the emperor plowed a
furrow and the empress gathered mulberry leaves. These rituals were admired
because they symbolically expressed the personal concern felt by emperor and
empress for the supply of their subjects' two most basic necessities: food and
clothing.[48] These paired rites symbolized not only the ideal division between
man's field work and woman's cloth making, but also between the social roles
that distinguished men from women. Gender identity was enacted in stylized
work roles. In these rituals, woman was portrayed as an equal counterpart to man;
each sex had proper and necessary roles in society. Ritual enacted ideal social
roles in the hope that people would alter their own lives to conform to these
formalized models, thereby making the world a more orderly and virtuous place.

Husband and wife were to have specific paired roles in other sacrifices as well.[49]
Records of Ritual describes in detail the male and female roles in an ideal sacrificial rite. According to this text, a palace official notified the ruler's wife eleven
days prior to the sacrifice. She then spent the next seven days loosely ordering
her thoughts, followed by three days of more intense concentration to become
suitably solemn. The ruler purified the outer apartments of the palace; his wife
purified the inner. Then they met in the grand temple for the sacrifice itself.[50]

> The ruler . . . stood at the top of the steps on the east; his wife in her head-dress
> and pheasant-embroidered robe stood in the eastern chamber. . . . When the victim
> was introduced, the ruler held it by the rope . . . the wives of the ruler's surname
> followed the wife with the basins; she presented the purified liquid; the ruler held
> in his hand the lungs; . . . and his wife put them on the dishes and presented them.[51]

Nor was the female role in state ritual limited to queen or empress. Other
palace ladies had ceremonial duties as well. *Rites of Zhou* summarized the ideal
ritual roles of a ruler's concubines. "In sacrifices they assist with the implements.
In guest rituals they follow the queen. In royal funerals they cry according to
rank."[52] Ritual not only affirmed a woman's ideal relationship with men but also
distinguished a hierarchy of female roles. Each rank of the various imperial ladies
came with distinct ritual duties, thereby formalizing the distinctions that should
have remained in place after the ceremony was completed.

The selective inclusion and exclusion of women in important state sacrifices propagated gender hierarchy. Women were never completely excluded from ritual practices. Allowing carefully defined female participation gave state rituals an air of universality and completeness. But excluding women from certain key rites or confining them to marginal roles concretely and publicly enacted the overall superiority of male over female. Performances within the ritually sensitive court, symbolic center of the cosmos, were thought to encourage a similarly hierarchical order on the world at large. The system of sacrifices thereby enacted a patrilineal view of ideal female identity. Women were seen as necessary to the legitimate social and cosmic order, but only when confined to properly restricted roles. And overall, female social roles were less important than male roles.

DEATH

Women had considerable responsibility for carrying out elaborate funeral and mourning rites for deceased relations.[53] Female participation was essential for a funeral's success. *Records of Ritual* implied that if an eldest son lacked a wife, he could not properly complete the mourning rituals over which he had to preside. For this reason he had the duty to always remain married, even if he reached the advanced age of seventy.[54] A different passage of the work concluded that because of the wife's vital role in funeral and mourning rituals, "could any husband dare not to show her respect?"[55] Mourning women were permitted to use a wooden staff, a tangible symbol of rank that women were normally denied.[56] Mourning rites thereby emphasized the importance of female roles within the patrilineal family.

Ritual texts specified that female roles in the funeral included receiving and escorting guests to their proper places, singing lamentations, impersonating a deceased woman, and clearing the vessels after the funeral feast.[57] Among her most important obligations, a woman had to display an appropriate degree of grief. Lamentations were formalized. *Etiquette and Ritual* ordered mourning families to gather each dawn and dusk for wailing; women were to mourn inside the hall housing the coffin while men remained outside.[58] Besides physical proximity to the deceased, the importance of women in mourning was emphasized by the many occasions when men were to remain silent while women wailed.[59] The public display of grief was primarily a female duty.

Female roles in the mourning system were vital components to a woman's personal identity. Mourning expressed ideal social hierarchies by clearly specifying a woman's relation to other members of the patrilineal kinship network. By forcing women to submit to these ideals at a sensitive time of liminal significance, the kinship hierarchies advocated by ritual specialists gained a degree of legitimacy. In this way, mourning customs embodied and conveyed patrilineal beliefs about what it was to be a woman.[60] Female mourning roles defined how a woman ought to have related to her family in happier times as well.

Female obligations toward the deceased did not end with the funeral. Of all the sacrifices, periodic rites in honor of the ancestors held pride of place. Spirits of the deceased were widely believed to only accept sacrifices from patrilineal descendants and their wives.[61] Assiduously maintaining sacrifices to the dead during one's own lifetime ensured that one's descendants were likely to continue the custom. In this way, the ancestral sacrifices provided the living with a powerful sense of solace. They knew that after their own death, their descendants would sacrifice to them as they had sacrificed to the spirits of those before them. Those who lacked male heirs fretted about their own eventual incarnation as a forgotten shade denied proper ancestral rites.[62]

Beliefs concerning ancestral sacrifices gave women as much interest in the continuation of these rites as men. In a particularly extreme example, each family of the state of Qi reportedly withheld their eldest daughter from marriage so that she could devote herself to tending the ancestral shrine and perhaps also practice shamanism. This regional custom lasted into the Han.[63] More widespread was the reverse practice of linking a woman's observance of ancestral sacrifices to the marriage ceremony.[64] Prior to marriage, a woman was to be carefully instructed in the proper conduct of the ancestral sacrifices.[65] The marriage ceremonies formally concluded only after a bride had visited her new husband's ancestral shrine. Ritualists, stressing this act, argued that a woman who died after completing the marriage ceremony but before presenting herself within her husband's ancestral shrine should be buried with her parents rather than her spouse.[66] According to this view, the marriage ceremony was only the beginning of a proper wedding. Only participation in her husband's ancestral cult gave a wife full membership in her husband's family.[67] Sacrificing to her husband's ancestors was a fundamental performance of the wifely role and key to membership in the patrilineal family.

After a lifetime of service to the spirits of others, a woman was to be accorded respect at the time of her death. Female graves were to receive appropriate veneration.[68] Even after death, a woman maintained the social roles linking her to the living members of the patrilineal family. Women were not mourned as individuals but according to their specific kinship roles. According to tradition, the most important kinship position a deceased woman could hold was mother. In ancient times, people who bewailed a man with abandon were said to mourn him "as they would wail for their mothers."[69] Inscriptional evidence from the Han confirms that, as ritual texts mandated, many men observed proper mourning for their mothers.[70] Some mourned extravagantly. For example, at the funeral of the mother of Ju Meng, a Han strongman famed for redressing wrongs, "those who came from remote places to attend the funeral rode in about a thousand carriages."[71] After a mother's death, sons were to observe the taboo against ever speaking in conjunction the characters used to write her name.[72] Women also received posthumous ritual respect for their role as wife. *Etiquette and Ritual* went so far as to prohibit a husband from remarrying within three years of his spouse's death.[73]

There seem to have been conflicting opinions as to how the degrees of mourning for women should be calculated. *Records of Ritual* specified that the mourning rites for a woman should be determined according to her husband's rank.[74] Alternatively, Mencius argued that a son could offer a deceased mother funeral rites more lavish than those for his father if his rank had increased in the interval between the deaths of his two parents.[75] Mencius's reasoning implies that a woman's posthumous status was linked to the rank of her son, not her husband. Regardless of which system of calculation was used, neither derived a woman's ritual status from any quality or attribute innate to herself. Her relationship to one of the men closest to her (whether husband or son) determined her posthumous social status. Woman's posthumous identity remained tied to patrilineal kinship roles.

Confucius decreed equality in the amount of time a child should mourn father and mother, setting both at three years. He reasoned that because three years marks the length of time a child is "nursed" (*huai*) by parents, the child consequently owes them three years of similar devotion.[76] Later authorities reversed Confucius's gender egalitarianism. One ritual specialist argued that paying more respect to a deceased father than mother stands as a hallmark of civilization; only savages mourn both equally.[77] According to this system, as long as the father remained alive, a child was to reduce the degree of mourning for his mother in recognition that "in the sky there are not two suns, nor in the land two kings, nor in the state two rulers, nor in a family two equally honorable."[78]

These sorts of ideas marked a rise in patrilineal values, which sought to revise all major social roles according to a particular interpretation of ideal kinship hierarchy. Generally speaking, over time mourning ideals increasingly adhered to patrilineal views of female identity. Even those who favored tracing the degree of mourning through the husband told the son that he could not mourn his deceased mother if she had been divorced from his father.[79] Emperor Xuan extended this line of thinking in an edict pronouncing that if a widow remarried, a son by her original husband was not to mourn her. "If a woman does not nourish her parents-in-law, and does not attend to the sacrifices (to her husband's ancestors), . . . the son is not in duty bound to a mother who has left."[80] Both of these mourning rules reinforced patrilinealism. According to this reasoning, a son's relation to his mother derived from her social role as spouse to his father rather than directly through his own blood tie.[81]

Other mourning grades also located the deceased woman within kinship role hierarchies.[82] For example, some believed that a man's mourning for his deceased wife should decrease if his mother were still alive.[83] This view asserted the primacy of mothers-in-law over daughters-in-law, a standard patrilineal view. *Etiquette and Ritual* similarly emphasized the inferiority of a concubine in relation to a wife by requiring extremely light mourning for a deceased concubine from the closest family members.[84]

Mourning rules further strengthened patrilineal kinship ties by reinforcing the distance between a married woman and her natal family. For example, a widowed woman who died without a male heir was to have her funeral presided over by one of her husband's relatives. If no relatives of her husband could be found, a neighbor might substitute. Under no circumstances was her funeral to be arranged by her natal family.[85] This rule used mourning to assert the absolute division of a married (or widowed) woman from the family of her birth, a basic patrilineal principle. Marriage theoretically severed blood ties, and mourning was used to maintain this distinction.

Other rites contradicted the belief that a married woman was absolutely severed from her blood relations. These rites symbolized the mainstream popular practice allowing a woman to maintain important ties to her natal family. Ritual texts stated that a woman was to wear mourning (to a lesser degree) for her parents and brothers.[86] A man did not wear mourning for his wife's relatives, though he was to wail in the back of his ancestral temple when they died.[87] Most intriguing are a pair of funeral rules instructing families on how to treat deceased married female blood relatives. *Etiquette and Ritual* required light mourning for married paternal aunts and daughters; *Records of Ritual* demanded that a hemp sash be worn on the death of a woman who had married out of the family.[88] Although differing slightly as to which degree of mourning was to be assumed, both texts took a similar approach to the death of married female relatives. The families of husband and wife maintained ritual links with each other that periodically renewed awareness of the bond that marriage had first established. While allowing a married woman to maintain some ritual links to her natal family, her roles in these rites simultaneously reemphasized the primacy of her bonds to her husband's family. Contradictory mourning roles both strengthened patrilineal values within the family and reinforced bonds between kin groups allied by marriage.

Upon death, a woman related to society in new ways. A posthumous name and special titles of kinship described relations with the deceased, symbolizing her new roles.[89] Yet after death, a wife remained part of her husband's family. A woman's spirit had to be appeased with remembrance and sacrifice. Instead of having independent temples for their spirits, most women had their spirit tablets housed in the shrines of their husbands' ancestors. There a woman's spirit could receive periodic sacrifice from her husband, sons, daughters-in-law, and more remote descendants.[90] Even in death, ritual emphasized a woman's wifely role as the most important component of her social identity.

Not all sacrifices to the spirits of deceased women were conducted out of love or magnanimity. The female dead could be dangerous, so they required remembrance and appeasement. The Eastern Han lustration festival seems to have been a rite for appeasing the spirits of dead girls.[91] Although female spirits could sometimes remain among the living, most of them gradually faded away along with memories of the deceased. Ancestral sacrifices to women continued to remind family members of abstract patrilineal virtues such as filial devotion to one's mother.[92] Furthermore, extended mourning followed by periodic ancestral sacrifices eased the process of grieving by giving a child or husband time to slowly adjust to the loss of a loved one. Just as ritual gave structure and meaning to a woman's life by ordering it according to fixed roles, it also changed her death from a sudden event into an extended and explicable process. A woman's identity was grounded in the kinship system. As family and descendants forgot her, she gradually ceased to exist.

8

Cosmology

Cosmology may seem far removed from daily life in early imperial China, but in fact it was intimately connected with a wide range of matters. Statecraft, music, medicine, sculpture, and many other arts, both decorative and utile, sought guidance from cosmological theory. Thinkers used cosmological metaphors to organize and interpret the large bodies of empirical knowledge that had steadily accumulated through China's already lengthy history. Confident in the value of cosmological theory, scholars used it to account for the causes of the phenomena they observed.

Cosmological systems included gendered elements. However, cosmology imputed meaning to female identity differently from other standard modes of early thought. The most common way early Chinese understood femininity was through social logic. In this commonsense view of gender, female identity consisted of the sum of women's myriad social roles. This social definition of the female consisted of more than simple binary opposition to the male. Each sex assumed multiple positions in a complex social system that required each person to play many different gendered roles simultaneously. Gender identity became an elaborate composite of the entire range of social roles each woman or man played.

In contrast to the multivalent complexity of the social view of gender, cosmology took a simpler approach. Cosmologists associated a series of abstract binary concepts with male and female. Instead of saying "woman is x" and "man is y" or envisioning gender as a range of affiliated social roles, they preferred to draw parallels between gender identity and several extremely abstract binary concepts. None of these ideas was precisely synonymous with gender. Yin, Earth, and *kun* did not mean female; nor did yang, Heaven, and *qian* mean male. They believed that gender was different yet analogous to other pairs of metaphysical concepts ordering our world.

Most important, cosmologists emphasized the binary aspect of gender.

143

Although comparing several cosmological pairs might seem complicated at first glance, this method actually simplified gender by reducing it to a series of binary contrasts. Thinkers could now abstract male and female from their affiliated social roles and contrast the sexes directly.[1] Compared with the complex ambiguity of everyday gender identity, which was closely tied to overlapping social roles, abstract binary concepts such as Heaven and Earth were relatively simple.

Because cosmology was direct, it became a powerful tool in the hands of those advocating patrilineal kinship values. Instead of trying to establish an endless array of hierarchies among the multitude of gendered social roles, they could order society according to a simple ideal hierarchy of man and woman. In this way, cosmology became a persuasive medium for expressing antifemale rhetoric.

BINARY THOUGHT

Dualism was a basic mode of thought in early China.[2] Thinkers of various schools based competing systems of cosmology on the common idea that our universe consists of an all-inclusive unity containing an interacting duality. According to this view, the cosmos is a dynamic process that emerges from continuous interaction between two complementary elements. The names of these concepts have changed many times in Chinese intellectual history, yet a fascination with unity formed of dualities has endured.[3] Generally speaking, the abstract thought of all cultures tends to simplify ideas into direct opposites; China was no exception to this trend.[4] Given the binary orientation of so much early Chinese thought, it was inevitable that thinkers would apply dualistic systems to gender.

Cosmologists held that because binary difference is at the heart of the cosmic order, the sexes had to maintain proper relations with each other.[5] But how should this occur? Duality does not necessarily imply equality. Two terms can relate to each other either equally or unequally. So there were two inherent possibilities to the cosmological model of binary gender: viewing both sexes as necessary hence equal or relating them as a hierarchy.

Instead of equal duality (which can be symbolically expressed by the terms A and B), many dichotomies relate to each other according to exclusion (A and not-A).[6] In early imperial China, did the female-associated elements of abstract dichotomies (such as Heaven/Earth, *qian/kun*, yin/yang, and even man/woman) derive their definitions positively (B is B) or negatively (B is not-A)? This question holds the key to understanding cosmological notions of female identity in that era. Answering this ontological problem will reveal whether the early Chinese feminine was defined positively as a presence in and of itself or negatively as an absence of maleness. In many intellectual systems, unequal differences are related hierarchically rather than laterally. Binary structures tend to evolve from the egalitarian "A/B" into the hierarchy "A/not-A."[7] China was no exception.

In addition to tendencies arising from the structure of binary reasoning, the uses of cosmology in Han society and politics also influenced the representation of female identity within these systems. Learned officials might not have been able to topple a hated empress dowager, but they could propagate cosmological systems that exalted masculine elements and denigrated the feminine.[8] Because of the controversial involvement of women in government, cosmological debates became increasingly important in Han dynasty statecraft. Scholars used cosmology to bolster male interests at court and in society as a whole. By redefining gender as a simple hierarchy, cosmology became a way to justify male domination of key social hierarchies.

Three pairs of ideas formed the main conceptual analogues to gender in early imperial cosmology: Heaven/Earth, *qian/kun* and yin/yang. Originally these pairs were embedded in three separate cosmological systems. Over time, they became intertwined parts of a comprehensive worldview. Obviously, understanding these three sets of ideas and their relations to gender is no easy task. We must look carefully at the historical development and associations of each pair as well as how they related to each other. Only then can we begin to reconstruct early imperial views of the cosmic feminine.

HEAVEN/EARTH

Heaven and Earth were exceptionally important concepts in ancient government and religion as well as abstract cosmology. This pair also became closely associated with gender. The Earth of cosmology differs considerably from the Earth of religious ritual. This Earth was not a personified being but rather one element in a larger abstract system. As such, elemental Earth (*di*) became paired with the ancient concept of Heaven (*tian*) to form a duality central to early imperial models of the cosmos.

Eastern Zhou and Han texts began associating Heaven and Earth with a wide range of things. They often appeared as a duality of interacting physical elements whose changing relations affect the entire world. Early Daoism portrayed Heaven and Earth as fundamental elements of universal creation. The *qi* (vital force, energy) of Heaven and Earth were believed to produce and influence the myriad material things.[9] In this interpretation, Heaven and Earth seem almost like physical forces, disinterested in how they affect the world's creatures.[10] Later thinkers praised the natural regularity of this pair's interactions and used the divination system of the *Classic of Changes* to predict their transformations.[11]

Going one step further, other thinkers moralized Heaven and Earth by relating this cosmic pair to humankind. Many pre-Qin philosophers explored the relationship between Heaven and humanity.[12] During the Western Han it became common to speak of a triad consisting of Heaven, Earth, and Human Being.[13] By introducing humanity into this previously binary relation, the relation of Heaven and Earth took on moral characteristics as a cosmological paradigm for human ethics. In this view, human social roles ought to imitate the orderly interaction of Heaven and Earth.[14] The redoubtable combination of moral and physical powers attributed to Heaven and Earth led Emperor Wu to include this pair in the Han state cult, which favored sacrifices to abstract elemental forces rather than personified gods.[15]

Advocates of elemental Earth *(di)* attributed many powers to it. Some grew out of fertility cults worshiping Mother Earth. By conflating separate traditions that viewed Earth as a deity and an abstract element, the elemental concept gained detail and appeal. Daoist texts emphasized Earth as that from which everything is born and to which all eventually returns.[16] Dong Zhongshu, though chiefly remembered for exalting Heaven, nevertheless credited Earth as the ultimate creator of rain, clouds, and wind.[17] Some thinkers also credited Earth as being the guiding force behind ritual performances. *Records of Ritual* states, "Rites are regulated according to Earth."[18] Wang Chong explained this idea by observing, "The five sacrifices of the household originate out of a reverence for Earth."[19] Various Warring States and Han cosmologies credited the element Earth (of the Heaven/Earth dichotomy) with various powers: giving birth to the multitudinous things making up our world, making the rain vital for nourishing agriculture, and inspiring ritual.

Despite the important powers of Earth, most thinkers preferred to exalt Heaven *(tian)*. This line of thought has far greater antiquity than reverence for elemental Earth. During the Shang and Western Zhou dynasties, Heaven appeared almost interchangeably with the supreme god, Shangdi. Earth was not yet paired with Heaven in inscriptions or texts.[20] During the Warring States era, Earth began to be paired with Heaven for the sake of cosmological symmetry. Nevertheless, as the older and greater element in this new pair, Heaven remained the privileged term.

Practical factors bolstered Heaven's position. Early Western Han Confucianism stressed kinship and ethics. Dong Zhongshu helped take Confucianism in a cosmological direction by stressing Heaven as the source of the ruler's legitimacy.[21] Mainstream cosmology and political theory emphasized the ruler as a representative of humanity in his vital relationship with Heaven. But Earth still had its advocates. Scholarship in the Han oscillated between the New Text faction (which saw human beings, represented by the ruler, accountable to Heaven) and the Old Text school (which advocated worshiping Earth and influencing that elemental deity through the correct performance of sacrifices).

Dong Zhongshu's Confucian cosmology exemplified an increasingly popular new view of Heaven.[22] Besides seeing Heaven as a cosmological element in opposition to Earth, Dong also believed Heaven to embody the entire physical universe. His Heaven was cognizant and in some limited ways anthropomorphic.[23] Dong usually described Heaven in absolute terms without mentioning Earth. When he did relate Heaven and Earth to each other, Earth was portrayed as "humble," "serving," and "below."[24] Other Confucian-inspired thinkers also exalted Heaven. Wang Chong ascribed human destiny and mastery of the hundred spirits to Heaven.[25] The Daoist tradition also glorified Heaven. Laozi exalted the "Way (*dao*) of Heaven" (not that of Earth) as the heart of his cosmological scheme.[26] Both Confucianism and Daoism produced highly favorable and detailed impressions of Heaven.

When Earth became explicitly paired with Heaven, it inevitably seemed secondary to a concept that was older, highly exalted, and more popular. For example, the *Laozi* commanded that human beings model themselves on Earth, Earth on Heaven, and Heaven on the Way (*dao*).[27] In this way Daoism began to depict Heaven and Earth as a hierarchy. Other Eastern Zhou texts described Heaven as "above" and Earth as "below." This comparison might seem to be an innocuous description of physical position until we recall that "above" and "below" were commonly used to describe relative social status in early China.[28]

Various texts expressed the hierarchy of Heaven/Earth in many ways: Heaven "taking precedence" (*xian*) over Earth, "exalted" (*chong*) Heaven and "humble" (*bei*) Earth, and Heaven represented by the number "three" and Earth by "two" in numerological mysticism.[29] As Heaven and Earth became connected as an integral pair in the cosmological systems of different schools, their relationship became asymmetrical. To state the situation symbolically: instead of an A/B relation based on ontological parity, during the early empire the Heaven/Earth dichotomy took on the unequal form A/not-A.

The essential, explicit hierarchy of Heaven and Earth in abstract cosmology had important implications as the pair became associated with gender. In remote antiquity, when the concept of Heaven as yet lacked links with Earth, Heaven was either ungendered or else invested with the identity of both sexes. A poem in the ancient *Classic of Odes* declares, "Oh, distant, great Heaven, / you are called (our) 'father and mother.' "[30]

Heaven became overtly masculine as it grew closer to feminine Earth.[31] Some began to see this pair in parental terms: "Heaven and Earth are the father and mother of the myriad things."[32] Associating Heaven/Earth with the father/mother roles of patrilineal kinship allowed thinkers to apply these concepts to politics and ethics in new ways. For example, when the ruler honored Heaven as his father and Earth as his mother, political cosmology combined with patrilineal kinship values.[33]

Some who compared Heaven and Earth to parents used sexually suggestive language to emphasize the parallel. The phrase "Heaven emanates and Earth produces" has clear sexual connotations.[34] Other texts were more specific in comparing sexual intercourse of man and woman with cosmic union. "Heaven and Earth come together, and all things take shape and find form. Male and female mix their seed, and all creatures take shape and are born."[35] This sexually charged language imbued Heaven and Earth with unambiguous gender identities. Heaven and Earth also became affiliated with the bond between husband and wife.[36] The "Eastern Capital Rhapsody" from the early Eastern Han describes how Heaven and Earth "created anew the relation of husband and wife" in this new era of peace and stability.[37]

To summarize, during the Eastern Zhou and Han, Heaven and Earth became associated with a series of paired social roles. Some were unrelated to gender, including father/son, ruler/subject, and social superior/inferior. Others were consciously gendered, such as man/woman, husband/wife, and male and female sex partners.[38] What these diverse social pairs had in common was their inequality. Confucianism, patrilineal values, and political practices all viewed these social pairs as hierarchies. Relating them to the abstract cosmological duality Heaven/Earth, and portraying Heaven/Earth as a hierarchy, justified the view that society should be organized around unequal relationships. Cosmology provided a theoretical rationale for social inequality.

Some thinkers began to use cosmological reasoning to reorganize gender relations. Assuming the superiority of Heaven over Earth, they argued that the parallel relation of man and woman should conform to this hierarchy so that society would mirror the cosmic order. From the Heaven/Earth hierarchy, these thinkers derived the corollary that social inferiors (such as women) must obey their superiors (men) in accord with the fundamental relation of Earth and Heaven. As *Records of Ritual* warns: "If no distinction were observed between males and females, disorder would arise and grow—such is the nature of the (different qualities of) Heaven and Earth."[39] Social theorists such as Ban Gu and Ban Zhao used these sorts of cosmological rationales to justify the inferiority of some female roles within the patrilineal kinship structure. The ideal wife obeys, serves, and aids her husband just as Earth remains subservient to Heaven.[40]

Ban Zhao provided a nuanced explanation of this analogy. "If people in action or character disobey the spirits of Heaven and of Earth, then Heaven punishes them. Likewise if a woman errs in the rites and in the proper mode of conduct, then her husband esteems her lightly."[41] Her phrasing makes the husband seem extremely generous and gentle in comparison with the stormy wrath of Heaven. Instead of physical punishment, the wife fears the far more subtle reprimand of her husband's disapproval. In this manner, the mechanism for controlling female behavior shifted away from the threat of brute force. The range of acceptable female behavior declined as grand cosmic hierarchies became a template for society.

Liu Xiang used the analogy between subservient Earth and woman to justify an ideal female life cycle under complete male control. "If a woman is not married, she regards her father and mother as Heaven. When she marries, she considers her husband as Heaven."[42] The unequal relation of Heaven and Earth thus came to affect views of gender identity in the increasingly metaphysical realm of Han dynasty thought. Opponents of female privilege at court and in the family could now use cosmology to justify female subservience.

QIAN/KUN

The pair *qian* and *kun* were equally important to Chinese cosmology. As key components in the complex system of the *Classic of Changes (Yijing)*, these concepts decisively influenced intellectual discourse. The privileged position of *qian/kun* in this canonical Confucian text lent the pair great persuasive weight in argument. Rhetorical conventions encouraged the educated elite to display their erudition by quoting the *Classic of Changes* at every opportunity.[43] In this manner, *qian* and *kun* became abstract analogues to many binary social concepts, including dichotomized gender.

While other ancient cultures commonly accounted for the great mysteries of existence and change through myth, early Chinese supplemented their sketchy mythological pantheon with the abstract system of divination embodied in *Classic of Changes*.[44] The famed trigrams and hexagrams (combinations of solid and broken lines) were probably not part of the original system. Originally diviners probably used numbers or drawings in their place.[45] The earliest portions of the *Changes* seem to have had little if any relation to gender. The use of trigrams and hexagrams and the addition of detailed commentaries brought gender into the system.

Classic of Changes consists of a confusing accretion of texts, editing changes, and commentaries. Any conclusions from the text must take this bewildering textual stratigraphy into account. In the earliest textual layer, the concepts behind the eight trigrams date from remote antiquity.[46] As for the main commentaries, the *Gunci* (also called the *Tuanci*) and the *Yaoci* (or *Xiangci*) seem to be the oldest. Estimates on their dates of compilation vary wildly from Western Zhou to Han. No one knows for certain when these texts were written. Finally, the *Ten Wings* (*Shiyi*) commentaries show the distinct influence of Confucian moral values. This evolution beyond terse divinatory epigrams to detailed moralizing suggests a relatively late date of composition, either Eastern Zhou or Western Han.[47] Although the ordering of the hexagrams in a manuscript unearthed at Mawangdui differs from that of the transmitted text, both arrangements show that *qian* and *kun* were considered complementary elements in the system from very early times.[48]

The written characters *qian* and *kun* have undergone major transformations.[49] The original form of *qian* lacked any immediate relation to abstract cosmology.[50] The character's transmitted form came into use sometime during the Han after this system had already become revered as an ancient source of cosmological, predictive, and moral insight. Its final orthography bears some relation to masculine qualities.[51]

As for *kun*, this concept kept its archaic written form far longer—until at least the twilight of the Eastern Han when the stone classics were inscribed.[52] The newer form of *kun* consisted of the radical for "earth" or "soil" (*tu*) together with a component indicating its sound.[53] This reference to Earth seems to have clear feminine associations and also resonates with the Heaven/Earth pair. But we must remember that *kun* probably did not originally have anything to do with Earth. It seems to have begun as an astrological concept. An ancient astrological term was imported into the divination system of the *Changes*, where its usage and meaning changed completely.[54]

So what do *kun* and *qian* mean? Given this twisted etymology, they do not specifically mean anything in and of themselves. They are highly abstract cosmological concepts borrowed from one divination system for use in another. So the characters represent abstract concepts in a larger divination system.[55] Only by positioning these two characters within the system and drawing subtle parallels with other pairs such as Heaven/Earth and man/woman did *qian/kun* evolve their present forms and implications. In other words, the meanings of *qian/kun* are relative not absolute, and more connotative than denotative.

Although there are parallels between Heaven/Earth and *qian/kun*, they are definitely not identical. Like Heaven/Earth, *qian/kun* attracted a wide range of connotations that increased over time as generation after generation of zealous commentators heaped on their own interpretations. Some of the wide-ranging connotations of *qian* included Heaven, son of Heaven, ruler, metal, jade, horse, head, father, ice, fruit, and struggle; *kun* manifested itself in Earth, shelter, cloth, ax, cow, belly, mother, and frugality.[56] Clearly *qian* and *kun* meant more than just masculine and feminine. The pair was associated with many concepts. Some were binary and others were not. Some were gendered and others were not. The complex range of associations loosely associated with *qian* and *kun* enriched the cosmological interpretation of female and male identity.

Although *qian* and *kun* were not synonymous with male and female, gender was an important aspect of their network of connotations. Father/mother, ruler/shelter, metal/cloth all had metaphorical gender implications. One passage in the early *Xici* commentary explicitly identified the way of *qian* as that which brings about the male and the way of *kun* as bringing about the female. In this way the *Xici* related *qian/kun* directly to masculinity and femininity.[57] However, this degree of clarity was the exception. Although gender connotations were an important aspect of this abstract pair, their precise relation to gender was often extremely nebulous.

Apart from their function within a larger divination system, *qian/kun* also constituted a self-contained duality set somewhat apart from less important elements in the *Changes*.[58] When compared with each other directly, the pair appeared as a hierarchy. For example, *qian* always came before *kun*.[59] The many concepts associated with *qian* and *kun* also suggested fundamental inequality. *Qian* rules, *kun* shelters; *qian* begins, *kun* completes; *qian* is represented by the number "216," *kun* by "144"; *qian* is above and *kun* below.[60] Most overtly, *qian* and *kun* came to represent patriarchal masculine and feminine stereotypes. Thus *qian* is strong while *kun* is weak, yielding, and submissive.[61] Like the Confucian view of woman, *kun*, because it is essentially responsive, implies the potential for cultivation and improvement.[62] Yet response implies a stimulus—one that comes from a man embodying *qian*. Although *qian* and *kun* may have been complementary, the two elements also clearly interacted as superior and inferior.

Some women could rise above the limitations implied by *kun*. A stele inscription dedicated to the Eastern Han woman Cao E, who dove into a river to retrieve her drowned father's corpse, celebrated her filiality by comparing her with both *qian* and *kun*.[63] In praising her as embodying both elements, her admirers sought to place Cao E beyond the weaknesses and passivity implied by *kun*. Her heroic behavior allowed her to transcend the female stereotypes promoted by cosmological theory. However, early imperial thinkers more often emphasized the fact that *qian* and *kun* were a hierarchy. Because this pair had strong associations with gender, they could argue that woman should be treated as man's inferior. By reasoning from cosmological theory, they could circumvent the privileges of many traditional female social roles.

YIN/YANG

Yin and yang were the third pair of cosmological abstractions that influenced gender concepts in early imperial China. Coincidentally, this duality is most famous in the West. Like *qian* and *kun*, these two terms also underwent a complex, convoluted development that complicated their relation to gender. Prior to their appearance in cosmology, yin and yang were mostly used to indicate contrasts of dark and light in the natural world.[64] But some Eastern Zhou thinkers began to use the pair in very new ways. Yin/yang began to refer to opposing cosmological forces that alternate in influence.[65] Philosophic schools seeking the vocabulary to express increasingly sophisticated cosmology and metaphysics redefined the existing terms yin and yang, which until then had referred to purely natural phenomena. Rather than develop completely new terminology for their novel intellectual systems, Eastern Zhou thinkers preferred to use existing terms. In this fashion yin/yang began to attract accretions of increasingly abstract meanings.

Thinkers of various schools depicted yin/yang as an interactive cosmological duality. Both Confucians and Daoists referred to these concepts, much as thinkers of different camps gave divergent interpretations to the common term "Way" (*dao*).[66] The third century B.C.E. philosopher Zou Yan of Qi raised yin/yang theory to new heights.[67] The pair became more explicit and detailed. Artworks began using binary symbolism related to yin/yang to express ineffable cosmological abstractions that included gender.[68]

As yin/yang thought became more elaborate, it could be put to many different uses. By the Han dynasty certain empirical systems of knowledge, such as medicine, may have reached a high degree of sophistication but lacked theoretical refinement commensurate with their practical achievements. In such cases, yin/yang theory presented a ready paradigm for explaining how something worked. Some thinkers gave yin/yang a materialistic interpretation as embodiments of the physical world.[69] Others applied the pair to psychological, moral, or metaphysical phenomena.[70] As the popularity of yin/yang increased, it became fashionable to use them to represent interactive dualistic categories encompassing all phenomena. Gender was only one of many binary relationships associated with the yin/yang model.[71]

By the Eastern Han, some thinkers saw the intercourse (*jiao*) of yin and yang as an analogue to the sexual intercourse of female and male, giving an explicit sexual dimension to this dichotomy.[72] Beyond the sexual act, yin/yang had other relations to gender identity as well. An early stratum of *Classic of Mountains and Lakes (Shanhaijing)* tells of a distant land of one-armed, triocular hermaphrodites, describing them as "having both yin and yang."[73] Here yin/yang was employed to describe the essence of gender identity. Dong Zhongshu repeatedly and explicitly stated that yin/yang is interchangeable with woman and man, going as far as to say, "Yin and yang can also be called male and female."[74] Ban Zhao similarly asserted that woman and man have different characteristics or behavior, just as yin and yang are of different natures.[75] So the relation of yin and yang to gender identity became extremely specific.

Other texts mentioned yin and yang in conjunction with particular social roles to be filled by woman and man. For example, the *Zhuangzi* compared yin/yang with mother/father.[76] Likewise, Ban Zhao connected the way of wife and husband with yin and yang.[77] Royal ladies, who symbolized womankind as a whole in court ritual, were also seen as specifically yin. *Rites of Zhou* defined "yin rituals" as those in which the queen participated.[78] Finally, a eulogy to a deceased Han empress referred to her as the "essence of Supreme Yin," an apt title for the official head of womankind.[79] These links between cosmological elements and social roles had major implications. As yin and yang became a template for proper gender roles in kinship and government, these ideas could be manipulated to influence social practices.

As yin and yang gained importance, their interpretations changed significantly. Yin and yang initially appeared as complementary paired concepts rooted in balanced alternation. Neither was superior or inferior. But as yin/yang became gender analogues, people began to see them as a hierarchy.[80] Their inequality could be used to justify gender hierarchy in society, often in contradiction of traditional values that allowed women to assume powerful roles such as mother.

Of course yin was not always depicted negatively. The *Zhuangzi*, which defined knowing the ultimate yin as having attained "the utmost," used yin as a catchword for withdrawal and stillness.[81] Daoist emphasis on the feminine (or in this case yin) might possibly be explained away as compensating for the excessive yang of an anticipated male readership prone to activism.[82] This view would seek to balance out the yin and yang tendencies within each individual to achieve a neutral balance. Liu Xiang summed up this view in his story about a woman of Chu who mused that whoever has yin will be rewarded with yang.[83]

However, most citations of yin in Han literature were far less complimentary. Although many other writers took up the theme of yin's inferiority to yang, the best development of this concept appears in the influential corpus of Dong Zhongshu. His cosmology was conditioned by a strong belief in the necessity of hierarchy. Dong claimed that yin and yang must be unequal because the equality of two paired elements is simply impossible.

> The eye is not able to perceive two things, nor
> is the ear able to hear two things . . .
> If one hand draws a square and the other draws a
> circle they will never be completed . . .
> Consequently the gentleman (junzi) takes the
> second as base and the first as exalted.[84]

His reasoning was simple. If all other paired concepts interact as a hierarchy, yin and yang must also be unequal. It was only necessary to determine the superior element in the pair. And for Dong Zhongshu, the answer to this question was obvious. He repeatedly referred to yang as exalted and yin as base.

Dong Zhongshu claimed that the hierarchy of yin and yang derives from the natural processes they represent. Ancient sages observing the unequal order of the natural world first recognized this relationship.[85] To Dong, the hierarchy of yin and yang was a natural fact that he called the "Way (dao) of Heaven."[86] He described the unequal relations of yin and yang as base and exalted, back and front, as well as humble and respected.[87] He even stripped credit for procreation from the feminine and bestowed it on yang, attributing "begetting" to yang and mere "completing" to yin.[88] Other authors burdened yin with stereotypically feminine inferior qualities such as weakness and gentleness.[89]

Dong Zhongshu went further to explicitly excoriate yin. Dong associated yin with evil (counter to morality), refractoriness (counter to the Confucian sense of order), and punishments (counter to Dong's advocacy of Confucian virtue over legalism).[90] Other thinkers also denigrated yin.[91] The later commentaries of the Classic of Changes, for example, depicted yin and yang respectively as harbingers of misfortune and auspiciousness.[92] In the ultimate association with the unfortunate, yin became the element representing death, whether of plants or human beings.[93]

Given the increasingly firm links between yin and woman, equating yin with the lowly and evil made this idea a powerful rhetorical tool for criticizing female privilege. Men fighting female power often attacked them using yin/yang theory. Dong Zhongshu declared that a husband, even if base, is nevertheless always yang; his wife, though perhaps noble, is always yin.[94] Consequently the wife must serve the husband just as yin serves yang.[95] Du Ye stated the analogy between cosmology and gender more broadly. "Although a man may be base, he is the yang of his family. Although a woman may be noble, she is still the yin of her state."[96]

By linking gender hierarchy to cosmology, the opponents of female influence invoked a far more frightening danger to female power than the simple inversion of patriarchal customs. Defying the proper order of the cosmos risked the terrifying prospect of natural chaos. *Records of Ritual* claimed that if women disobey men, they impede the correct progress of yin. This might cause a lunar eclipse.[97] Periodic eclipses were thus regular and convenient occasions for criticizing female power.

The use of yin/yang theory to demand female subservience also affected discussions of appropriate family relations. This pair represented not only abstract gender but also particular gendered kinship roles. Some people saw yin/yang as an ideal model for the roles of wife and husband.[98] Ban Gu fleshed out the specific details of this relationship.

> Why is it that according to the rites the man takes his wife, whereas the woman leaves her house? It is because the yin is lowly, and should not have the initiative; it proceeds to the yang in order to be completed.[99]

The marriages of imperial princesses seemed the most egregious violation of correct yin/yang hierarchy within the family. The marriage of a princess was called *shang* ("to serve") because the husband was to serve his wife in ritual contexts as the result of his relatively humble birth.[100] Wang Ji fervently condemned this custom, warning that chaos would result from inverting the correct positions of yin and yang.[101] Xun Shuang also criticized the ritual prerogatives imperial princesses had over their husbands. He denounced this inversion as contrary to the correct Way (*dao*) of both yin/yang and *qian/kun*.[102]

The use of yin/yang theory to criticize the ritual superiority of princesses shows how some officials used cosmological thought to counter privileged female roles. Other thinkers used similar reasoning to criticize all female participation in government. Han Ying warned, "One who does not understand government . . . allows yin to surpass yang."[103] Although yin had politically charged meanings other than gender, most often it was invoked as a metaphor for female political power.[104] For instance, when Emperor Cheng dismissed the childless Empress Xu from court, he did not cite the true reason: a pragmatic desire for a strong male heir. Instead he invoked the cosmological excuse of excessive yin at court.[105]

Xun Shuang used similar reasoning when protesting the large number of palace women. While others denounced the thousands of women in the palace for their meddling or extravagance, Xun complained that an excess of yin in the ritually sensitive court had caused terrible natural disasters.[106]

In summary, yin/yang closely resemble the parallel analogies of Heaven/Earth and *qian/kun* in their shifting relation to gender. Originally yin/yang lacked any link to gender. Even after yin/yang became an abstract cosmological pairing in Eastern Zhou philosophy, they were only tangentially related to gender. But increasingly complex intellectual systems appropriated existing binary terms and gave them new connotations. During the Han, although yin/yang reached beyond gender to encompass all major polarities in the universe, gender became a particularly important association. Cosmological assertions about gender then began to enter the mainstream of political and social discourse as tools for denouncing privileged female roles in society and government.[107]

To be sure, an apologist for the yin/yang model of gender (or any of the early Chinese cosmological pairs) can point to egalitarian aspects implicit in this way of thinking. Yin/yang can justify balance and unity as well as opposition. But when we look beyond the broadest statements of theory to see how this duality was actually applied to social and political discourse, it is apparent that yin was undeniably inferior to yang.

Advocates of the yin/yang model had cosmological grounds for systematically disparaging women. As the gender associations of yin/yang intensified, the dichotomy became more useful to those who wanted to justify female inferiority.[108] Yin increasingly changed from a positive element in the pair (A/B) to a negative definition based on exclusion from yang (A/not-A). By the Western Han, as yin took on strong connotations with the feminine, it had become the inferior element of the yin/yang pair. Yin/yang hierarchy transformed discourse about gendered social roles.

COSMOLOGICAL SYNCRETISM AND GENDER

The syncretism characterizing Han thought built up a dense network of interconnections between the cosmologic pairs affiliated with gender. Attempts to connect Heaven with yang and Earth with yin were most common. In some contexts Heaven alone was affiliated with both yin and yang, a reversion to the ancient primacy of Heaven in cosmological and religious thought.[109] But other texts related yin/yang with Heaven/Earth, usually by portraying Heaven/Earth as concrete analogues of abstract yin and yang.[110] Dong Zhongshu combined both precedents in his own complex system, sometimes mentioning yin/yang only in conjunction with Heaven and in other cases connecting it with both Heaven and Earth.[111] By the Eastern Han the link between these pairs permeated elite rhetoric. For example, *Discussions in the White Tiger Hall* explained that lucky omens appear when the ruler assists Heaven in harmonizing yin and yang.[112] Ban Zhao declared Heaven and Earth to be the models for human social roles. She specifically equated the relation of husband and wife with yin and yang.[113]

Yin and yang also became attached to the complex cosmology of *Classic of Changes*. The *Xici* commentary attributed to Confucius a quotation associating *qian* with yang and *kun* with yin.[114] Likewise, both the *Xici* and *Shuogua* commentaries tied *qian/kun* to Heaven/Earth. One passage brought together a gender-based triple link between Heaven/*qian*/father and Earth/*kun*/mother.[115] The *Shuogua* attempted to bring together all three prevailing grand cosmological dualities: Heaven/Earth, *qian/kun*, and yin/yang in a model of comprehensive syncretism.[116]

Gender had an important part in this intermixing of metaphysical dualities. Each of the three major cosmological pairs had different origins yet evolved along a similar course. Beginning as a pair of separate elements, one term gradually lost its independent value (A/B) and instead became defined as absence (A/not-A). This method defined the element negatively as what it is not instead of what it is. Of course this made the term the inferior element in the pair.

This redefinition coincided with the increased identification of each cosmological pair with gender, and the three pairs with each other. A long process of development gradually brought abstract representations of female identity into a hierarchy with the masculine. The introduction of gender, hierarchy, and syncretism into cosmology was complete by the Eastern Han. Although men were not always completely dominant in society, they could easily exalt the masculine within the much narrower confines of elite intellectual discourse. They might not be able to control the identity of women in daily life. Traditional social roles such as mother and empress gave some women important powers over men. But when cosmological theorists portrayed women primarily as the concrete embodiments of an abstract feminine essence, rather than as actors playing various social roles, they could systematically denigrate women in general. This redefinition of femininity as abstract essence rather than social role had enormous influence over gender discourse for the rest of imperial history.

Conclusion

The ways we live and think change constantly. To understand humanity, we have to bear in mind that people change over time. After confronting the mass of rhetoric about women from early imperial China, we will inevitably want to determine the significance of women's roles in Qin and Han society by comparing them with what came before and after. Early imperial rhetoric about women and their proper social roles had profound influence on later dynasties. The early empire was the first era in which Chinese lived under the imperial system of government that conditioned society for the next two millennia. Accordingly, many ideas and attitudes about women that began or matured in this period continued to influence society long afterward. Thinkers of later times viewed early imperial rhetoric as a significant precedent, legitimized by humbling antiquity and proximity to the origins of the imperial system. In subsequent eras, both reformers and reactionaries plumbed early writings for ideas to justify their own goals. Early imperial rhetoric continuously generated revivals, reinterpretations, and resistance in later dynasties. As such, ideas about women from the Qin and Han formed the ideological substrate for the remainder of imperial Chinese women's history.

When the past is viewed from such a distance that only the most general outlines of early life are still visible, it might seem that most aspects of women's lives remained fairly unchanged during the transition from the chaos of Zhou to the unified new empire. China was still a poor agricultural society, and most people lived simple lives dedicated mostly to procuring the necessities of life. Despite the new political system and social ideologies that arose with the advent of imperial government, most people remained tied to the timeless rhythms of sun and soil. Surrounded by family and neighbors, deferring to local custom, and obligated to sweat or perish, ordinary people were largely insulated from the rar-

159

efied abstractions that infatuated the elite scholars whose eyes we must use to see that era.

Of course not everything was changeless. Atop this sturdy substrate of agriculture and tradition, the details of life unceasingly altered. Many of these changes were minor. A fashionable hairstyle could come and go, leaving very little impact on the overall course of women's history. But other changes were far more significant. As the ways different groups understood and represented women steadily shifted through the centuries, female social roles began to change. In the long run, intellectual changes were extremely important. During the Han dynasty, some of the basic social paradigms affecting the ways people conceived of womanhood changed substantially. Once a new ideal of the feminine became widely accepted, the details of female life successively altered to conform to this new model. The particulars of daily life altered to follow the contours of fundamental abstract concepts.

The first major paradigm shift underlying changes in female life also happened to be the defining characteristic of the entire age. Qin Shihuangdi can be said to have created China as a nation when he conquered rival states and proclaimed himself emperor. The history of China as a single polity truly begins with the Qin unification. Although the ideal of a unified China had long existed in people's minds, the decayed Zhou monarchy was in no position to extract much more than empty tokens of deference from rulers of the myriad states. In the end, independent rulers contemptuously ignored even the titular Zhou king's empty ritual prerogatives. Qin swept away the last faded remnants of the Zhou system and brought true unity to China.

At the apex of the new imperial society, the ruler's consorts obtained powerful new roles. As the size and scope of government expanded, traditional female influence at court took on profound new significance. During the Han, the emperors' consorts and their families repeatedly seized the workings of government. Whenever they gained control of the helm of state, their power could be staggering. These women controlled the resources of a vast empire and held the power of life and death over a good portion of humanity. They were among the most powerful people who ever lived. The power of empresses dowager at the beginning of the imperial system seems particularly great, when compared with other periods of Chinese history. Some women in later eras were able to gain control of government, but, generally speaking, the statesmen of later dynasties learned from the mistakes of the Han. During the Eastern Han the extraordinary privileges of empresses dowager and their kin progressively destabilized the state, alienated the landed elite, and took power out of the hands of the bureaucracy. So the customs of later dynasties deliberately reduced female influence at court. The Han dynasty stands out as probably the longest period of intense female influence over the top reaches of government in the long history of China.

The impact of the new imperial state on ordinary people was both real and striking. Rule by a huge centralized state gradually began to affect women's lives at the grassroots level. The imperial state was powerful enough to rival kinship as the most powerful organization in society. Law increasingly replaced custom as the premier rule of social order. Once people were united as a single country, the lifestyles of people in distant parts of China began to converge. Political unification promoted cultural exchange and cross-fertilization. Ideas, customs, styles, and institutions from various parts of this vast new empire began a long process of amalgamation that has continued down to the present day.

This convergence of regional cultures during Qin and Han made women's lives in various parts of China increasingly similar. During the Zhou period, very different local customs regulated the lives of women in states as diverse as Lu and Chu. Under Qin and Han, these differences began to decrease. Of course major regional variations persisted throughout the Han. Even today, after more than two thousand years of continuous integration, regionalism is still an important force in Chinese culture. But the general trend had been established. Beginning with the Qin unification, the stories of women in different parts of China can increasingly be told in tandem.

A second important trend was the steady rise of patrilineal rhetoric. It seems somewhat ironic that this value system became popular among China's elite long after it declined as popular custom. Han dynasty patrilineal rhetoric was modeled on the distant practices of high antiquity. Kinship was the most important organizational force holding together early Zhou society, whose decentralized institutions were very simple compared with the large-scale bureaucratic organizations of Qin and Han. In distant antiquity, the central government was very weak. Therefore society had to be organized as a series of extended patrilineal descent groups in a system called *zongfa*. The customs and values of early Zhou society bolstered the kinship principles that held society's fundamental organizations together.

During the late Zhou, *zongfa* went into steep decline. The rise of centralized government made the previous system obsolete. Kinship groups shrank in size and influence. However, patrilineal values did not completely perish. Antiquarians, utopians, ritualists, and philosophers began looking back on the past as a golden age. By remembering the good and forgetting the bad, they turned high antiquity into their utopia. They believed that contemporary society could only become good and just by reviving ancient ideals. These thinkers revived outmoded kinship values to construct an elaborate new ethical system. Archaic customs were abstracted, standardized, and elaborated into a sophisticated mode of elite thought. After ancient kinship customs declined, their patrilineal ideals reemerged in a different form as an elite ideology.

Patrilineal values are most often associated with Confucianism. Sometimes scholars speak of the two kinds of thought as virtually synonymous. But Confucians were not the only ones to stress the importance of patrilineal ideals. Many thinkers who showed little interest in the humanistic Confucian project were nevertheless fascinated by the prospect of a utopian society with large extended families and harmonious hierarchies. Long after large families had declined as the predominant way of life, ideas based on the values of that extinct society became an influential elite ideology. Ritualists, cosmologists, jurists, social critics, and ordinary bureaucrats all showed increasing interest in patrilineal values during the Han. The eventual revival of large families during the Eastern Han bolstered this trend. Members of powerful clans and lineages used patrilineal values to hold their unwieldy kinship organizations together and demand respect from society.

The rise of patrilineal values changed the course of Chinese women's history. Local custom seems to have been relatively open and pragmatic regarding the social roles women could assume. Brute necessity imbued popular thinking with an attitude of flexibility. Because patrilinealism was grounded in ideology instead of experience, it was often rigid and unpragmatic. This way of thinking stressed the need to enforce a strict social hierarchy centered on kinship. People were not respected as autonomous individuals; patrilinealism preached that people should sacrifice their individual interests for the sake of an ideal system.

Social reform during the Han often consisted of attempts to impose archaic Bronze Age patrilineal values on a society that had become vastly different and more complex since these standards were the norm. Idealists failed to reorganize society according to ancient kinship values. Nevertheless, the impact of patrilinealism on social, political, and academic rhetoric was tremendous. Although patrilineal values were never fully implemented, specific aspects of these ideas gained wide currency as commonplaces that appeared in all kinds of discourse. Most importantly, this ideology popularized the idea that society should be a steep kinship hierarchy based on dominance and deference. Patrilineal ideas became fully integrated into Chinese intellectual life during the early imperial period and continued as a perennial staple of gender discourse in subsequent dynasties. Henceforth anyone who wanted to talk about women had to face the influential and venerated body of Han dynasty patrilineal rhetoric.

The impact of these ideas on the lives of ordinary women in the Han and after cannot be exaggerated. Although patrilinealism was never completely implemented, its ideas gradually transformed the way people thought about female social roles. It is impossible to classify the effects of patrilineal rhetoric on women as either completely positive or negative. Some female roles gained in prestige, most notably that of mother. Sons were expected to defer to their mothers, even after they were grown. Although theoretically a man's sons inherited the family property, we know that the wife of the deceased sometimes assumed true control of the household. Mothers seem to have enjoyed far greater privileges in the Han than in some later eras, such as the Song. But aside from the roles of mother and mother-in-law, patrilineal thought sought to depress the status of other female roles. For example, according to patrilineal theory a daughter-in-law should own no property and ought to dedicate her life to serving her senior in-laws.

The complex influence of patrilineal rhetoric on women's roles demonstrates why it makes little sense to talk about a singular "status of women" for the period. Each woman played many different social roles simultaneously. And the relative importance of these roles could change through the course of her life. For example, a bride assumed the roles of daughter-in-law and wife. After she bore a child, she acted as daughter-in-law, wife, and mother. Over time, the powers implicit in her maternal role increased. When her son married, she would become a mother-in-law. And if she outlived her husband and senior in-laws, her maternal role might make her head of the entire household. Because a woman's roles in the kinship hierarchy changed over the course of her life, it is impossible to say that woman's social position in the early imperial period was either high or low. Social status was based on role-playing, and social roles varied over the course of a lifetime. The status of each woman varied in relation to those around her.

A third shift in the ideas influencing views of women was far more abstract. Starting in the Eastern Zhou, some thinkers began to rethink the most basic concepts underpinning male and female identity. Traditionally, the concepts of male and female were understood via a set of gendered social roles. Kinship, work, ritual, and government were organized according to explicitly female and male roles. Under this role-based way of thinking, gender was rarely discussed in itself as something disembodied and abstract. Instead, gender was just one characteristic of many social roles. But beginning in the late Zhou, some thinkers began to think of gender apart from social roles as a separate metaphysical element. If we want to use the terminology that descended from Greek philosophy, we can say that they began to see gender as essence rather than attribute. They believed that the feminine and masculine have ontological presence. The female is not a characteristic of gendered things but is something real in itself. In other words, the feminine exists.

Essentialized gender appeared most visibly in cosmology. Highly abstract concepts such as Heaven and Earth, *qian* and *kun*, yin and yang all gained close affiliation with gender. They were not synonymous with gender. Each of these metaphysical concepts had gender as one of many characteristics. Nevertheless, some writers began to use these concepts as virtual synonyms for gender. In this way, male and female became incorporated into elaborate cosmological systems.

Although essentialized gender concepts had little actual influence on daily life in the early imperial era, this way of thinking nevertheless marked a major departure from previous ways of thinking about women. Previously, gender was understood largely as a set of behaviors superimposed on a particular physiology. In other words, gender was largely understood as a series of social roles. Woman was not just a biological entity but someone who acted as mother, weaver, wife, and housekeeper. Patrilinealism and pragmatic local custom may have differed on the relative importance and definitions of particular roles, but both types of thought were united in seeing femininity in terms of the roles women played. Both depicted gender largely as a set of characteristic behaviors enacted via gendered social roles.

Essentialized gender was something quite different. This belief held that regardless of what a woman did or what roles she might undertake, she nevertheless retained a changeless womanhood as the core of her identity. To this view, femininity is far more than just a personal or social characteristic. The feminine is one of the basic abstract elements constituting the cosmos and makes itself manifest in individual women. When theorists essentialized and reified gender in this way, they could creatively redefine womanhood. By separating women from the dense tangle of traditional kinship hierarchies and local custom, they could reinterpret the feminine.

Cosmological essentialism could be far more innovative than backward-looking patrilinealism. Advocates of patrilineal rhetoric often gained creative space to challenge contemporary practices by romanticizing and exaggerating the kinship customs of antiquity. Nevertheless, these thinkers remained committed to a core of inherited ideals that limited their inventiveness. For essentialists, however, seeing female and male as metaphysical elements freed them from the constraints implicit in social definitions of gender. They were at liberty to come up with new, different, and even novel notions of what it is to be a man or a woman.

During the Han dynasty, both patrilinealism and essentialism gained ground as increasingly important ways for understanding gender. Some thinkers managed to combine the two systems. But in the end, these two trends were clearly at odds with each other. Patrilinealism defined gender as a characteristic of social roles. Essentialism portrayed the feminine and masculine as metaphysical elements in a grand cosmic scheme that guides life in this world. Because patrilinealism was based on social roles, it allowed both relatively high and low positions for women in society. By failing to simplistically link gender identity to a fixed singular social status, patrilinealism took a fairly neutral view of the innate worth of women. In contrast, essentialism clearly favored male over female. This bias increased as gendered cosmological systems matured in complexity. By understanding masculine and feminine directly in relation to each other, instead of through a complex matrix of intermediate social roles, theorists began to make blanket judgments about the inherent worth of each sex. As time went on, the verdict became resoundingly clear. Although both feminine and masculine have important places in the cosmos, men are definitely superior to women.

Patrilinealists hoped to improve society by reviving what they thought were the customs of an ancient utopia. But their views of ancient society ultimately limited the scope of their efforts to change society. They could never completely disconnect their theories from traditional social practices, which allowed some women considerable privileges. In contrast, essentialists created elaborate metaphysical systems to explain the invisible structure of the cosmos and then used these schemes to justify radical social change. By transposing gender into an abstract realm beyond society, they could conceive of it in completely new terms. Because essentialized gender was a major component of cosmology, and the cosmos was seen as an ideal template for society, new metaphysical gender ideals could be used to justify extreme social change. Metaphysical reasoning led them to conclude that if the masculine-affiliated elements of the cosmos, such as Heaven, *qian*, and yang, are superior to feminine Earth, *kun*, and yin, then man is clearly superior to woman. Some Han dynasty thinkers used this thought to justify patriarchy. In subsequent centuries, men who wanted to limit female autonomy invariably referred to the essentialized gender dichotomy of early imperial cosmology.

Neither essentialism nor patrilinealism ever succeeded in completely dominating Chinese views of gender. Conceptions of male and female were always complex, contested, and somewhat contradictory. In later centuries, these two different trends sometimes combined in an uneasy alliance. In other cases they produced conflicting guidelines for gender relations. However, a third force almost always kept these abstract gender ideologies in check: the deeply rooted pragmatism tempering daily life. In the end, people who lived not far above bare subsistence had to be flexible about gender. Conflict among these three very different ways of thought formed the substrate of gender theory for the remainder of imperial history. Ceaseless interaction among the conflicting principles of pragmatism, patrilinealism, and essentialism fueled Chinese debates about gender for centuries to come.

Notes

INTRODUCTION

1. Ban Gu, *Hanshu*, annotated by Yan Shigu (Beijing: Zhonghua, 1962), 72:3063.

2. Major Western advocates for the theory of matriarchy include Lewis Henry Morgan, *Ancient Society; or, Researches in the Lines of Human Progress from Savagery, through Barbarism to Civilization* (New York: H. Holt, 1877); Ralph Manheim, trans., *Myth, Religion, and Mother Right: Selected Writings of J. J. Bachofen* (Princeton: Princeton University Press, 1967); Frederick Engels, *The Origin of the Family, Private Property, and the State*, ed. Eleanor Burke Leacock (New York: International Publishers, 1972); Karl Wittfogel, "The Society of Prehistoric China," *Zeitschrift für Sozialwissenschaften* 8 (1939): 138–86.

Western critiques of this theory include R. H. Barnes, introduction to Josef Kohler, *On the Prehistory of Marriage: Totemism, Group Marriage, Mother Right*, trans. R. H. Barnes and Ruth Barnes (Chicago: University of Chicago Press, 1975), 23–29; Kathleen Gough, "An Anthropologist Looks at Engels," in *Woman in a Man-Made World*, ed. Nona Glazer-Malbin and Helen Youngelson Waehrer (Chicago: Rand McNally, 1972), 156–68; Joan Bamberger, "The Myth of Matriarchy: Why Men Rule in Primitive Society," in *Women, Culture, and Society*, ed. Michelle Zimbalist Rosaldo and Louise Lamphere (Stanford: Stanford University Press, 1974), 263–80; Nanneke Redclift, "Rights in Women: Kinship, Culture, and Materialism," in *Engels Revisited: New Feminist Essays*, ed. Janet Sayers, Mary Evans, and Nanneke Redclift (London: Tavistock Publications, 1987), 113–44.

For a representative Chinese study employing the theory of matriarchy, see Li Genpan, Huang Chongyue, and Lu Xun, *Zhongguoshi shehui jingji yanjiu* (Beijing: Zhongguo Shehui Kexue, 1987), 321–56.

3. Wang Ningsheng, "Yangshao Burial Customs and Social Organization: A Comment on the Theory of Yangshao Matrilineal Society and Its Methodology," *Early China* 11–12 (1985–1987): 21 n. 1; Xia Zhiqian, "Was There Ever a Matriarchy?" *Chinese Sociology and Anthropology* 25 (1993): 12.

4. Most of the early Western observations on Chinese women's history took a relatively ahistorical approach. Florence Ayscough, *Chinese Women Yesterday and Today*

(Shanghai: Modern Book Company, n.d.); Christopher Lucas, *Women of China* (Hong Kong: Dragonfly Books, 1965). Many of the stereotypes about the ahistorical "Chinese woman" have been derived from the writings of late imperial scholars. This line of traditional scholarship is summarized in [Zhu Tan] Chu T'an, *Ban Zhao* (Taipei: Shangwu, 1977), 7–9.

5. The best of the studies remain sensitive to the limitations of the material. For a sensible treatment of the classics, see Richard W. Guisso, "Thunder over the Lake: The Five Classics and the Perception of Women in Early China," in *Women in China: Current Directions in Historical Scholarship,* ed. Richard W. Guisso and Stanley Johannesen (Youngstown, N.Y.: Philo, 1981), 47–61.

6. Elisabeth J. Croll, *Changing Identities of Chinese Women: Rhetoric, Experience, and Self-Perception in Twentieth-Century China* (Hong Kong: Hong Kong University Press/Zed, 1995), 2.

7. David L. Hall and Roger T. Ames, *Thinking from the Han: Self, Truth, and Transcendence in Chinese and Western Culture* (Albany, N.Y.: State University of New York Press, 1998), 81–82.

8. For example, there is the concluding essay of Albert Richard O'Hara, *The Position of Woman in Early China: According to the Lieh Nü Chuan, "The Biographies of Chinese Women"* (Taipei: Mei Ya, 1971), 255–85. Users of this terminology in Taiwan have included [Li Zefen] Li Tse-fen, "Han dai funü de diwei," in Li, *Xian Qin ji liang Han lishi lunwenji* (Taipei: Shangwu, 1981), 153–73. For an example from mainland China, see "The Position and Value of Chinese Women," in Hu Kun, *Lanse de yinying: Zhongguofunü wenhua guanzhao* (Xian: Shaanxi Renmin Jiaoyu, 1989), 47ff.

9. Robert H. Lowie, *Primitive Society* (New York: Boni & Liverright, 1920), 187; Martin King Whyte, *The Status of Women in Preindustrial Societies* (Princeton: Princeton University Press, 1978), 95–108, 116–18; Michelle Rosaldo, "The Use and Abuse of Anthropology: Reflections on Feminism and Cross-Cultural Understanding," *Signs* 5, no. 3 (1980): 389–417; Sherry Ortner, "Is Female to Male as Nature Is to Culture?" in *Women, Culture, and Society,* ed. Michelle Zimbalist Rosaldo and Louise Lamphere (Stanford: Stanford University Press, 1974), 67–87, uses specifically Chinese examples to persuasively reject the idea of a unitary "status" of women.

10. Croll, *Changing Identities of Chinese Women,* 2–3.

11. Technically, an unmarried woman was called *nü* and a married woman *fu.* Zhao Fengjie, *Zhongguo funü zai falü shang zhi diwei* (1929; reprint, Taipei: Shihuo, 1973), 25–26. A woman was also called by numerous terms according to kinship, as explained in Zheng Xuan, *Liji Zheng zhu* (n.p.: Laiqingge, 1937), 10:9a–9b (*Dazhuan*); James Legge, trans., *The Sacred Books of China: The Texts of Confucianism,* pts. 3–4, *The Li Ki,* in *The Sacred Books of the East,* ed. F. Max Muller, vols. 27–28 (Oxford: Oxford University Press, 1885), 28–62; Ban Gu, *Baihutong,* in *Baojingtang congshu,* ed. Lu Wenchao (1784; reprint, Beijing: Zhili, 1923); Tjoe Som Tjan, *Po Hu T'ung: The Comprehensive Discussions in the White Tiger Hall, A Contribution to the History of Classical Studies in the Han Period* (Leiden: Brill, 1949–1952), 2:589. The ritual system also had many names for referring to women

according to rank. Zhang, *Liji* (*Quli*), 1:24a; Legge, *Li Ki*, 27:112–13. After a woman died, she could be referred to by a different set of names. Zheng, *Liji* (*Quli*), 1:26a–26b; Legge, *Li Ki*, 27:117–18.

12. Erving Goffman, *The Presentation of Self in Everyday Life* (Garden City, N.Y.: Doubleday, 1959).

CHAPTER 1

1. The best overview of the period available in English is Cho-yun Hsü and Katheryn M. Linduff, *Western Chou Civilization* (New Haven: Yale University Press, 1988).

2. For a good discussion of the social and political dynamism most characteristic of the Eastern Zhou, see Cho-yun Hsü, *Ancient China in Transition: An Analysis of Social Mobility, 722–222 B.C.* (Stanford: Stanford University Press, 1965).

3. The most comprehensive and systematic introduction to all major aspects of Qin and Han history is Denis Twitchett and Michael Loewe, eds., *The Cambridge History of China*, vol. 1, *The Ch'in and Han Empires, 221 B.C.–A.D. 220* (Cambridge: Cambridge University Press, 1986).

CHAPTER 2

1. Zheng (*Liji*, 10:9a–9b) and Legge (*Li Ki*, 28:62 [*Dazhuan* 6]) discuss kinship terminology for women. For a discussion of the names, ranks, and titles applied to early women, as well as their relation to social identity, see Lisa Ann Raphals, *Sharing the Light: Representations of Women and Virtue in Early China* (Albany: State University of New York Press, 1998), 227–32. Ban (*Baihutong*, 3b:7a) and Tjan (*Po Hu T'ung*, 2:561–62) provide one explanation of the meaning of terms for "husband" (*fu*) and "wife" (*fu*).

2. Patricia Ebrey, "Women, Marriage, and the Family," in *Heritage of China: Contemporary Perspectives on Chinese Civilization*, ed. Paul S. Ropp (Berkeley: University of California Press, 1990), 198.

3. Zheng, *Liji*, 7:11b; Legge, *Li Ki*, 27:392 (*Liyun* 4:16).

4. D. C. Lau, *Mencius* (Harmondsworth, U.K.: Penguin, 1970), 66 (1B.5). Historians in China today have substituted Engels's periodization of the stages in the development of human marriage for the traditional Confucian evolutionary view. For Engels's theory, see his *Origin of the Family*, 87–146. An application of Engels's periodization to the development of prehistoric and ancient Chinese marriage appears in Li Hengmei, "Woguo yuanshi shehui hunyin xingtai yanjiu," *Lishi yanjiu* 180, no. 2 (1986): 95–109. Unfortunately, Engels's ideas on marriage are overly rigid, too dependent on the paradigm of Darwinian evolution, and uninformed by the flood of subsequent anthropological data.

5. These points are explored in detail in Wong Sun-ming, "Confucian Ideal and Reality: Transformation of the Institution of Marriage in T'ang China (A.D. 618–907)"

(Ph.D. diss., University of Washington, 1979), 21–45; [Liu Zenggui] Liu Tseng-kui, *Handai hunyin zhidu* (Taipei: Huashi, 1980), 201–3. For an excellent survey of Han divorce, see Jack L. Dull, "Marriage and Divorce in Han China: A Glimpse at 'Pre-Confucian' Society," in *Chinese Family Law and Social Change in Historical and Comparative Perspective*, ed. David C. Buxbaum (Seattle: University of Washington Press, 1978), 23–74.

6. Wong, "Confucian Ideal and Reality," 8. Even after the Tang, conformity of popular custom to Confucian theory was still very uneven.

7. Ellen R. Judd, "*Niangjia*: Chinese Women and Their Natal Families," *Journal of Asian Studies* 48, no. 3 (1989): 525–26.

8. Zhao Yi, *Gaiyu congkao* (Shanghai: Shangwu, 1957), 42:926.

9. Zheng, *Liji*, 10:4a; Legge, *Li Ki*, 28:49 (*Sangfu xiaoji* 2:7).

10. Han Ying, *Hanshi waizhuan*, in *Yingyin Wenyuange siku quanshu*, vol. 83 (Taipei: Taiwan Shangwu, 1983), 4:4a; James Robert Hightower, *Han Shih Wai Chuan: Han Ying's Illustrations of the Didactic Applications of the Classic of Songs* (Cambridge, Mass.: Harvard University Press, 1952), 132.

11. Ban, *Baihutong*, 2A:9a; Tjan, *Po Hu T'ung*, 2:444–45.

12. Huang Jinshan, "Handai jiating chengyuan de diwei he yiwu," *Lishi yanjiu* 192, no. 2 (1988): 38; [Liu Zenggui] Liu Tseng-kui, "Shilun Handai hunyin guanxi zhong de lifa guannian," in *Zhongguo funüshi lunji xuji*, ed. [Bao Jialin] Pao Chia-lin (Taipei: Daoxiang, 1991), 11–13. For a general introduction to Chinese concubinage, see Wang Shaoxi, *Xiaoqieshi* (Shanghai: Shanghai Wenyi, 1995).

13. [Yang Yunru] Yang Yun-ju, "Chunqiu shidai zhi nannü fengji," in *Zhongguo funüshi lunwenji*, ed. [Li Youning] Li Yu-ning and [Zhang Yufa] Chang Yu-fa, 2d ed. (Taipei: Taiwan Shangwu, 1988), 22.

14. Huang, "Handai jiating chengyuan," 37.

15. Cheng Shude, *Jiuchao lükao* (Beijing: Zhonghua, 1963), 114; Li Jing, *Qinlü tonglun* (Jinan: Shandong Renmin, 1985), 506.

16. Ban, *Baihutong*, 2B:5b; Tjan, *Po Hu T'ung*, 2:473.

17. Zheng, *Liji*, 2:2a; Legge, *Li Ki*, 27:122 (*Tangong* 1:A:4).

18. Dull ("Marriage and Divorce") presents copious examples.

19. Zheng, *Liji*, 4:15b–16a, 5:20b, 7:1b; Legge, *Li Ki*, 27:243–244 (*Wangzhi* 5:13), 27:298 (*Yueling* 4:A:10), 27:365 (*Liyun* 1:2); Han, *Hanshi waizhuan* 4:8a; Hightower, *Han Shih Wai Chuan*, 140; Qian Tang, *Lienüzhuan jiaozhu* (Shanghai: Zhonghua, n.d.), 6:4b; O'Hara, *Position of Woman*, 162.

20. A. F. Hulsewé, *Remnants of Han Law*, vol. 1, *Introductory Studies and an Annotated Translation of Chapters 22 and 23 of the History of the Former Han Dynasty* (Leiden: Brill, 1955), 48.

21. [Dong Jiazun] Tung Chia-tsun, "Cong Han dao Song guafu zaijia xisu kao," in *Zhongguo funüshi lunwenji*, ed. [Li Youning] Li Yu-ning and [Zhang Yufa] Chang Yü-fa, 2d ed. (Taipei: Taiwan Shangwu, 1988), 39–44; Yang, "Chunqiu shidai zhi nannü fengji," 22; Yang Shuda, *Handai hunsang lisu kao* (Shanghai: Shangwu, 1933), 53ff.; Li, "Han dai funü de diwei," 153–58.

22. Hu (*Lanse de yinying*, 137–50) discusses the emergence of ideals of female virginity and widow chastity. For the popularity of Song widow remarriage despite Neo-Confucian disapproval, see Patricia Buckley Ebrey, *Family and Property in Sung China: Yuan Ts'ai's Precepts for Social Life* (Princeton: Princeton University Press, 1984), 99.

23. Li, *Qinlü*, 505–6; Niu Zhiping, "Gudai funü zhenjieguan," *Lishi yuekan* 26, no. 3 (1990): 20–21. Dull ("Marriage and Divorce," 65) notes that Han authorities, unlike those in the Qin and post-Han periods, did not seem to distinguish between the remarriage of women without children and those with children.

24. Zheng, *Liji*, 8:9a–9b; Legge, *Li Ki*, 27:439 (*Jiaotesheng* 3:7).

25. [Dong], "Cong Han dao Song guafu zaijia xisu kao," 42; Niu, "Gudai funü de zhenjieguan," 20. This motivation seems to have held true over time. J. Holmgren draws similar conclusions regarding a later period in "Observations on Marriage and Inheritance Practices in Early Mongol and Yuan Society: With Particular Reference to the Levirate," *Journal of Asian History* 20 (1986): 127–92.

26. Joanna Handlin, "Lü K'un's New Audience: The Influence of Women's Literacy on Sixteenth-Century Thought," in *Women in Chinese Society*, ed. Margery Wolf and Roxane Witke (Stanford: Stanford University Press, 1979), 14.

27. Patricia Buckley Ebrey, *The Inner Quarters: Marriage and the Lives of Chinese Women in the Sung Period* (Berkeley: University of California Press, 1993), 194–200; Ebrey, "Woman, Marriage, and the Family," 220.

28. Qian, *Lienüzhuan jiaozhu*, 2:4b–5b; O'Hara, *Position of Woman*, 60; Fan Ye, *Houhanshu*, annotated by Li Xian (Beijing: Zhonghua, 1962), 26:904–5; Liu, *Handai hunyin zhidu*, 25–26.

29. James Legge, trans., *The Chinese Classics*, vol. 5, pts. 1–2, *The Ch'un Ts'ew, with the Tso Chuen* (Hong Kong: Legge, 1872), 92–93 (*Zhuang* 15); Qian, *Lienüzhuan jiaozhu*, 4:4b–6a, 8a–10a; O'Hara, *Position of Woman*, 112–16, 122–26; Fan, *Houhanshu*, 84:2798–99.

30. Fan, *Houhanshu*, 84:2798–99.

31. Traditionally *Lienüzhuan* is attributed to Liu Xiang. But some textual critics have suggested that Liu Xiang's son Liu Xin may have penned the work's prefaces and encomias.

32. Mark Elvin, "Female Virtue and the State in China," *Past and Present* 104 (1984): 111–52; [Dong Jiazun] Tung Chia-tsun, "Lidai jiefu lienü de tongji," in *Zhongguo funüshi lunji*, ed. [Bao Jialin] Pao Chia-lin (Taipei: Daoxiang, 1978), 112; Hu, *Lanse de yinying*, 137–50.

33. For example, on the vulnerability of Song widows, see Ebrey, *Inner Quarters*, 190–91.

34. Gan Bao, *Soushenji* (Beijing: Zhonghua, 1969), 6:77.

35. Stuart A. Queen and John B. Adams, *The Family in Various Cultures* (Philadelphia: Lippincott, 1952), 130–31.

36. Makino Tatsumi, "Kandai ni okeru kazuku no ōkisa," in Makino, *Shina kazoku kenkyū* (Tokyo: Seikatsu, 1944), 148; Ochi Shigeaki, "Thoughts on the Understanding of

the Han and the Six Dynasties," *Memoirs of the Research Department of the Tōyō Bunko* 35 (1977): 1–73.

37. Makino, *Shina kazoku kenkyū*, 147, 175; Liu, *Handai hunyin zhidu*, 62. These smaller Han families were nevertheless larger than the norm for preindustrial Europe. J. C. Russell, "Population in Europe, 500–1500," in *Fontana Economic History of Europe*, ed. Carlo M. Cipolla (Glasgow: Collins, Fontana, 1972), 1:1–70.

38. Ch'ü T'ung-tsu, *Han Social Structure*, ed. Jack L. Dull (Seattle: University of Washington Press, 1972), 8; Michael Loewe, *Records of Han Administration* (Cambridge: Cambridge University Press, 1967), 1:113, 2:83–91, includes household registers and passports listing at least five cases of an unmarried sister living with her older brother.

39. Guo Moruo, Wen Yiduo, and Xu Weiyu, *Guanzi jijiao* (Beijing: Kexue, 1956), 64:974–75; W. Allyn Rickett, *Guanzi: Political, Economic, and Philosophical Essays from Early China* (Princeton: Princeton University Press, 1985), 1:317 (*Zhong Kuang*). This early Han text echoes Lau, *Mencius*, 98 (3A.3).

40. Zheng, *Liji*, 15:17b–18a; Legge, *Li Ki*, 38:295 (*Fangji* 30).

41. This law and its implications receive detailed treatment in Huang, "Handai jiating chengyuan," 35.

42. Qiu Jun, *Daxue yanyi bu* (Taipei: Taiwan Shangwu, 1971), 53:19b; Huang, "Handai jiating chengyuan," 37.

43. Lau, *Mencius*, 186 (7A.22).

44. Lau, *Mencius*, 135 (4B.30). Ebrey (*Family and Property*, 96–97) shows that this conflict was still a major problem during the Song.

45. Hightower, *Han Shih Wai Chuan*, 276; Han, *Hanshi waizhuan*, 8:12a.

46. Fan, *Houhanshu*, 81:2684–86.

47. Ban, *Hanshu*, 48:2244. Suicide among women in contemporary China is often linked to pressure from in-laws. This gives some indication of the similar pressures a woman in earlier times faced when entering a strange household. Margery Wolf, "Women and Suicide in China," in *Women in Chinese Society*, ed. Margery Wolf and Roxane Witke (Stanford: Stanford University Press, 1979), 111–41.

48. Wu Zhaoyi, *Yutai xinyong jianzhu*, in *Wenxue congshu*, ed. Yang Jialuo, pt. 1, vol. 2 (Taipei: Shijie, 1956), 1:24–32; Hans H. Frankel, "The Chinese Ballad 'Southeast Fly the Peacocks,' " *Harvard Journal of Asiatic Studies* 34 (1974): 248–71; Anne Birrell, *New Songs from a Jade Terrace: An Anthology of Early Chinese Love Poetry* (Harmondsworth, U.K.: Penguin, 1986), 53–62.

49. Ban, *Hanshu*, 48:2244, 72:3077; Ch'ü, *Han Social Structure*, 118; Huang, "Handai jiating chengyuan," 42–43; Li, *Qinlü*, 504; James L. Watson, "Anthropological Overview: The Development of Chinese Descent Groups," in *Kinship Organization in Late Imperial China 1000–1940*, ed. Patricia Buckley Ebrey and James L. Watson (Berkeley: University of California Press, 1986), 285.

50. Ban, *Hanshu*, 72:3065 n. 2 (commentary of Jin Zhuo); Fujikawa Masakazu, *Kandai ni okeru reigaku no kenkyū* (Tokyo: Kazama, 1968), 335; Liu, *Handai hunyin zhidu*, 22, 57.

51. Ban, *Hanshu*, 72:3064.

52. Fan, *Houhanshu*, 10A:407–14.

53. Ban, *Hanshu*, 98:4018.

54. Anne Behnke Kinney, "Infant Abandonment in Early China," *Early China* 18 (1993): 107–38; [Li Changnian] Li Chang-nien, "Nüying shahai yu Zhongguo liangxing bujun wenti," in *Zhongguo funüshi lunji*, ed. [Bao Jialin] Pao Chia-lin (Taipei: Daoxiang, 1978), 212–20; Bernice J. Lee, "Female Infanticide in China," in *Women in China*, ed. Richard W. Guisso and Stanley Johannesen (Youngstown, N.Y.: Philo, 1981), 163–77.

55. Lien-sheng Yang, "The Concept of *Pao* as a Basis for Social Relations in China," in *Chinese Thought and Institutions*, ed. John Fairbank (Chicago: University of Chicago Press, 1957), 291–309, 395–97. For examples of *bao* in early times, see Ouyang Xun, *Yiwen leiju*, (Taipei: Zhongwen, 1980), 33:581–84.

56. Takeo Doi, *The Anatomy of Dependence*, trans. John Bester (Tokyo: Kodansha, 1973).

57. For an injunction that a mother should obey her grown son, see Jia Gongyan, *Yili zhushu ji buzheng* (Taipei: Shijie, 1970), 31:9b; John Steele, *The I-li or Book of Etiquette and Ceremonial* (London: Probsthain, 1917), 2:20. For an actual example of a mother issuing orders to a grown son, see Ban, *Hanshu*, 90:3671–72.

58. Legge, *Li Ki*, 27:453 (*Neize* 1:10); Zheng, *Liji*, 8:15a.

59. Ebrey, *Family and Property in Sung China*, 84.

CHAPTER 3

1. Jan Pahl, *Money and Marriage* (New York: Macmillan, 1989).

2. Legge, *Li Ki*, 27:458 (*Neize* 1:19), changing "any one" to "anyone." Zhang, *Liji*, 8:17a–17b.

3. Legge, *Li Ki*, 28:295 (*Fangji* 30); Zheng, *Liji*, 15:18a. Also Zhang, *Liji*, 8:17a–17b; Legge, *Li Ki*, 27:458 (*Neize* 1:19). The implications of such passages are discussed in Huang, "Handai jiating chengyuan," 33; Zhao, *Funü zai falü*, 75.

4. Watson, "Anthropological Overview," 283.

5. For wife: Yokota Kenzan, *Sengoku saku seikai* (Tokyo: Fujisan, 1915), 10:22; J. I. Crump Jr., *Chan-Kuo Ts'e* (Oxford: Clarendon, 1970), 583. For mother: Yokota, *Sengoku saku seikai*, 1:16, 3B:56, 7B:15; Crump, *Chan-Kuo Ts'e*, 35, 142, 426. For a more general statement on the land holdings of Han imperial ladies, see Wei Hong, "Hanjiuyi," in *Pingjinguan congshu*, ed. Sun Xingyan (n.p.: Huailu, 1885), *ce* 4, B:4b.

6. Ban, *Hanshu*, 97A:3948.

7. Fan, *Houhanshu*, 23:812.

8. Fan, *Houhanshu*, 84:2795.

9. Dorothy Ko, *Teachers of the Inner Chambers: Women and Culture in Seventeenth-Century China* (Stanford: Stanford University Press, 1994), 139. In later periods, such as

the Song, it was not unusual for a woman to step in to manage the family assets when her husband was incapable or dead. Ebrey, *Family and Property in Sung China*, 118.

10. A. F. Hulsewé, *Remnants of Ch'in Law: An Annotated Translation of the Ch'in Legal and Administrative Rules of the 3rd Century B.C. Discovered in Yun-meng Prefecture, Hu-pei Province, in 1975* (Leiden: Brill, 1985), 51. Moreover, Katrina C. D. McLeod and Robin D. S. Yates, "Forms of Ch'in Law: An Annotated Translation of the *Feng-chen shih*," *Harvard Journal of Asiatic Studies* 41, no. 1 (1981): 137 n. 72, examining the question of whether a wife's property could be impounded for a husband's crime, suggest that a wife could hold property independent of her husband.

11. Fan, *Houhanshu*, 83:2769.

12. Shigeru Katō, "A Study on the *Suan-fu*, the Poll Tax of the Han Dynasty," *Memoirs of the Research Department of the Tōyō Bunko* 1 (1926): 52. All ages are given in *sui*.

13. Hulsewé, *Remnants of Han Law*, 45, 60.

14. The ceremony for presentation of the *pin* was called *nazheng* ("presentation of betrothal presents"). Dull, "Marriage and Divorce," 45. Bernhard Karlgren, *The Book of Odes: Chinese Text, Transcription, and Translation* (Stockholm: Museum of Far Eastern Antiquities, 1950), 65–66 (no. 101), describes the husband presenting a ritualized bride price of shoes and cap pendants to his bride's family during the marriage ceremony. This ancient custom became fossilized into Han ritual as the rarely practiced *nacai* ceremony of a presentation of gifts from the groom's parents to those of the bride. Dull, "Marriage and Divorce," 42–43.

15. Takigawa Kametarō, *Shiki kaichū kōshō* (1932–1934; reprint, Taipei: Zhongxin, 1977), 89:2, 117:6; Fan, *Houhanshu*, 84:2781; Cheng, *Jiuchao lükao*, 3:67; Dull, "Marriage and Divorce," 47–48.

16. Ebrey, *Family and Property in Sung China*, 116–18.

17. Ebrey, *Inner Quarters*, 101.

18. Yunmeng Qin Mu Zhujian Zhengli Xiaozu, "Yunmeng Qinjian shiwen (3)," *Wenwu* 342, no. 8 (1976): 33; Hulsewé, *Remnants of Ch'in Law*, 168 (D 149); Li, *Qinlü*, 505.

19. Hulsewé, *Remnants of Ch'in Law*, 169.

20. Zheng, *Liji*, 12:20b; Legge, *Li Ki*, 28:170–171 (*Zaji* 2:B:34); Cheng, *Jiuchao lükao*, 67; Hulsewé, *Remnants of Ch'in Law*, 168 (D 149); Li, *Qinlü*, 505.

21. Ebrey, *Inner Quarters*, 107.

22. Li, *Qinlü*, 512–13.

23. Li, *Qinlü*, 513.

24. Huang, "Handai jiating chengyuan," 36.

25. In 129 B.C.E. Zhao Wangsun granted his daughter a share of property equal to that given his son. Takigawa, *Shiki kaichū kōshō*, 117:66. Women could also bequeath property. An Eastern Han stele inscription records the will of a childless widow. Hong Gua, *Lishi* (Shanghai: Sibu Congkan, 1935), 12:11a–13a.

26. Takigawa, *Shiki kaichū kōshō*, 129:16; Nancy Lee Swann, *Food and Money in Ancient China: The Earliest Economic History of China to A.D. 25, Han Shu 24*, with related texts,

Han Shu 91 and Shih-chi 129 (Princeton: Princeton University Press, 1950), 431; Ch'ü, *Han Social Structure*, 54–55.

27. Bret Hinsch, "Women, Kinship, and Property as Seen in a Han Dynasty Will," *T'oung Pao* 84 (1998): 1–20; Yangzhou Bowuguan, "Jiangsu Yizheng Xupu 101 hao Xi Han mu," *Wenwu* 368, no. 1 (1987): 1–13; Chen Ping and Wang Quanjin, "Yizheng Xupu 101 hao Xi Han mu 'xianling quanshu' chukao," *Wenwu* 368, no. 1 (1987): 20–25, 36.

28. Ebrey, *Family and Property in Sung China*, 85.

29. Lau, *Mencius*, 59 (1A.7), 66–67 (1B.6); D. C. Lau, *Confucius: The Analects (Lun Yü)* (Harmondsworth, U.K.: Penguin, 1979), 81 (6.4); Zheng, *Liji*, 7:1b; Legge, *Li Ki*, 27:365 (*Liyun* 1:2). Guisso comments on this passage in "Thunder over the Lake," 57. Some contemporary scholars have accepted this idealized distinction as an accurate depiction of women's roles in the early economy. Ch'ü, *Han Social Structure*, 28.

30. Judith K. Brown, "A Note on the Division of Labor by Sex," *American Anthropologist* 72, no. 5 (1970): 1073–78; Elizabeth Wayland Barber, *Women's Work, The First 20,000 Years: Women, Cloth, and Society in Early Times* (New York: W.W. North, 1994), 29–30.

31. Liu, *Handai hunyin zhidu*, 14.

32. Liu, *Handai hunyin zhidu*, 14, 62; Takigawa, *Shiki kaichū kōshō*, 117:5–6.

33. References to women cooking for the family include Zheng, *Liji*, 9:2a; Legge, *Li Ki*, 28:4 (*Yusao* 1:19); Qian, *Lienüzhuan jiaozhu*, 1:8a, 5:2a; O'Hara, *Position of Woman*, 34, 129. For archeological evidence, see Shen Zhongchang, *Sichuan Handai taoyong* (Beijing: Chaohua Meishu, 1963), pl. 41.

34. Firewood: Han, *Hanshi waizhuan*, 9:6b–7a; Hightower, *Han Shih Wai Chuan*, 302. Carrying water: Shen, *Sichuan Handai taoyong*, pl. 16; Xun Bing, *Sichuan Handai diaosu yishu* (Beijing: Zhongguo Gudian Meishu, 1959), pl. 16. Sauces: Zheng, *Liji*, 1:27b; Legge, *Li Ki*, 27:119 (*Quli* 2:B:20). Brewing: Zheng, *Liji*, 1:27b; Legge, *Li Ki*, 27:119 (*Quli* 2:B:20); Qian, *Lienüzhuan jiaozhu*, 1:11a; O'Hara, *Position of Woman*, 42; Takigawa, *Shiki kaichū kōshō*, 117:6. Grain preparation: Shen (*Sichuan Handai taoyong*, 7) features a grain pounder figurine that seems to be female.

35. Wei, *Hanjiuyi*, B:2a. At funeral feasts women followed their usual role by clearing the meal away, as specified in Jia, *Yili zhushu ji buzheng*, 50:18b; Steele, *I-Li*, 2:214. At festivals, royal harem women were not to remove the meal. The fact that this directive had to be specified suggests that it went contrary to the usual practice at royal courts. See Zheng, *Liji*, 9:10a; Legge, *Li Ki*, 28:20 (*Yusao* 3:13).

36. Bedding: Zheng, *Liji*, 8:23b; Legge, *Li Ki*, 27:470 (*Neize* 1:14); Qian, *Lienüzhuan jiaozhu*, 6:8a; O'Hara, *Position of Woman*, 170. Brushing pillows and mats: Qian, 4:7a; O'Hara, *Position of Woman*, 118. Sweeping: Qian, 2:10b, 4:7a, 6:8a; O'Hara, *Position of Woman*, 73, 118, 170; Zheng, *Liji*, 1:27a; Legge, *Li Ki*, 27:119 (*Quli* 2:B:20); Yamazaki Makoto and Yamato Shigeru, *Chūgoku joseigaku gairon* (Tokyo: Aki, 1987), 81 (*Nüjie*, introduction); Nancy Lee Swann, *Pan Chao: Foremost Woman Scholar of China* (New York: Century, 1932), 82.

37. Xun, *Sichuan Han dai diaosu yishu*, pl. 17; Qian, *Lienüzhuan jiaozhu*, 6:5a; O'Hara, *Position of Woman*, 163; Han, *Hanshi waizhuan*, 1:1b; Hightower, *Han Shih Wai Chuan*, 13.

38. Qian, *Lienüzhuan jiaozhu*, 6:8a; O'Hara, *Position of Woman*, 170; Edward Schafer, "The Development of Bathing Customs in Ancient and Medieval China and the History of the Foliate Clear Palace," *Journal of the American Oriental Society* 76, no. 2 (1956): 56–81.

39. Qian, *Lienüzhuan jiaozhu*, 1:2a, 2:9a, 8:10a; O'Hara, *Position of Woman*, 18, 70, 242–43; Fan, *Houhanshu*, 83:2776; [Xu Zhuoyun] Hsü Cho-yun, "Cong Zhouli zhong tuice yuangu de funü gongzuo," in *Zhongguo funüshi lunji*, ed. [Bao Jialin] Pao Chia-lin (Taipei: Daoxiang, 1978), 55.

40. Derk Bodde, *Festivals in Classical China: New Year and Other Annual Observances during the Han Dynasty, 206 B.C.–A.D. 220* (Princeton: Princeton University Press, 1975), 202.

41. Li Shan, *Wenxuan Li Shan zhu* (Shanghai: Sibu Beiyao, n.d.), 7:8a (*Jietianfu*); David R. Knechtges, *Xiao Tong: Wen Xuan, or Selections of Refined Literature* (Princeton: Princeton University Press, 1982), 2:43. Although this third-century poem postdates the Han, there seems to have been a great deal of ritual continuity between the late Eastern Han and subsequent periods.

42. Cho-yun Hsü, *Han Agriculture: The Formation of Early Chinese Agrarian Economy (206 B.C.–A.D. 220)*, ed. Jack L. Dull (Seattle: University of Washington Press, 1980), 118–19.

43. Women not only wove cloth but also plaited useful objects out of straw. Ban, *Hanshu*, 84:3411.

44. Ebrey, *Inner Quarters*, 148–49.

45. "Women's work": *fugong, fushi*, [Xu], "Yuangu de funü gongzuo," 53; Yamazaki, *Chugoku joseigaku*, 4:94 (*Nüjie*); Swann (*Pan Chao*, 86) defines women's work (*fugong*) broadly as including sewing, weaving, cleaning, and serving guests alcohol and food. Most other contexts for this and similar terms, however, restrict the definition of "women's work" to textile production.

46. Mulberry: Qian, *Lienüzhuan jiaozhu*, 6:10a–11a, 8:1a–1b; O'Hara, *Position of Woman*, 174–77, 216; Ban, *Baihutong*, 2B:13a–13b; Tjan, *Po Hu T'ung*, 2:493; Yang Zongrong, *Zhanguo huihua ziliao* (Beijing: Zhongguo Gudian Yishu, 1957), pl. 20; Lucy Lim, *Stories from China's Past: Han Dynasty Pictorial Tomb Reliefs and Archeological Objects from Sichuan Province, People's Republic of China* (San Francisco: Chinese Culture Foundation of San Francisco, 1987), 152; Liu Zhiyuan et al., *Sichuan Handai huaxiangzhuan yu Handai shehui* (Beijing: Wenwu, 1983), 43, shows an image of women playing music and dancing during the mulberry harvest. Spinning: Han, *Hanshi waizhuan*, 5:10a; Hightower, *Han Shih Wai Chuan*, 176. Weaving: Han, *Hanshi waizhuan*, 2:12a; Hightower, *Han Shih Wai Chuan*, 60; Qian, *Lienüzhuan jiaozhu*, 2:5a; O'Hara, *Position of Woman*, 60; Zheng, *Liji*, 8:27b; Legge, *Li Ki*, 27:479 (*Neize* 2:36); Édouard Chavannes, *La Sculpture sur pierre en Chine au temps des deux dynasties Han* (Paris: Ernest Leroux, 1893), pl. 3; Song Boyin and Li Zhongyi, "Cong Han huaxiangshi tansuo Handai zhiji gouzao," *Wenwu* 137, no. 3

(1962): 23–24. Dyeing: Zheng, *Liji*, 5:13a; Legge, *Li Ki*, 27:278 (*Yueling* 2:C:9). Sewing: Qian, *Lienüzhuan jiaozhu*, 1:11a, 8:10b; O'Hara, *Position of Woman*, 42, 244. Myth featured accounts of the "first sericulturalist," Lady Xiling (also called Leizu), the wife of the primal Yellow Emperor, as well as the involvement of the Zhou ancestress Jiang Yuan in the beginnings of mulberry and hemp cultivation. Dieter Kuhn, "Tracing a Chinese Legend: In Search of the Identity of the 'First Sericulturalist,' " *T'oung Pao* 70, nos. 4–5 (1984): 216–18; Qian, *Lienüzhuan jiaozhu*, 1:2a; O'Hara, *Position of Woman*, 18. In addition, the hemp cap is referred to as representing the first of woman's handicrafts in Ban, *Baihutong*, 4B:2b; Tjan, *Po Hu T'ung*, 2:615.

47. Yunmeng Qinmu Zhujian Zhengli Xiaozu, "Yunmeng Qinjian shiwen (2)," *Wenwu* 242, no. 7 (1976): 5; Hulsewé, *Remnants of Ch'in Law*, 61 (A59).

48. About 400 B.C.E. an official in Wei estimated the average family's annual clothing costs at 1,500 cash. Because he spoke of clothing in terms of monetary value, we know that there was already a textile market. Furthermore, the annual cash value of grain needed by the average household was only slightly higher than that for clothing. Ban, *Hanshu*, 24A:1125; Swann, *Food and Money in Ancient China*, 140–43; Hsü, *Han Agriculture*, 79, 235–36. These figures suggest that, even disregarding the female role in field work, women may have produced almost half of the average household's output. These numbers do not seem unrealistic. Scholars have long known that in the earliest stages of industrial development the output of women and children is often more easily marketable than that of men. Sheila Rowbotham, *Hidden from History: 300 Years of Women's Oppression and the Fight against It* (London: Pluto, 1973), 55–56.

49. A. F. Hulsewé, " 'Contracts' of the Han Period," in *Il Diritto in Cina, Teoria e applicazione durante le dinastie imperiali e problematica del diritto Cinese contemporareo*, ed. Lionello Lanciotti (Florence: L.S. Olschki, 1978), 11–38.

50. Ban, *Hanshu*, 24B:1181; Swann, *Food and Money in Ancient China*, 339.

51. Wu Ronghui, "Qin de guanfu shougongye," in *Yunmeng Qin jian yanjiu*, ed. Zhonghua Shuju Bianjibu (Beijing: Zhonghua, 1981), 46. Wei (*Hanjiuyi*, B:1b–2a) describes the uses of court-produced textiles. The palace "drying house," where the less pleasant jobs of dyeing and boiling the cloth were conducted, also doubled as a hospital and prison for the palace ladies. Hans Bielenstein, "Lo-yang in Later Han Times," *Bulletin of the Museum of Far Eastern Antiquities* 48 (1976): 53–54.

52. Takigawa, *Shiki kaichū kōshō*, 129:14; Swann, *Food and Money in Ancient China*, 429.

53. Ban, *Hanshu*, 59:2652.

54. Shi Shenghan, *Simin yueling jiaozhu* (Beijing: Zhonghua, 1965), 9 (1.5) (*Zhengyue*).

55. Jing, *Guanzi*, 9:10b; Rickett, *Guanzi*, 1:371 (*Wen*). Tao Ying of Lu, widowed while still young, "since she was without strong brothers (to provide for her), spun for a living." Qian, *Lienüzhuan jiaozhu*, 4:8a; O'Hara, *Position of Woman*, 121. For other examples, see O'Hara, 118, 124.

56. Swann, *Food and Money in Ancient China*, 129; Ban, *Hanshu*, 24A:1121. Also see Han, *Hanshi waizhuan*, 2:2a; Hightower, *Han Shih Wai Chuan*, 39.

57. Angelina W.K. Yuen-Tsang, *Towards a Chinese Conception of Social Support: A*

Study on the Social Support Networks of Chinese Working Mothers (London: Ashgate, 1997), 137–48.

58. Qian, *Lienüzhuan jiaozhu*, 6:13a–13b; O'Hara, *Position of Woman*, 182–83.

59. Yokota, *Sengoku saku seikai*, 3A:36–37; Crump, *Chan-Kuo Ts'e*, 83–84.

60. Lau, *Mencius*, 186 (7A.22); Ban, *Hanshu*, 24A:1120; Swann, *Food and Money in Ancient China*, 124–25.

61. Lin Yin, *Zhouli jinzhu jinyi* (Taipei: Taiwan Shangwu, 1972), 1:10, 2:79–83.

62. Fan, *Houhanshu*, 10A:413.

63. Swann, *Food and Money*, 434; Ban, *Hanshu*, 91:3687.

64. For some examples, see Ban, *Hanshu*, 65:2853; Fan, *Houhanshu*, 71:2308. Han, *Hanshi waizhuan*, 2:11b; Hightower, *Han Shih Wai Chuan*, 59; Qian, *Lienüzhuan jiaozhu*, 2:9a; O'Hara, *Position of Woman*, 70. The dealings of Han dynasty Chinese with the nomadic Xiongnu further acquainted them with female merchants. Many of the most successful Xiongnu merchants were women. Yü Ying-shih, *Trade and Expansion in Han China: A Study in the Structure of Sino-Barbarian Economic Relations* (Berkeley: University of California Press, 1967), 99. The importance of women to the world of commerce was reflected in Han thought. Some authorities believed that markets themselves were yin in nature, hence, associated with femininity in general and the ruler's consort in particular. Michael Loewe, "The Cult of the Dragon and the Invocation for Rain," in *Chinese Ideas about Nature and Society: Studies in Honour of Derk Bodde*, ed. Charles LeBlanc and Susan Blader (Hong Kong: Hong Kong University Press, 1987), 211–12; [Xu], "Yuangu de funü gongzuo," 59–60.

65. A. F. Hulsewé, "A Lawsuit of A.D. 28," in *Studia Sino-Mongolica: Festschrift Für Herbert Franke*, ed. Wolfgang Bauer (Wiesbaden: Steiner, 1979), 26–28.

66. Knechtges, *Wen Xuan*, 1:203; Li, *Wenxuan*, 2:8b (*Xijingfu*).

67. Qian, *Lienüzhuan jiaozhu*, 6:5b–6b; O'Hara, *Position of Woman*, 165–67.

68. Cart: Qian, *Lienüzhuan jiaozhu*, 6:4b–5a; O'Hara, *Position of Woman*, 161–62. Head: Qian, *Lienüzhuan jiaozhu*, 2:9b; O'Hara, *Position of Woman*, 72. Arm: Qian, *Lienüzhuan jiaozhu*, 2:9b; O'Hara, 72. For a woman carrying firewood, see Ban, *Hanshu*, 64A:2791.

69. Ban, *Hanshu*, 2:89.

70. Takigawa, *Shiki kaichū kōshō*, 30:10.

71. [Zhou Cecong] Chow Tse-tsung, *Guwuyi yu "liushi" kao: Zhongguo langman wenxue tanyuan* (Taipei: Lianjing, 1986), 141–56, 181–184.

72. Mircea Eliade, *Shamanism: Archaic Techniques of Ecstasy*, trans. Willard R. Trask (New York: Bollingen Foundation/Pantheon, 1964), 215. For a study of early Chinese practitioners of healing and magic, see Kenneth J. DeWoskin, *Doctors, Diviners, and Magicians of Ancient China: Biographies of Fang-shih* (New York: Columbia University Press, 1983).

73. Ban, *Hanshu*, 25A:1220.

74. Donald Harper, "The 'Wu Shih Erh Ping Fang' Translation and Prolegomena" (Ph.D. diss., University of California, 1982), 612.

75. Kang Zhengguo, *Fengsao yu yanqing: Zhongguo gudian shici de nuxing yanjiu* (Zheng-zhou: Henan Renmin, 1988), 62–71.

76. Legend takes the involvement of women in healing back to the time of Shun, whose two wives E Huang and Nü Ying concocted an antidote to poison and saved his life. Qian, *Lienüzhuan jiaozhu*, 1:1b; O'Hara, *Position of Woman*, 15.

77. Qian, *Lienüzhuan jiaozhu*, 8:4a; O'Hara, *Position of Woman*, 224; Shuihudi Qin Mu Zhujian Zhengli Xiaozu, *Shuihudi Qinmu zhujian* (Beijing: Wenwu, 1978), 274; Takigawa, *Shiki kaichū kōshō*, 122:26. The Qin bondwoman may not have been a full-time physician but merely an older woman who had already had several children and therefore was called on to apply her personal experience in examining the victim of a miscarriage.

78. Lin, *Zhouli*, 2:45, 48.

79. Ban, *Hanshu*, 40:2057, 92:3701.

80. Wei, *Hanjiuyi*, B:2b; Ch'ü, *Han Social Structure*, 143; Wang Tingqia, "Runiang, baomu ji qita," *Lishi yuekan* 26, no. 3 (1990): 25–26.

81. Remains of terra-cotta figures depicting female servants are numerous. For example see Shen, *Sichuan Handai taoyong*, pls. 30–32, 34, 35, 38, 39.

82. For ancient female entertainers, see Bodde, *Festivals in Classical China*, 152–53; [He Zhihao] Ho Chih-hao, *Zhongguo wudaoshi* (Taipei: Zhonghua Dadian, 1970), 90–95, 100; Ma Daying, *Handai caizhengshi* (Beijing: Caizheng Jingji, 1983), 305–6; Li, *Wenxuan*, 2:15b–16a, 2:17a, 8:8a–8b; Knechteges, *Wen Xuan*, 1:229–31, 1:237, 2:107. For female slave entertainers, see Ban, *Hanshu*, 97A:3962; C. Martin Wilbur, *Slavery in China during the Former Han Dynasty, 206 B.C.–A.D. 25* (Chicago: Field Museum, 1943), 180.

83. For discussion of several early precedents to full-fledged prostitution, see [Guo Licheng] Kuo Li-ch'eng, *Zhongguo funü shenghuo shihua* (Taipei: Hanguang Wenhua, 1983), 179–85; [Gao Mai] Kao Mai, "Zhongguo changji zhidu zhi lishi de soujiu," in *Zhongguo funüshi lunji*, ed. [Bao Jialin] Pao Chia-lin (Taipei: Daoxiang, 1978), 119; Wang Shunu, *Zhongguo changjishi* (Shanghai: Shenghuo, 1934), 30–31; R. H. Van Gulik, *Sexual Life in Ancient China: A Preliminary Survey of Chinese Sex and Society from ca. 1500 B.C. till 1644 A.D.* (Leiden: Brill, 1961), 65 n. 2. [Song Dexi] Sung Te-hsi, "Tangdai de jinü," in *Zhongguo funüshi lunji xuji*, ed. [Bao Jialin] Pao Chia-lin (Taipei: Daoxiang, 1991), 67–68, discusses the origins of Chinese prostitution.

CHAPTER 4

1. Zhao, *Funü zai falü*, 9; Legge, *Ch'un Ts'ew, with the Tso Chuen*, 789 (*Ding* 14).

2. Du You, *Tongdian* (Shanghai: Tushu Jicheng, 1902), 166:2b. However, *budao* remained a category for other types of crimes during the Han. [Wang Jianwen] Wang Chien-wen, "Xi Han luling yu guojia zhengdangxing: Yi lulingzhong de 'budao' wei zhongxin," *Xinshixue* 3, no. 3 (1992): 1–36.

3. Hulsewé, *Remnants of Han Law*, 73.

4. Ban, *Hanshu*, 76:3205.

5. Jing, *Guanzi*, 1:11b; Rickett, *Guanzi*, 1:101 (*Lizheng*).

6. Ban Gu et al., *Dongguan Hanji* (Fujian: Buzheng, 1895), 20:4a.

7. Bielenstein, "Lo-yang in Later Han Times," 50.

8. Fan, *Houhanshu*, 10A:417.

9. Ban, *Hanshu*, 12:356; Fan, *Houhanshu*, 1A:35; Hulsewé, *Remnants of Han Law*, 78.

10. Ban, *Hanshu*, 4:122.

11. Qian, *Lienüzhuan jiaozhu*, 5:7b–8a; O'Hara, *Position of Woman*, 143–44.

12. Shuihudi Qinmu Zhujian Zhengli Xiaozu, *Shuihudi Qinmu zhujian*, 185; Li, *Qinlü*, 505.

13. Yunmeng Qinmu Zhujian Zhengli Xiaozu, "Yunmeng Qinjian shiwen (3)," 29; Hulsewé, *Remnants of Qin Law*, 141 (D 64).

14. Yamazaki, *Chūgoku joseigaku*, 3:90–91 (*Nüjie*); Swann, *Pan Chao*, 86.

15. Cheng, *Jiuchao lükao*, 114.

16. For example, see Ban, *Hanshu*, 77:3268; Fan, *Houhanshu*, 23:819, 34:1182.

17. Yunmeng Qinmu Zhujian Zhengli Xiaozu, "Yunmeng Qinjian shiwen (3)," 30; Hulsewé, *Remnants of Ch'in Law*, 148–49 (D 87).

18. Yunmeng Qinmu Zhujian Zhengli Xiaozu, "Yunmeng Qinjian shiwen (3)," 29; Hulsewé, *Remnants of Ch'in Law*, 137 (D 49, D 50).

19. Lau, *Analects*, 121 (13.18).

20. Han, *Hanshi waizhuan*, 4:9b; Hightower, *Han Shih Wai Chuan*, 143–44.

21. Ban, *Hanshu*, 8:251.

22. Ban, *Hanshu*, 47:2215.

23. Karlgren, *Book of Odes* 10 (no. 17); Qian, *Lienüzhuan jiaozhu*, 4:1a; O'Hara, *Position of Woman*, 102–3.

24. Dull, "Marriage and Divorce," 24.

25. For a fragment of *Jueyu* regarding marriage, see Li Fang, *Taiping yulan* (Beijing: Zhonghua, 1960), 640:8a. Also see Dull, "Marriage and Divorce," 68; Wong, "Confucian Ideal and Reality," 67.

26. Hulsewé, *Records of Han Law*, 55.

27. Dong Yue, *Qiguokao* (Beijing: Zhonghua, 1956), 12:367; Timoteus Pokora, *Hsin-Lun (New Treatise) and Other Writings by Huan T'an (43 b.c.–28 a.d.)* (Ann Arbor: University of Michigan Press, 1975), 207.

28. Cheng, *Jiuchao lükao*, 115; Wong, "Confucian Ideal and Reality," 81.

29. Yunmeng Qinmu Zhujian Zhengli Xiaozu, "Yunmeng Qinjian shiwen (3)," 29; Hulsewé, *Remnants of Ch'in Law*, 140 (D 61).

30. Asaf Ali Asghar Fyzee, *Outlines of Muhammadan Law* (Oxford: Oxford University Press, 1955), 126–28.

31. Yunmeng Qinmu Zhujian Zhengli Xiaozu, "Yunmeng Qinjian shiwen (3)," 33; Hulsewé, *Remnants of Ch'in Law*, 168 (D 148).

32. Development of this legal concept is described in Li, *Qinlü*, 506; Hulsewé, *Remnants of Ch'in Law*, 168.

33. Hulsewé, *Remnants of Ch'in Law*, 167–68.

34. Li, *Qinlü*, 505.

35. Han divorce receives detailed treatment in Dull, "Marriage and Divorce," 54 passim.

36. Dull, "Marriage and Divorce," 71.

37. Dull, "Marriage and Divorce," 67–68.

38. Wang Fu, *Qianfulun* (n.p.: Congshu Jiqing, 1937), 5:136–38. Wang states that officials investigating a case of a woman leaving her first husband to marry another allowed her to stay with her second husband.

39. Jing, *Guanzi*, 8:9a; Rickett, *Guanzi*, 1:332 *(Xiao Kuang)*.

40. Hulsewé, *Remnants of Han Law*, 74, 298–99; Cheng, *Jiuchao lükao*, 68–69.

41. Yunmeng Qinmu Zhujian Zhengli Xiaozu, "Yunmeng Qinjian shiwen (3)," 36–37; McLeod and Yates, "Forms of Ch'in Law," 159–60 (5.22); Hulsewé, *Remnants of Ch'in Law*, 205 (E 23).

42. Cheng, *Jiuchao lükao*, 1:116.

43. Cheng, *Jiuchao lükao*, 1:110.

44. Yunmeng Qinmu Zhujian Zhengli Xiaozu, "Yunmeng Qinjian shiwen (3)," 29; Hulsewé, *Remnants of Ch'in Law*, 8, 139 (D 56).

45. Fan, *Houhanshu*, 67:2216; Cheng, *Jiuchao lükao*, 1:109.

46. Ch'ü, *Han Social Structure*, 23; Hulsewé, *Remnants of Han Law*, 89; Cheng, *Jiuchao lükao*, 1:109.

47. Hulsewé, *Remnants of Han Law*, 89.

48. H. Y. Feng and J. K. Shryock, "The Black Magic in China Known as *Ku*," *Journal of the American Oriental Society* 55 (1935): 1–30.

49. Yunmeng Qinmu Zhujian Zhengli Xiaozu, "Yunmeng Qinjian shiwen (3)," 37; McLeod and Yates, "Forms of Ch'in Law," 161 (5.23); Hulsewé, *Remnants of Ch'in Law*, 206 (E 24).

50. Hulsewé, *Remnants of Han Law*, 167; Michael Loewe, "The Case of Witchcraft in 91 B.C.: Its Historical Setting and Effect on Han Dynasty History," *Asia Major*, n.s. 15 (1970): 159–96.

51. Du Guichi, *Hanlü jizheng* (n.p.: Falüguan, n.d.), 1:6a; Cheng, *Jiuchao lükao*, 61–62.

52. Hulsewé, *Remnants of Han Law*, 120.

53. Loewe, "The Case of Witchcraft."

54. Hulsewé, *Remnants of Han Law*, 121.

55. Hulsewé, *Remnants of Han Law*, 123.

56. Fujikawa, *Kandai ni okeru reigaku*, 471–72.

CHAPTER 5

1. For the relation between kinship and female power in government, see [Xing Yitian] Hsing I-t'ien, "Muquan waiqi, rusheng: Wang Mang xian Han de jidian jieshi," *Lishi yuekan* 14, no. 3 (1989): 38.

2. Qian, *Lienüzhuan jiaozhu*, 8:2b–3a; O'Hara, *Position of Woman*, 220.

3. For example, see Fan, *Houhanshu*, 28A:955–56; Pokora, *Hsin-Lun*, 233.

4. Like their male counterparts, women would regularly usurp ritual prerogatives of higher ranks; for example, see Gushihou Gudai Yihao Mu Fajue Zu, "Henan Gushihou Gudui yihao mu fajue jianbao," *Wenwu* 296, no. 1 (1981): 7; Ma Yong, "Lun Changsha Mawangdui yihao Hanmu chutu bohua de mingcheng he zuoyong," *Kaogu* 125, no. 2 (1973): 118–25.

5. Hung-hsiang Chou, "Fu-X Ladies of the Shang Dynasty," *Monumenta Serica* 29 (1970–1971): 346–47, 355–57. For some Zhou examples, see Ouyang, *Yiwen leiju*, 51:930.

6. Wei, *Hanjiuyi*, B:4b; Ch'ü, *Han Social Structure*, 269 n. 89.

7. Cheng, *Jiuchao lükao*, 47.

8. Yokota, *Sengoku saku seikai*, 1:16, 3B:56–57, 7B:15; Crump, *Chan-Kuo Ts'e*, 35, 142, 426.

9. Ouyang, *Yiwen leiju*, 15:277. For the rank and prerogatives of Han princesses, see Fujikawa, *Kandai ni okeru reigaku*, 315–23, 325–26, 333. For an overview of Han female aristocratic titles, see Li, "Handai funü de diwei," 166–68.

10. Sometimes Han dynasty women held marquisates outright. Yu Shinan, *Beitang shuchao* (Taipei: Hongye, 1974), 48:7B; Michael Loewe, "The Orders of Aristocratic Rank of Han China," *T'oung Pao* 48, no. 1–3 (1960): 125 n. 2. These cases were clearly exceptional. For the usual system see Liu, *Handai hunyin zhidu*, 22. This Han practice may have had its roots in the Zhou. Han texts claim that the ranks of Zhou royal consorts corresponded exactly to equivalent male aristocratic grades. Kamata Shigeo, *Shin Kan seiji seido no kenkyu* (Tokyo: Nihon Gakujutsu, 1962), 551–52. But this supposed Zhou system may have been just another fabrication of Han authors who manufactured useful precedents and attributed them to the Zhou. Regardless of the actual origins of this practice, the ranks of consorts during the Han became explicitly equated with male aristocratic titles. Fujikawa, *Kandai ni okeru reigaku*, 405–6; Loewe, "Orders of Aristocratic Rank," 162. During the Eastern Han, Emperor Guangwu pared the number of ranks for imperial consorts back to five. Kamata, *Shin Kan seiji seido*, 552.

11. Yu, *Beitang shuchao*, 48:8a; Du, *Tongdian*, 34:6a; Ch'ü, *Han Social Structure*, 269 n. 89; 475 n. 351.

12. Yu, *Beitang shuchao*, 48:7b; Zhao, *Funü zai falü*, 114; Loewe, "Orders of Aristocratic Rank," 114.

13. Ban, *Baihutong*, 2A:12b; Tjan, *Po Hu T'ung*, 2:453.

14. A. Soper, "King Wu Ting's Victory over the 'Realm of Demons,'" *Artibus Asiae* 17, no. 1 (1954): 55–60.

15. Qian, *Lienüzhuan jiaozhu*, 3:8b–9a; O'Hara, *Position of Woman*, 96–97.

16. Yan Wanli, *Shangjunshu xin jiaozheng* (Shanghai: Sibu Beiyao, n.d.), 3:8a–8b; J. J. L. Duyvendak, *The Book of Lord Shang: A Classic of the Chinese School of Law* (London: Arthur Probsthain, 1928), 250–51.

17. This phenomenon was not unique to the early imperial period. Female-led rebellions continued long after the Han. For some Ming and Qing examples of loyalist move-

ments and rebellions led by women, see Mary Backus Rankin, "The Emergence of Women at the End of the Ch'ing," in *Women in Chinese Society*, ed. Margery Wolf and Roxane Witke (Stanford: Stanford University Press, 1979), 40–41 n. 4.

18. Okusaki Yūji, "Aka mayu no seikai," in *Chūgoku kodai shi kenkyū* 5 (1982): 142–43, 155–56; A. Soper, "The Purpose and Date of the Hsiao-t'ang-shan Offering Shrine: A Modest Proposal," *Artibus Asiae* 36, no. 4 (1974): 250, 262.

19. An excellent treatment of Chinese and Vietnamese textual and oral sources relating to the Tru'ng rebellion is Bui Quang Tung, *Le soulèvement des soeurs Tru'ng à travers les textes et le folklore viêtnamien* (Saigon: Imprimerie Nouvelle d'Extrême-Orient, 1961). Gotō Kinpei, "Chō shimai no hanran," *Chūgoku kodai shi kenkyū* 3 (1969): 211–48, adds detailed archeological evidence to the textual sources.

20. This system can be most clearly appreciated in its mature manifestation under the Northern Song dynasty. Priscilla Ching-Chung, "Palace Women in the Northern Sung: Their Social Organization," *Bulletin of Sung-Yuan Studies* 15 (1979): 79–97.

21. A statement attributed to Duke Huan of Qi sums up the basic trend: "Let the wife rule the inner apartments and [the official] Guan Zhong manage outer affairs." Qian, *Lienüzhuan jiaozhu*, 2:2a; O'Hara, *Position of Woman*, 52.

22. Lin, *Zhouli*, 2:76–77.

23. Kamata, *Shin Kan seiji seido no kenkyū*, 544–45. Kamata also discusses the origins of the terms *huanghou* and *huangtaihou* during the Qin, 553.

24. Kamata, *Shin Kan seiji seido no kenkyū*, 548–50.

25. Kamata, *Shin Kan seiji seido no kenkyū*; Loewe, "Orders of Aristocratic Rank," 162; Hulsewé, *Remnants of Han Law*, 43.

26. *Hanshu* 19 and *Houhanshu* 36.

27. Ban, *Hanshu*, 19A:730–34.

28. Ma, *Handai caizhengshi* 310, 312. This bureaucratization appears to have been repeated during the Han in the households of powerful kings and marquises. For example, the funerary banner from Mawangdui depicts a lady next to two subservient minor officials.

29. The power of imperial consorts and their kin under the Han broke with precedent. Palace ladies rarely gained political prominence under the Zhou. Some scholars have argued that because the ruling Liu family suddenly arose from lowly status, Han imperial kinship practices were from a different social stratum than those of China's traditional ruling class. Liu, *Handai hunyin zhidu*, 79. Whether or not there was a new kinship system, the break with Zhou aristocratic customs allowed palace ladies new and powerful political roles.

30. Ban, *Hanshu*, 68:2937–40.

31. Yang Lien-sheng, "Female Rulers in Imperial China," *Harvard Journal of Asiatic Studies* 23 (1960–1961): 51.

32. Takigawa, *Shiki kaichū kōshō*, 85:12.

33. Homer H. Dubs et al., *The History of the Former Han Dynasty: By Pan Ku* (Baltimore: Waverly, 1938–1955), 1:192; Yang, "Female Rulers in Imperial China," 53.

34. Ch'ü (*Han Social Structure*, 73) discusses the positions of Sima Qian and Ban Gu toward the "reign" of Emperor Hui.

35. Qin Bo, "Xi Han huanghou yuxi he ganlu ernian tongfanglu de faxian," *Wenwu* 204, no. 5 (1973): 26–29.

36. Gan Shu, "Lingnan Handai wenhua baoku—Guangzhou Xianggang Nan Yue wangmu," *Lingnan wenshi* 10 (n.d.): 15–17.

37. Yang, "Female Rulers in Imperial China," 54.

38. Ch'ü, *Han Social Structure*, 61. Du, *Tongdian*, 34:5b–6b, traces the history of the palace women's institutions. Olga Lang, *Chinese Family and Society* (New Haven: Yale University Press, 1946), 52, argues ahistorically that the powers of empresses dowager were essentially anomalous and did not represent the true traditional position of women in China.

39. Ban, *Baihutong*, 3A:13b; Tjan, *Po Hu T'ung*, 2:515.

40. Zhao Yi, *Ershier shi zhaji* (Shanghai: Shangwu, 1957), 3:5b–6a; Kamata, *Shin Kan seiji seido*, 556–57.

41. Ban, *Hanshu*, 77:3251–52. For the process used to select imperial women, see Fujikawa, *Kandai ni okeru reigaku*, 406–11.

42. Ch'ü, *Han Social Structure*, 78.

43. Liu, *Handai hunyin zhidu*, 85–88.

44. Ban, *Hanshu*, 97B:3998–99.

45. Ban, *Hanshu*, 7:217. For a study of some of the struggles between rival empresses dowager, see Rafe de Crespigny, "The Harem of Emperor Huan: A Study of Court Politics in Later Han," *Papers on Far Eastern History* 12 (1975): 1–42.

46. Liu, *Handai hunyin zhidu*, 180–81; [Jin Fagen] Chin Fa-ken, "Dong Han danggu renwu de fenxi," in *Gu yuanzhang Hu Shi xiansheng jinian lunwenji* (Taipei: Zhongyang Yanjiuyuan, Lishi Yuyan Yanjiusuo, 1962): 505–58.

47. Knechtges, *Wen Xuan*, 1:239; Li, *Wenxuan*, 2:17b (*Xijingfu*).

48. Liu, *Handai hunyin zhidu*, 135.

49. Zhao, *Ershier shi zhaji*, 3:12a–13b.

50. Takigawa, *Shiki kaichū kōshō*, 9:13–16.

51. Michael Loewe, *Crisis and Conflict in Han China, 104 b.c. to a.d. 9* (London: George Allen & Unwin, 1974), chap. 2, provides a lucid summary of these events.

52. Loewe (*Crisis and Conflict*, chap. 4) details the fall of the Huos.

53. Fan, *Houhanshu*, 78:2523.

54. De Crespigny, "The Harem of Emperor Huan," 3.

55. Ōzora Fujino, *Chūgoku no kokyu* (Tokyo: Tatsukei, 1977), 42; Jack L. Dull, "A Historical Introduction to the Apocryphal (Ch'an-wei) Texts of the Han Dynasty" (Ph.D. diss., University of Washington, 1966), 286.

56. Hightower, *Han Shih Wai Chuan*, 242 n. 1; Kamata, *Kandai seiji seido*, 564–65. Tactics varied. Some officials even drew on Taoism and (late in the Eastern Han) Buddhism for their moralistic attacks. See Kenneth Chen, *Buddhism in China: A Historical Survey* (Princeton: Princeton University Press, 1964), 35.

57. Legge, *Tso Chuen*, 727 (*Zhao* 28); Jing, *Guanzi*, 21:5a, 5:10a, 8:4b, 11:11a; Rickett, *Guanzi*, 1:143 (*Banfa*), 247 (*Zhongling*), 322–23 (*Xiao Kuang*), 433 (*Sicheng*).

58. Qian, *Lienüzhuan jiaozhu*, 7:1b–2a; O'Hara, *Position of Woman*, 187–89. For precedents of this view in Eastern Zhou works, see Raphals, *Sharing the Light*, 15–18. For a discussion of its expression in Han rhetoric, see Raphals, *Sharing the Light*, 61–70.

59. Raphals, *Sharing the Light*, 12–14.

60. O'Hara, *Position of Woman*, 98; Qian, *Lienüzhuan jiaozhu*, 3:9b–10a.

61. Qian, *Lienüzhuan jiaozhu*, 7:1a–2a; O'Hara, *Position of Woman*, 186, 188; Bernhard Karlgren, "Legends and Cults in Ancient China," *Bulletin of the Museum of Far Eastern Antiquities* 18 (1946): 327, 340.

62. Qian, *Lienüzhuan jiaozhu*, 7:1b–2a; O'Hara, *Position of Woman*, 187–89.

63. Takigawa, *Shiki kaichū kōshō*, 4:62–65; Qian, *Lienüzhuan jiaozhu*, 7:2b–3a; O'Hara, *Position of Woman*, 190; Huang Hui, *Lunheng jiaoshi* (Taipei: Taiwan Shangwu, 1983), 5:206; Alfred Forke, *Lun-Heng*, pt. 1, *Philosophical Essays of Wang Ch'ung* (1911; reprint, New York: Paragon, 1962), 2:163.

64. Ōzora (*Chūgoku no kokyu*, 42) discusses the importance of cosmological interpretations by Han officials in criticizing palace ladies. He theorizes that the development of this critical attitude led to a decline in the importance of consorts and their families after the Han. For examples of the detailed, eloquent, stridently antifemale rhetoric of Han officials, see Ban, *Hanshu*, 85:3456–65, 85:3473–74, 97B:3977–81; Fan, *Houhanshu*, 28A:956, 62:2051–57. These diatribes include multiple cosmological, philosophical, moral, and historical rationales.

CHAPTER 6

1. Yokota, *Sengoku saku seikai*, A:1–2; Crump, *Ch'an-Kuo Ts'e*, 54; Huang, *Lunheng jiaoshi*, 26:1067; Forke, *Lun-Heng*, 2:118.

2. Jia, *Yili zhushu ji buzheng*, 6:20b; Steele, *I-Li*, 1:36.

3. For example, *Zuozhuan* faults two men for believing what their women say. Legge, *Tso Chuen*, 629 (*Zhao* 10).

4. Guisso, "Thunder over the Lake," 59–60.

5. Lau, *Mencius*, 195 (7B.9).

6. Wing-tsit Chan, *A Source Book in Chinese Philosophy* (Princeton: Princeton University Press, 1963), 100 (*Zhongyong* 12).

7. Han, *Hanshi waizhuan*, 2:2b–3a; Hightower, *Han Shih Wai Chuan*, 40–41; Ouyang, *Yiwen leiju*, 15:282. Ban Zhao mentions *xiannü* (sagacious women). Yamazaki, *Chūgoku joseigaku*, 7:102 (*Nüjie*); Swann, *Pan Chao*, 89.

8. Qian, *Lienüzhuan jiaozhu*, 1:4a–4b; O'Hara, *Position of Woman*, 23–24; Li, *Taiping yulan*, 360:5b–6a.

9. Qian, *Lienüzhuan jiaozhu*, 1:9b–10a, 1:13a–13b, 8:3b, 8:5a–5b; O'Hara, *Position of Woman*, 37–38, 46–48, 221–22, 226–27.

10. Qian, *Lienüzhuan jiaozhu*, 1:10a–11b; O'Hara, *Position of Woman*, 39–42; Fan, *Houhanshu*, 84:792–93; Zheng, *Liji*, 6:6a–6b; Legge, *Li Ki*, 27:327 (*Zengziwen* 1.26) states that a ruler's son was taught by a male teacher outside the palace and by a governess within it, showing a place for education of men by women under this idealized vision of the Zhou.

11. Raphals, *Sharing the Light*, 34–35.

12. For the development of the theme of women as counselors to men, see Raphals, *Sharing the Light*, 27–59.

13. Hightower, *Han Shih Wai Chuan*, 135; Han, *Hanshi waizhuan*, 4:5b.

14. Fan, *Houhanshu*, 10B:438. For a detailed explanation of the context of Liang's patronage, see Dull, "Apocryphal (Ch'an-wei) Texts of the Han Dynasty," 342.

15. Fan, *Houhanshu*, 30A:1048–50.

16. Takigawa, *Shiki kaichū kōshō*, 49:14; 121:7, 15, 17–18. Ōzora (*Chūgoku no kokyu*, 40) discusses Lady Feiyan (consort of Emperor Cheng) and her attraction to the arts of immortality attributed to the mythical figure Pengzu.

17. Michael Loewe, *Chinese Ideas of Life and Death: Faith, Myth, and Reason in the Han Period (202 B.C.–A.D. 220)* (London: George Allen & Unwin, 1982), 144–58.

18. Takigawa, *Shiki kaichū kōshō*, 107:9.

19. Roger T. Ames, "Taoism and the Androgynous Ideal," in *Women in China: Current Directions in Historical Scholarship*, ed. Richard W. Guisso and Stanley Johnannesen (Youngstown, N.Y.: Philo, 1981), 21 n. 1, 23; Max Kaltenmark, *Lao Tzu and Taoism*, trans. Roger Greaves (Stanford: Stanford University Press, 1969), 59; Van Gulik, *Sexual Life in Ancient China*, 44.

20. Kaltenmark (*Lao Tzu and Taoism*, 60) attributes the feminine orientation of Taoism to the influence of shamanism. Edward Schafer, *The Divine Woman: Dragon Ladies and Rain Maidens in T'ang Literature* (San Francisco: North Point Press, 1980), 42, emphasizes the tradition of ancient female water deities.

21. For example, Ban Zhao credits her father and particularly her mother with giving her a literary education. Yamazaki, *Chūgoku joseigaku*, 81 (*Nüjie*, introduction); Swann, *Pan Chao*, 82. Furthermore, Ban Zhao takes credit for educating her own daughters, showing continuity in a mother-to-daughter tradition of education. Yamazaki, *Chūgoku joseigaku*, 81; Swann, *Pan Chao*, 82. Elite female literary education did not begin during the Eastern Han. At the end of the second century B.C. a sister of Emperor Wu, Princess Yian, had a personal tutor even after reaching adulthood. Ban, *Hanshu*, 65:2851.

22. Yamazaki, *Chūgoku joseigaku shi*, 2:87–88 (*Nüjie*); Swann, *Pan Chao*, 84–85.

23. Such was the view of late imperial readers. See Susan Mann, "Learned Women in the Eighteenth Century," in *Engendering China: Women, Culture, and the State*, ed. Christina K. Gilmartin et al. (Cambridge, Mass.: Harvard University Press, 1994), 30.

24. Ko, *Teachers of the Inner Chambers*, 53–54.

25. Katherine Carlitz, "Desire, Danger, and the Body: Stories of Women's Virtue in Late Ming China," in *Engendering China*, 124.

26. Mann, "Learned Women," 30.

27. Ko, *Teachers of the Inner Quarters*, 18–19, 54–55, 124–25.

28. O'Hara, *Position of Woman*, 66, 87; Qian, *Lienüzhuan jiaozhu*, 2:7a, 3:5b.

29. Fan, *Houhanshu*, 84:2796.

30. Takigawa, *Shiki kaichū kōshō*, 10:28.

31. Huang, *Lunheng jiaoshi*, 28:1120; Forke, *Lun-Heng*, 1:448. Gu Jiegang, "Wude zhongshi shuoxia de zhengzhi he lishi," *Qinghua xuebao* 6 (1930): 74.

32. Ban, *Hanshu*, 75:3155.

33. Ma Zong, *Yilin* (Shanghai: Sibu Beiyao, n.d.), 3:9b; Yu, *Beitang shuchao*, 98:7b; Pokora, *Hsin-Lun*, 103.

34. Huang, *Lunheng jiaoshi*, 29:1158; Forke, *Lun-Heng*, 1:462.

35. [Zhu], *Ban Zhao*, 23–24; Swann, *Pan Chao*, 61–73 assess Ban Zhao's precise contributions to *Hanshu*.

36. O'Hara, *Position of Woman*, 245. Changing "Book" to "Classic" and "Spring-Autumn" to "Spring and Autumn." Qian, *Lienüzhuan jiaozhu*, 8:11a.

37. O'Hara, *Position of Woman*; Qian, *Lienüzhuan jiaozhu*; Hu Wenkai, *Lidai funü zhuzuo kao* (Shanghai: Shangwu, 1957), 5.

38. Hu, *Lidai funü zhuzuo kao*, 1.

39. For a useful survey of Han dynasty women's literature, see Huang Yanli, *Handai funü wenxue wujia yanjiu* (Kaifeng: Henan Daxue, 1993).

40. For Xu Shu, see Hu, *Lidai Funü zhuzuo kao*, 2. For Cai Yan, see Hu, *Lidai Funü zhuzuo kao*, 5–6. Another collection, seemingly of poetry, was entitled *Collected Works of Miss Kong (Kongshiji)*. The only facts now known about her are her name, the name of her husband, and that she lived during the Eastern Han. No clues to the contents of this work survive. Hu, *Lidai Funü zhuzuo kao*, 2.

41. [Zhang Xiurong] Chang Hsiu-jung, *Han Tang guizu yu cainü shige yanjiu* (Taipei: Wenshizhe, 1985), 20.

42. O'Hara, *Position of Woman*, 233; Qian, *Lienüzhuan jiaozhu*, 8:7a. For her life and works see O'Hara, *Position of Woman*, 231–35; Qian, 8:6b–7b; Hu, *Lidai Funü zhuzuo kao*, 1–2.

43. Ban, *Hanshu*, 96B:3903; Zhang, *Cainü shige*, 15.

44. Yamazaki, *Chūgoku joseigaku*, 81 (*Nüjie*, introduction); Swann, *Pan Chao*, 82–83.

45. [Zhu], *Ban Zhao*, 32–33 discusses the influence of this text. Fan, *Houhanshu*, 84:2792 notes that Ma Rong ordered his wife and daughters to study this work, showing that it had already acquired an enthusiastic readership before the end of the Eastern Han.

46. [Zhu], *Ban Zhao*, 37.

47. Lily Xiao Hong Lee, "Ban Zhao (c. 48–c. 120): Her Role in the Formulation of Controls Imposed upon Women in Traditional China," in *The Virtue of Yin: Studies on Chinese Women* (Broadway, N.S.W.: Wild Peony/Honolulu: University of Hawaii Press, 1994), 21–22.

48. Chinese education was not unique in this regard. Other systems of female educa-

tion have had similar intent. Anna Davin, " 'Mind That You Do as You Are Told': Reading Books for Board School Girls, 1870–1902," *Feminist Review* 3 (1979): 89–92.

49. Yu-shih Chen, "The Historical Template of Pan Chao's *Nu Chieh*," *T'oung Pao* 82 (1996): 229–57.

50. [Zhu] (*Ban Zhao*, 39–52) assesses the influence of Ban Zhao on subsequent authors.

51. Yamazaki, *Chūgoku joseigaku*, 5:96, 6:99 (*Nüjie*); Swann, *Pan Chao*, 87–88; 97 n. 51.

52. Other Eastern Han and Wei works, either lost or surviving only as fragments, include three books similarly titled *Admonitions for Women (Nüjie)* by Du Du, Xun Shuang, and Zhuge Liang, as well as Cheng Xiao's *Collection of Female Models (Nüdianpian)* and Cai Yong's *Instructions for Women (Nüxun)*. Yamazaki, *Chūgoku joseigaku*, 24–25. For Xun Shuang and Cheng Xiao's works, see Ouyang, *Yiwen leiju*, 23:419. For Cai Yong's book, see Yu, *Beitang shuchao*, 109:8b. Zhuge Liang's book has been referred to by several alternate titles: *Collection of Female Masters (Nüshipian)*, *Admonitions for Women (Nüjie)*, and *Collection of Women's History (Nüshipian)*.

53. [Zhu], *Ban Zhao*, 30–32; Hu, *Lidai Funü zhuzuo kao*, 2–5.

54. Marina H. Sung, "The Chinese Lieh-nü Tradition," in *Women in China: Current Directions in Historical Scholarship*, ed. Richard W. Guisso and Stanley Johannesen (Youngstown, N.Y.: Philo, 1981), 64. An excellent guide to the origins and development of the women's biographical tradition in China from its beginnings to late imperial times is Muramatsu Ei, *Chūgoku Retsujoden: Senzennen no rekishi no naka de* (Tokyo: Chūō, 1968).

55. Yamazaki (*Chūgoku joseigaku*, 24) discusses the form and transmission of the text. Raphals (*Sharing the Light*, 299–304) summarizes each woman's occupations and expertise.

56. Raphals, *Sharing the Light*, 82–86; Lee, "Ban Zhao," 22.

57. Lee, "Ban Zhao," 25.

58. Liu ("Shilun Handai de hunyin," 16–19) discusses the interplay of concepts of widow chastity versus widow remarriage during the Han.

59. Fan, *Houhanshu*, 28A:956. Elvin ("Female Virtue," 116, 135) cites this as the beginning of the custom of rewarding virtuous women with state-sponsored symbols.

60. Fan, *Houhanshu*, 84:2797.

61. Chang Qu, *Huayang guozhi* (Taipei: Hongye, 1972), 10A:16a–16b.

62. Wu Hong [Wu Hung], *The Wu Liang Shrine: The Ideology of Early Chinese Pictorial Art* (Stanford: Stanford University Press, 1989), 171–73. For other early examples of this visual tradition, see F. S. Drake, "Sculptured Stones of the Han Dynasty," *Monumenta Serica* 8 (1943): 289, 293.

63. Yamazaki, *Chūgoku joseigaku*, 24.

64. Jan Fontein and Tung Wu, *Unearthing China's Past* (Boston: Museum of Fine Arts, Boston, 1973), 96–100; Museum of Fine Arts, Boston, *Asiatic Art in the Museum of Fine Arts, Boston* (Boston: Museum of Fine Arts, Boston, 1982), 98–99.

65. Wu, *Wu Liang Shrine*, 149–50.

CHAPTER 7

1. A concise and useful summary of ritual theory in the West appears in Howard J. Wechsler, *Offerings of Jade and Silk: Ritual and Symbol in the Legitimation of the T'ang Dynasty* (New Haven: Yale University Press, 1985), 20–21.

2. Jack Goody, "Religion and Ritual: The Definitional Problem," *British Journal of Sociology* 12 (1961): 159. Various anthropologists have attributed numerous other traits to ritual, including regularity, repetition, dramatic performance, collectivity, and the use of symbols (Wechsler, *Offerings of Jade and Silk*, 22–23). The English terms "ritual", "rite", "ceremony", and "etiquette" are all similar but express subtle differences. For a clear explanation of these distinctions, see John J. Honigmann, "Ceremony," in *A Dictionary of the Social Sciences*, ed. Julius Gould and William L. Kolb (New York: Free Press, 1964); and E. R. Leach, "Ritual," in *Dictionary of the Social Sciences*, 607–8. This English terminology differs somewhat from the terms used by early Chinese to discuss similar matters. So the fit between contemporary English and early Chinese concepts is imperfect.

3. Victor Turner, *The Forest of Symbols* (Cornell: Cornell University Press, 1967).

4. Hall and Ames, *Thinking from the Han*, 95, 98.

5. Yang ("Chunqiu shidai zhi nannü fengji," 36) sees *li* as a product of the post-Spring and Autumn period.

6. Yang ("Chunqiu shidai zhi nannü fengji," 47; Nishima Sadao, *Chūgoku keizaishi kenkyū* (Tokyo: Tōkyō Daigaku Bungakubu, 1966), 51. For example, a Western Han prefect ordered those under his jurisdiction to follow ritual in performing weddings and funerals (Ban, *Hanshu*, 76:3210).

7. Beijing Daxue Xunzi Zhushi Zu, *Xunzi xinzhu* (1979; reprint, Taipei: Liren, 1983), 19:369–70.

8. *Zhouli* (*Rites of Zhou*) purports to outline Western Zhou government. The imperial librarian Liu Xin edited the book in the early Eastern Han, and it received wide circulation. It was probably written during the Warring States period. The author romanticizes the Western Zhou as a time of stability and harmony. *Zhou li* is useful in reconstructing some of the ritual ideals of late Eastern Zhou and Han thinkers. Herrlee Glessner Creel, *The Origins of Statecraft in China* (Chicago: University of Chicago Press, 1970), 478–80. Zhang Xincheng, *Weishu tongkao* (Shanghai: Shangwu, 1954), 1:282–327, includes various opinions on the dating and authenticity of the text. [Zhang], 1:282 notes that Sima Qian mentions the *Offices of Zhou* (*Zhouguan*), a text that the Tang scholar Yan Shigu identified with the *Zhouli*. Liang Qichao believed that *Zhouli* was written by an idealistic individual in the period from the late Warring States to early Western Han, reacting to late Zhou political chaos and hence idealizing the Western Zhou. [Zhang], 1:313.

Yili (*Etiquette and Ritual*) is a practical guide that minutely describes how to perform various rituals. It probably derives from aristocratic rites of the Chunqiu period and later. The precise regularity of these rites betrays wishful idealization. This text probably came together after the disappearance of at least some of the rituals described. Liang Qichao points out the similarities between rituals described in *Yili* and *Zuozhuan*. [Zhang], 1:279. *Yili* was probably compiled during Zhanguo period. Creel, *Origins of Statecraft in China*, 45–486; Zhang, *Weishu tongkao*, 1:269–80. Sima Qian refers to the *Yili* as *Shili (Rituals of Gentlemen)*. These seem to be alternate names for the same text, so it existed in the reign of Emperor Wu.

    Liji (Records of Ritual) seems to have been redacted into its final form sometime in the first century B.C. Its many short texts were written at various times for different purposes. This eclectic anthology consists of miscellaneous ritual texts deemed significant by the anonymous Han compiler. Tradition may be correct in attributing some of the main currents of thought in *Liji* to a "school of Confucius." The book exhibits many Confucian-inspired values. It seems to be the written reflection of a long tradition of oral ritual learning passed down through generations of ritual specialists who included Confucius and his disciples. As a Han work of editing, *Liji* is a valuable compilation of ritual lore thought to be worthy of preservation and study during the early empire. Creel, *Origins of Statecraft*, 486; Zhang, *Weishu tongkao*, 1:327–41.

    9. Ebrey, *Family and Property in Sung China*, 36, 50.

    10. See Michael Loewe, "The Concept of Sovereignty," in *The Cambridge History of China*, vol. 1, *The Ch'in and Han Empires 221 B.C.–A.D. 220*, ed. Denis Twitchett and Michael Loewe (Cambridge: Cambridge University Press, 1986), 726–46; Wechsler, *Offerings of Jade and Silk*, 25–26.

    11. Hsü, *Ancient China in Transition*, 19–23; Norbert Elias, *The History of Manners*, trans. Edmund Jephcott (1978; reprint, New York: Pantheon, 1978), 1:99–108. Ancient Chinese rites similar to Western "manners" prohibited women from standing while riding in a carriage, squatting, or staring upward.

    12. Liu, *Handai hunyin zhidu*, 81, 84.

    13. Liu, *Handai hunyin zhidu*, 28–29.

    14. Ban, *Hanshu*, 1B:81, 43:2126.

    15. For the interest of various Han scholars in these texts see Zhang, *Weishu tongkao*, 1:269, 1:282–83, 1:327–28.

    16. Zhao, *Funü zai falü*, 25–26.

    17. Zheng Zhong, a scholar of the early Eastern Han, even composed a text entitled *Marriage Rituals (Hunli)*, now lost. Dull, "Marriage and Divorce," 37.

    18. Dull, "Marriage and Divorce," 23 passim; Wong, "Confucian Ideal and Reality," 8.

    19. Legge, *Tso Chuen*, 121 (*Zhuang* 32), 162 (*Xi* 15); Liu, *Handai hunyin zhidu*, 49.

    20. Han, *Hanshi waizhuan*, 2:2b–3a; Hightower, *Han Shih Wai Chuan*, 40–41.

    21. Dull ("Marriage and Divorce," 39–41) examines this question in detail. Also Liu, *Handai hunyin zhidu*, 49; Wong, "Confucian Ideal and Reality," 96.

    22. Liu, *Handai hunyin zhidu*, 50.

    23. Crump, *Chan-Kuo Ts'e*, 532; Yokota, *Sengoku saku seikai*, 9A:32.

    24. These sentiments are echoed in Yokota, *Sengoku saku seikai*, 9A:32; Crump, *Chan-Kuo Ts'e*, 532; Jing, *Guanzi*, 1:7a, 20:12b; Rickett, *Guanzi*, 88 (*Xingshijie*).

    25. Dull, "Marriage and Divorce," 39.

26. Lin, *Zhouli*, 4:144.

27. Zheng, *Liji*, 1:3a, 8:27b, 8:27b–28a; Legge, *Li Ki*, 27:65 (*Quli* 1.A.27), 27:478 (*Neize* 2.35), 27:479 (*Neize* 2.37); Dull, "Marriage and Divorce," 25–26.

28. Huang, *Lunheng jiaoshi*, 18:804; Forke, *Lun-Heng*, 1:471–72.

29. Li, *Qinlü*, 503.

30. Liu, *Handai hunyin zhidu*, 48–49; Ōzora, *Chūgoku no kokyu*, 46–52.

31. Ban, *Hanshu*, 2:91. All ages are given in Chinese *sui* rather than Western "years." Thus "age fifteen" refers to fifteen *sui*.

32. Liu, *Handai hunyin zhidu*, 47–48; Dull, "Marriage and Divorce," 26–28.

33. J. Hajnal, "Two Kinds of Pre-Industrial Household Formation Systems," in *Family Forms in Historic Europe*, ed. Richard Wall et al. (Cambridge: Cambridge University Press, 1983), 65–104.

34. Dull, "Marriage and Divorce," 38–51; Fujikawa, *Kandai ni okeru reigaku*, 412–16; Liu, *Handai hunyin zhidu*, 50–51.

35. Dull, "Marriage and Divorce," 49–51.

36. Dull, "Marriage and Divorce," 48–49; Dull, "Apocryphal (Ch'an-wei) Texts," 381. The ceremony of the bride's journey had ancient roots. Karlgren, *Book of Odes*, 6–7 (no. 9), 16–17 (no. 28), 25–26 (no. 39). Emphasis on the wedding feast seems to have been a much later innovation.

37. Zheng, *Liji*, 15:2b, 20:2b–3a; Legge, *Li Ki*, 28:59 (*Jingjie* 7), 28:430 (*Hunyi* 3).

38. Zheng, *Liji*, 15:2b, 20:2b–3a; Legge, *Li Ki*, 28:259 (*Jingjie* 7), 28:430 (*Hunyi* 3).

39. Zheng, *Liji*, 15:3b; Legge, *Li Ki*, 28:261 (*Aigongwen* 1).

40. W. S. F. Pickering, *Durkheim on Religion: A Selection of Readings and Bibliographies* (London: Routledge & K. Paul, 1975).

41. Emily Ahern, *Chinese Ritual and Politics* (Cambridge: Cambridge University Press, 1981).

42. Legge, *Li Ki*, 28:238 (*Jitong* 4); Zheng, *Liji*, 14:17b.

43. Lin, *Zhouli*, 2:71, 98.

44. Song dynasty scholar Nie Chongyi discusses this question in detail in his *Sanlitu* (Edo: Sūmon Dō, 1761), 2:1a. Nie explains that this discrepancy arose from the fact that queens did not participate in every major ancient state sacrifice, whereas kings did. Also see Jing, *Guanzi*, 1:14a; Rickett, *Guanzi*, 1:109 (*Lizheng*); Zhou Xibao, *Zhongguo gudai fushishi* (Beijing: Zhongguo Xiju, 1984), 51–52.

Rites of Zhou personified the woman ritualist as the "female invocator" (*nüzhu*) overseeing minor palace rituals (Lin, *Zhouli*, 2:78). Li (*Taiping yulan*, 735:2b) quotes the now lost Jin dynasty *Wuyan* mentioning a "shaman invocator" (*wuzhu*) in ancient Chu, perhaps a model for the female invocator of the *Zhouli*. Similarly a shamaness (*nüwu*) took part in the Qin grand sacrifice to various local deities throughout the empire, thereby participating in the ritual and religious unification of the Han realm to match its political unification (Takigawa, *Shiki kaichū kōshō*, 6:36).

For other sacrifices in which women participated, see Karlgren, *Book of Odes*, 161–63 (no. 209); Qian, *Lienüzhuan jiaozhu*, 1:11b; O'Hara, *Position of Woman*, 43; Fan, *Houhanshu*, 84:2787.

45. Bodde, *Festivals in Classical China*, 388–89.

46. For example, Tjan (*Po Hu T'ung*, 2:652) bars the queen from participating in the suburban sacrifice.

47. This rite receives detailed treatment in Bodde, *Festivals in Classical China*, 263–68. Bodde (329) theorizes that the empress did not actually take part in the sacrifice to the First Sericulturalist but rather collected mulberry leaves after the sacrifice. For other descriptions of the ritual, see Zheng, *Liji*, 5:6b, 5:7a–7b, 14:10b–11a, 14:17b–18a; Legge, *Li Ki*, 27:263 (*Yueling* 1.C.6), 27:265 (*Yueling* 1.C.12), 28:223–24 (*Jiyi* 2.7), 28:239 (*Jitong* 5); Ban, *Baihutong*, 2B:13a; Tjan, *Po Hu T'ung*, 493; Wei, *Hanjiuyi*, B:1b–2a; Nie, *Sanlitu*, 2:3b–4a. Jane E. Harrison, *Ancient Art and Ritual* (Oxford: Oxford University Press, 1951), discusses ritual as a stylized performance of daily activities.

48. Han, *Hanshi waizhuan*, 3:22b; Hightower, *Han Shih Wai Chuan*, 124. Bodde (*Festivals in Classical China*, 229) provides an alternate moralistic explanation.

49. Zheng, *Liji*, 14:17b; Legge, *Li Ki*, 28:238 (*Jitong* 4). For a specific ancient example, see Karlgren, *Book of Odes*, 161–63 (no. 209).

50. Zheng, *Liji*, 1418b; Legge, *Li Ki*, 28:240 (*Jitong* 7).

51. Legge, *Li Ki*, 28:240–41 (*Jitong* 7); Zheng, *Liji*, 14:18b.

52. Lin, *Zhouli*, 2:76.

53. Mencius praised the wives of Hua Zhou and Qi Liang, asserting that the intensity of their mourning transformed the funeral practices of an entire state. Lau, *Mencius*, 175 (4B.6). The wife of one Qian Lou directed his funeral by herself. Qian, *Lienüzhuan jiaozhu*, 2:7b–8a; O'Hara, *Position of Woman*, 68. The *Zhouli* puts low-ranking royal ladies in charge of mourning at the funerals of officials (Lin, *Zhouli*, 2:77).

54. Zheng, *Liji*, 6:2b; Legge, *Li Ki*, 27:316 (*Zengziwen* 1.7).

55. Zheng, *Liji*, 15:5b; Legge, *Li Ki*, 28:266 (*Aigongwen* 12).

56. Zheng, *Liji*, 10:7a, 13:4b–5a; Legge, *Li Ki*, 28:57 (*Sangfu xiaoji* 2.45), 28:180–81 (*Sang daji* 1.19–21). Denial of the staff to young women not in mourning is specified in Jia, *Yili zhushu ji buzheng*, 28:2a; Steele, *I-li*, 2:10.

57. Escorting: Zheng, *Liji*, 13:4a; Legge, *Li Ki*, 28:179 (*Sang daji* 1.18). Impersonating: Jia, *Yili zhushu ji buzheng*, 43:5b; Steele, *I-li*, 2:119. Feast: Jia, *Yili zhushu ji buzheng*, 50:18b; Steele, *I-li*, 2:214.

58. Jia, *Yili zhushu ji buzheng*, 37:12a; Steele, *I-li*, 1:69.

59. Zheng, *Liji*, 12:7b; Legge, *Li Ki*, 28:143 (*Zaji* 1.B.25); Jia, *Yili zhushu ji buzheng*, 27:10a, 10b, 13a, 14a; Steele, *I-li*, 2:63, 65, 74, 76.

60. Stanley Jeyaraja Tambiah, *Culture, Thought, and Social Action: An Anthropological Perspective* (Cambridge, Mass.: Harvard University Press, 1985), 146, 155–57.

61. Karlgren, "Legends and Cults in Ancient China," 215.

62. A childless widow of Chu devoted the latter years of her life to sacrifices to the dead. Perhaps she hoped that someone would eventually follow her example and undertake the same rituals to her own doomed spirit after her decease (Qian, *Lienüzhuan jiaozhu*, 4:9b; O'Hara, *Position of Woman*, 125). Fear of lacking male descendants led the Eastern Han poet Xu Shu, who lacked male progeny, to adopt a son after her husband's death (Hu, *Funü zhuzuo*, 2).

63. Guo, *Guanzi jijiao*, 20:314; Ban, *Hanshu*, 28B:1661; Li, "Yuanshi shehui hunyin xingtai," 96; Fujino Iwatomo, *Fukei bungaku ron: So ji o chushin to shite* (Tokyo: Daigaku, 1951), 20.

64. Dull, "Marriage and Divorce," 49–51.

65. Zheng, *Liji*, 20:3b; Legge, *Li Ki*, 28:432 (*Hunyi* 10).

66. Zheng, *Liji*, 6:5a; Legge, *Li Ki*, 27:322 (*Zengziwen* 1.21).

67. Ch'ü, *Han Social Structure*, 34–35; Liu, *Handai hunyin zhidu*, 57. For women's roles in the actual ceremony, Legge (*Tso Chuen*, 543 [*Xiang* 28]) gives an early view of women offering aquatic plants to the ancestors. Details of the sacrifice, including women's roles, appear in Zheng, *Liji*, 7:19b–20a, 9:15a, 14:6a; Legge, *Li Ki*, 27:411–12 (*Liqi* 2.15); 28:33 (*Mingtangwei* 11); 28:212 (*Jiyi* 6). For female costume worn during this ceremony, see Nie, *Sanlitu*, 2:2a, 2:3a. Women might have participated in musical performances in the Han imperial ancestral cult. See [He], *Zhongguo wudaoshi*, 51.

Gradually the observance of ancestral sacrifices shifted from temple to tomb. Yang Kuan, "Qin Shi Huang lingyuan buju jiegou de tantao," *Qin tong guan kaiguan sannian wenji* 10 (1982): 7–14, suggests that walls at the tomb park of Qin Shihuangdi marked the quarters of officials and palace ladies who lived at the site to attend to regular sacrifices.

68. Duke Xiang of Song is praised for the abundance of sacrificial foods he placed at the tomb of his wife. Zheng, *Liji*, 2:1b; Legge, *Li Ki*, 27:154 (*Tangong* 1.C.19). Confucius is said to have wept bitterly when his mother's tomb collapsed. Zheng, *Liji*, 2:2b; Legge, *Li Ki*, 27:123 (*Tangong*); Huang, *Lunheng jiaoshi*, 20:877; Forke, *Lun-Heng*, 1:197. Legends arose that looters of women's tombs were incinerated by magical fires or suffocated by a mysterious stench (Huang, *Lunheng jiaoshi*, 21:905; Forke, *Lun-Heng*, 1:218–19).

69. Hafo Yanjing Xueshe Yinde Bianzuanchu, *Zhuangzi yinde* (Beiping: Hafo Yanjing Xueshe, 1947), 3:8; A. C. Graham, *Chuang Tzu: The Inner Chapters* (London: George Allen & Unwin, 1981), 65.

70. For example, the tablet of Wu Kaiming reads, "In the first year of the Yongjia era (A.D. 145), his mother died, and he retired from office (for mourning)" (Wu, *Wu Liang Shrine*, 25).

71. Takigawa, *Shiki kaichū kōshō*, 124:9.

72. Zheng, *Liji*, 3:14b; Legge, *Li Ki*, 27:190 (*Tangong* 2.C.7); Zheng, *Liji*, 12:15b. Legge, *Li Ki*, 28:161 (*Zaji* 2.B.1), further specify that a husband or son was to avoid using any taboo characters in a deceased mother's name.

73. Jia, *Yili zhushu ji buzheng*, 30:7a; Steele, *I-li*, 2:15–16. Respect for deceased wives even influenced Zhou state ritual. Diplomatic missions arriving during a period of mourning for the ruler's wife saw their reception ceremonies curtailed. And envoys of other states would come to offer condolences to a ruler even on the death of a concubine. Jia, *Yili zhushu ji buzheng*, 23:19a; Steele, *I-li*, 1:228; Hsü, *Ancient China in Transition*, 118.

74. Zheng, *Liji*, 12:7a; Legge, *Li Ki*, 28:142 (*Zaji* 1.B.19).

75. Lau, *Mencius*, 72–73 (1B.16).

76. Lau, *Analects*, 147 (17.21). *Huai* denotes breast-feeding and connotes close emotional attachment. It seems that Confucius gives both parents credit for "nursing" the child, implying an emotional rather than purely physical use of this term.

77. Jia, *Yili zhushu ji buzheng*, 30:9a; Steele, *I-li*, 2:19.

78. Zheng, *Liji*, 20:17a–17b; Legge, *Li Ki*, 28:467 (*Sangfu sizhi* 6). Jia, *Yili zhushu ji buzheng*, 30:7a; Steele, *I-li*, 2:15–16; Ch'ü, *Han Social Structure*, 52. In Zheng, *Liji*, 2:7b; Legge, *Li Ki*, 27:131 (*Tangong* 1.A.28) a son who mourns for his mother beyond the time fixed by ritual is rebuked by Confucius for being excessively demonstrative.

79. Zheng, *Liji*, 2:2a; Legge, *Li Ki*, 27:122 (*Tangong* 1.A.4); Jia, *Yili zhushu ji buzheng*, 30;7b; Steele, *I-li*, 2:16.

80. Dai Sheng, *Shiqu lilun*. In *Yuhanshan fangji yishu*, ed. Ma Guohan (1872; reprint, Taipei: Wenhua, 1967), 2:1060, 2b; Tjan, *Po Hu T'ung*, 1:130–31.

81. Mourning relations reinforced the mother–son bond (Steele, *I-li*, 2:13). Jia, *Yili zhushu ji buzheng*, 30:6b says, "A son mourns for his stepmother as he does for his mother." This rule also implies that ritual specialists saw the son's link to his mother as deriving primarily from her position as his father's wife.

82. For a summary of mourning grades and their relation to kinship, see Han-yi Feng [Feng Han-chi], *The Chinese Kinship System* (Cambridge, Mass.: Harvard University Press, 1967), 38–43; Ch'ü, *Han Social Structure*, 313–17 n. 274.

83. Jia, *Yili zhushu ji buzheng*, 30:12a; Steele, *I-li*, 2:24.

84. Jia, *Yili zhushu ji buzheng*, 33:16b–17a; Steele, *I-li*, 2:37. A concubine could raise her mourning status by wet nursing her master's heir. Jia, 33:17b; Steele, 2:35.

85. Zheng, *Liji*, 12:16a–16b; Legge, *Li Ki*, 28:162–63 (*Zaji* 2.B.6).

86. Jia, *Yili zhushu ji buzheng*, 31:9b, 31:11b, 23:14a; Steele, *I-li*, 2:20, 23–24, 29.

87. Zheng, *Liji*, 18:4a; Legge, *Li Ki*, 28:372 (*Bensang* 20).

88. Jia, *Yili zhushu ji buzheng*, 31:14a; Steele, *I-li*, 2:28; Zheng, *Liji*, 18:5a; Legge, *Li Ki*, 28:374 (*Bensang* 30).

89. Zheng, *Liji*, 1:26a–26b; Legge, *Li Ki*, 27:117–18 (*Quli* 2.B.13–14); Ban, *Baihutong*, 1A:16b–17b; Tjan, *Po Hu T'ung*, 2:373–74.

90. Zheng, *Liji*, 10:5a, 10:6a–7a, 12:4a; Legge, *Li Ki*, 28:51, 55–57 (*Sangfu xiaoji* 2.19, 33–34, 42–43); 281137 (*Zaji* 1.A.22); Fujikawa, *Kandai ni okeru reigaku*, 471. However, prior to the Han some women had independent shrines (Legge, *Tso Chuen*, 19 [Yin 5]). Qin Huitian, *Wuli tongkao* (1880; reprint, Taipei: Xinxing, 1970), 6223ff., 6226ff., discusses the ancestral shrines of Han empresses. For the veneration of women's shrines by relatives, see Zheng, *Liji*, 3:16a–16b, 7:16a–16b; Legge, *Li Ki*, 27:194 (*Tangong* 2.C.15); 27:404 (*Liqi* 1.23); Ban, *Dongguan Hanji*, 21:4a.

91. Bodde, *Festivals of Classical China*, 281–83.

92. C. K. Yang, *Religion in Chinese Society: A Study of Contemporary Social Functions of Religion and Some of Their Historical Factors* (Berkeley: University of California Press, 1961), 52–53, 285–86.

CHAPTER 8

1. Alison H. Black, "Gender and Cosmology in Chinese Correlative Thinking," in *Gender and Religion: On the Complexity of Symbols*, ed. C. W. Bynum et al. (Boston: Beacon, 1989), 184.

2. Gender was not always seen as binary. There were rare references to hermaphroditism, sex change, and asexual reproduction in Zhou and Han texts. Hafo Yanjing Xueshe, *Zhuangzi yinde*, 14:40; Graham, *Chuang Tzu*, 134; Hao Yixing, *Shanhaijing jianshu* (Shanghai: Sibu Beiyao, n.d.), 3:1b; Huang, *Lunheng jiaoshi*, 2:57–58; Forke, *Lun-Heng*, 1:327; Tjan, *Po Hu T'ung*, 1:112.

3. Liu Jingshan, "An Exploration of the Mode of Thinking in Ancient China," *Philosophy East and West* 35, no. 4 (1985): 387–96.

4. Raphals, *Sharing the Light*, 141.

5. Guisso, "Thunder over the Lake," 48.

6. Nancy Jay, "Gender and Dichotomy," *Feminist Studies* 7, no. 1 (1981): 47–48.

7. Jay, "Gender and Dichotomy," 54. Hall and Ames (*Thinking from the Han*, 96–97) discuss the workings of this process in early Chinese thought.

8. Hu (*Lanse de yinying*, 5–6) believes that yin/yang was equated with female/male because scholar-officials began to use cosmology to fight the influence of ladies at court. Hu (10–21) uses feminist analysis to discuss the emergence of cosmological systems with superior male and inferior female elements as "patriarchal ideology."

9. Zheng, *Liji*, 5:3a; Legge, *Li Ki*, 27:255 (*Yueling* 1.A.14); Huang, *Lunheng jiaoshi*, 5:244, 18:786; Forke, *Lun-Heng*, 1:101, 2:186.

10. [He Rongyi] Ho Jung-I, *Daodejing zhuyi yu xijie* (Taipei: Wuna, 1985), 1:1, 5:61; D. C. Lau, *Lao-tsu: Tao Te Ching* (Harmondsworth, U.K.: Penguin, 1963), 57, 61; Robert G. Henricks, *Lao-Tzu Te-Tao Ching: A New Translation Based on the Recently Discovered Ma-Wang-Tui Texts* (New York: Ballantine, 1989), 188–89, 196–97. Note that the Mawangdui versions omit mention of Heaven and Earth in the first chapter of the *Laozi*. Instead they pair the "beginning" (*shi*) and the "mother" (*mu*). It is tempting to interpret this pair as implying a sexual union of male and female. But the prominent female component in the orthography of *shi* would make it an odd choice to represent elemental masculinity. Instead it seems to be a union of two female elements, each representing primal fertility. Also see Hafo Yanjing Xueshe, *Zhuangzi yinde*, 6:19; Graham, *Chuang Tzu*, 93.

11. Beijing Daxue Xunzi Zhushi Zu, *Xunzi xinzhu*, 3:38; Chen Menglei, *Zhou yi qianshu* (Shanghai: Guji, 1983), 7:13b; Richard Wilhelm and Cary F. Baynes, *The I Ching or Book of Changes* (Princeton: Princeton University Press, 1977), 293.

12. [Hu Zifeng] Hu Tzu-feng, *Xian Qin zhuzi yishuo tongkao* (Taipei: Wenshizhe, 1974), 127–60.

13. Lai Yanyuan, *Chunqiu fanlu jinzhu jinyi* (Taipei: Taiwan Shangwu, 1984), 17:443; Chen, *Zhouyi*, 7:85b (*Xici*); Wilhelm, *I Ching*, 351–52; Ban, *Hanshu*, 24B:1164; Swann, *Food and Money*, 270.

14. Lai, *Chunqiu fanlu jinzhu*, 10:278; Beijing Daxue Xunzi Zhushi Zu, *Xunzi xinzhu*, 9:152; Chen, *Zhouyi*, 7:16b, 51b (*Xici*); Wilhelm, *I Ching*, 295, 320; Huang, *Lunheng jiaoshi*, 3:122; Forke, *Lun-Heng*, 1:134.

15. Loewe (*Crisis and Conflict*, 154–92) summarizes the struggle between what Loewe anachronistically terms the "modernist" faction (which favored worship of the Five Powers, Grand Unity, and *houtu*) and the "reformist" faction (advocating worship of heaven

and earth). A concise summary appears in Cheng Te-k'un, "Yin-Yang Wu-Hsing and Han Art," *Harvard Journal of Asiatic Studies* 20, no. 1–2 (1957): 169–71.

16. Hafo Yanjing Xueshe, *Zhuangzi yinde*, 11:26; Graham, *Chuang Tzu*, 178. This passage seems to emphasize the inability of living beings to escape the fate of returning to humble *tu* instead of exalting *tu* itself. A similar passage appears in Wei Zhao, *Guoyu* (Shanghai: Guoxue Jiben Congshu, 1935), 21:233 (*Yueyu xia*). See Fung Yu-lan, *A Short History of Chinese Philosophy* (New York: Macmillan, 1948), 1:33. However, this passage uses *di* rather than *tu* and is built around the Heaven/Earth/human being triad and thus seems to exalt *di* rather than make a bleak comment on mortality.

17. Lai, *Chunqiu fanlu jinzhu*, 10:278. A similar passage in Zheng, *Liji*, 15:12b; Legge, *Li Ki*, 28;282 (*Kongzi xianju* 7) calls Earth the source of the wind and thunder. Dong also rebutted the arguments of those who saw heaven as the master of rain. He reasoned that Earth creates rain and then humbly gives Heaven the credit (Lai, *Chunqiu fanlu jinzhu*, 10:279). Many important thinkers believed that heaven controlled rain and related phenomena. Karlgren, *Book of Odes*, 164 (no. 210); Jing, *Guanzi*, 20:1b; Rickett, *Guanzi*, 1:63 (*Xingshijie*); Zheng, *Liji*, 15:12b; Legge, *Li Ki*, 28:282 (*Kongzi xianju* 8); Huang, *Lunheng jiaoshi*, 15:650; Forke, *Lun-Heng*, 1:109.

18. Zheng, *Liji*, 11:10a; Legge, *Li Ki*, 28:100 (*Yueji* 1.23). This statement is an elaboration of an initial contention that ritual orders Heaven and Earth. Therefore, ritual is related to Heaven as well.

19. Forke, *Lun-Heng*, 1:510; Huang, *Lunheng jiaoshi*, 25:1044. These sacrifices are those to the outer door, inner door, well, hearth, and inner court.

20. Guo Moruo, "You guan Yijing de xin," *Zhongguoshi yanjiu* 1 (1979): 5.

21. [Zhou Lin'gen] Chou Lin-ken, *Zhongguo zhonggu lijiaoshi* (Taipei: Haiyang Xueyuan, 1969), 51–55.

22. The textual history of writings attributed to Dong Zhongshu is complex. Some scholars contend that many sections were written later and subsequently attributed to Dong. Regardless of the date of authorship assigned to these works, it is clear that there was a general trend during the Han and after toward exalting Heaven and denigrating Earth.

23. Fung, *Short History of Chinese Philosophy*, 2:19, 29–30.

24. Lai, *Chunqiu fanlu jinzhu*, 17:429, 434–35.

25. Huang, *Lunheng jiaoshi*, 24:1006; Forke, *Lun-Heng*, 1:526.

26. [He], *Daodejing zhuyi yu xijie*, 73:587; Lau, *Lao-tsu*, 135; Henricks, *Lao-Tzu Te-Tao Ching*, 172–73. Also see [He], *Daodejing zhuyi yu xijie*, 77:611; Lau, *Lao-tsu*, 139; Henricks, *Lao-Tzu Te-Tao Ching*, 180–81.

27. [He], *Daodejing zhuyi yu xijie*, 25:215; Lau, *Lao-tsu*, 82; Henricks, *Lao-Tzu Te-Tao Ching*, 236–37.

28. Chen Mengjia, "Wuxing zhi qiyuan," *Yanjiu xuebao* 24 (1938): 35–38, analyzes a relevant Warring States inscription on a bronze sword. For other examples, see Beijing Daxue Xunzi Zhushi Zu, *Xunzi xinzhu*, 9:141; Han, *Hanshi waizhuan*, 7:13b–4a; Hightower, *Han Shih Wai Chuan*, 246.

29. Zheng, *Liji*, 8:9b; Legge, *Li Ki*, 27:440 (*Jiaotesheng* 3.8); Graham, *Chuang Tzu*, 257, 261; Chen, *Zhouyi*, 7:28a (*Xici*), 8:1b (*Shuogua*); Wilhelm, *I Ching*, 262, 303; Lai, *Chunqiu fanlu jinzhu*, 13:327; Michael Nylan and Nathan Sivin, "The First Neo-Confucianism: An Introduction to Yang Hsiung's 'Canon of Supreme Mystery' (*T'ai hsuan ching*, c. 4 B.C.)," in *Chinese Ideas about Nature and Society: Studies in Honour of Derk Bodde*, ed. Charles LeBlanc and Susan Blader (Hong Kong: Hong Kong University Press, 1987), 43.

30. Karlgren, *Book of Odes*, 147–48 (no. 198). Traces of this view are preserved in the *Taipingjing*, which generally places a much higher value on *tian* than on *di*. This text states, "Heaven begets human beings." Wang Ming, *Taipingjing hejiao* (Beijing: Zhonghua, 1960), 67:242.

31. For example, Huang, *Lunheng jiaoshi*, 6:302; Forke, *Lun-Heng*, 1:296.

32. Graham, *Chuang Tzu*, 182; Hafo Yanjing Xueshe, *Zhuangzi yinde*, 19:48; Lai, *Chunqiu fanlu jinzhu*, 17:430.

33. Ban, *Baihutong*, 1A:1a; Tjan, *Po Hu T'ung*, 1:218; Huang, *Lunheng jiaoshi*, 15;679, 25:1052; Forke, *Lun-Heng*, 1:517, 2:339.

34. Lai, *Chunqiu fanlu jinzhu*, 13:327, 17:443; Hightower, *Han Shih Wai Chuan*, 97 n. 3.

35. Wilhelm, *I Ching*, 342–43; Chen, *Yijing*, 7:73b. Changing "earth" to "Earth." Also see Huang, *Lunheng jiaoshi*, 3:153, 18:775; Forke, *Lun-Heng*, 1:92, 322.

36. Wang Chong in particular praised this analogy. Huang, *Lunheng jiaoshi*, 6:288, 11:492, 18:776, 18:783; Forke, *Lun-Heng*, 1:93, 99, 261, 287. Also see Wang, *Taipingjing hejiao*, 35:30.

37. Knechtges, *Wen Xuan*, 1:151; Li, *Wenxuan*, 1:13b.

38. Chen, *Yijing*, 8:30b. Similar human associations began to accrue to the element *tu* of the five phases system as *tu* became moralized and conflated with *di*. Tomiya Itaru and Yoshikawa Tadao, eds., *Kansho gogyōshi* (Tokyo: Heibon, 1986), 74.

39. Legge, *Li Ki*, 28:104 (*Yueji* 1.32). Capitalizing "Heaven" and "Earth." Zheng, *Liji*, 11:11b.

40. Jia, *Yili zhushu ji buzheng*, 30:9b; Steele, *I-li*, 2:20; Yamazaki, *Chūgoku joseigaku*, 5:96 (*Nüjie*); Swann, *Pan Chao*, 87; Ban, *Baihutong*, 2A:1a, 2A;7b–8a; Tjan, *Po Hu T'ung*, 2:429, 442; Ch'ü, *Han Social Structure*, 41 n. 39.

41. Swann, *Pan Chao*, 87; Yamazaki, *Chūgoku joseigaku*, 5:96 (*Nüjie*).

42. O'Hara, *Position of Woman*, 44 (*Nüjie*). Changing "heaven" to "Heaven." Qian, *Lienüzhuan jiaozhu*, 1:12a.

43. For an exhaustive study of this rhetorical convention, see Hu, *Xian Qin zhuzi yishuo tongkao*.

44. Helmut Wilhelm, *Heaven, Earth, and Man in the Book of Changes: Seven Eranos Lectures* (Seattle: University of Washington Press, 1977), 31.

45. Zhang Zhengliang, "Boshu 'Liushisi gua' ba," *Wenwu* 334, no. 3 (1984): 9; Li Jingchi, *Zhouyi tanyuan* (Beijing: Zhonghua, 1978), 280–81.

46. Edward Louis Shaughnessy, "The Composition of the *Zhouyi*" (Ph.D. diss., Stanford University, 1983), 17–26, summarizes previous efforts at dating the early strata of the *Yijing*. On page 49 Shaughnessy concludes a probable date of 830–800 B.C.E.

47. There is a vast, contentious, highly contradictory scholarly literature dedicated to dating the various parts of the *Yijing*. A useful general description of each commentary appears in [Gao Huaimin] Kao Huai-min, *Xian Qin yixueshi* (Taipei: Dongwu Daxue, 1975), 238–79. Two respected scholars who recently attempted to date the various commentaries (with extremely different results) are Ozawa Bunshirō, *Kandai ekigaku no kenkyū* (Tokyo: Meitoku, 1970); and Li, *Zhouyi tanyuan*, 2–5, 229. A silk manuscript from Mawangdui was probably copied during the reign of Emperor Wen. Yu Haoliang, "Boshu 'Zhou yi,'" *Wenwu* 334, no. 3 (1984): 24. This manuscript has led some scholars to propose a relatively late date for most of the commentaries; the *Guaci*, *Yaoci*, and most of the *Ten Wings* were apparently composed after the Mawangdui manuscript was copied. The *Xici* commentary, however, appears in the manuscript and hence dates from Emperor Wen's reign or before. Zhang Zhengliang, "Zuotan Changsha Mawangdui Hanmu boshu," *Wenwu* 220, no. 9 (1974): 48.

48. The transmitted version places *qian* and *kun* as first and second of the sixty-four hexagrams; but the Mawangdui text has *qian* first and *kun* thirty-third. The logic of this arrangement becomes clear if the sixty-four hexagrams of the Mawangdui version are arranged in a circle. In this pattern *qian* appears opposite the circle from *kun*, showing a binary relation as apparent as the consecutive order in the transmitted text. Mawangdui Han Mu Boshu Zhengli Xiaozu, "Mawangdui boshu 'Liushisi gua' shiwen," *Wenwu* 334, no. 3 (1984): 1–8; Yu, "Boshu 'Zhouyi,'" 17. A different result occurs when the order of only the eight upper and lower trigrams of the Mawangdui text are examined. The upper trigrams place *qian* and *kun* as numbers one and eight in the system, again appearing opposite each other in a circular arrangement. When the eight lower trigrams are arranged in a circle, however, they appear next to each other in a consecutive array that anticipates the eventual order of *qian* and *kun* in the transmitted text. Zhou Shirong, "Zuotan Changsha Mawangdui Hanmu boshu," *Wenwu* 220, no. 9 (1974): 49; Yu, "Boshu 'Zhouyi,'" 17. A Han editor working after the time when the Mawangdui manuscript was copied probably changed the order. Placing *qian* and *kun* next to each other as the first and second hexagrams clarified their relation to each other. Perhaps this editor saw a circular arrangement of the hexagrams out of vogue or simply too arcane for readers interested in the *Changes* as a moral rather than divinatory guide. Shaughnessy ("Composition of the *Zhouyi*," 172–73, 266–85) interprets the shared dragon imagery of *qian*/*kun* as proof that they were complementary concepts.

49. Originally *qian* was written with a homonym meaning "lock bolt" or "linchpin" (**g'ian*, now pronounced *jian*). *Kun* took the form of a character similar to that now meaning "river" (*chuan*), although this archaic variant was also pronounced *kun* (or, anciently, **k'wen*). Bernhard Karlgren, *Grammata Serica Recensa* (Stockholm: Museum of Far Eastern Antiquities, 1972), 57, 80, 117. Both archaic forms appear in the Mawangdui manuscript; the transmitted *qian* and archaic *kun* appear in the *Yijing* stele engraved 175–83 c.e.; and of course the current orthography for *qian* and *kun* appear in the transmitted text (Yu, "Boshu 'Zhouyi,'" 16). These changes in the written form of the characters were probably just shifts between homonyms with the same denotation. Apparently

there was no shift in the underlying concepts accompanying the change from archaic to transmitted written forms of *qian* and *kun* (Yu, "Boshu 'Zhouyi," 15–16).

50. Early meanings of the archaic written form include a wooden pole used to carry a bronze tripod and the linchpin of a wheel. Duan Yucai, *Shuowen jiezi zhu* (Shanghai: Guji, 1981), 14:6b. Shirakawa theorizes that the meaning "bolt of a lock" might possibly be related to the eventual masculine associations of *qian* because of the phallic shape of traditional Chinese lock bolts. Shirakawa Shizuka, *Setsumon shingi* (Kobe: Hakukaku Bijutsukan, 1969–1974), 14A:2832.

51. The "banner staff" component on the left portion of the character suggests the masculine. Shirakawa, *Setsumon shingi*, 14B:2954; Wilhelm, *Heaven, Earth, and Man*, 36. Some philologists have suggested interpretations such as "dry," "arising," and "sprouting" for this character's original meaning, though these seem to be later accretions (Shirakawa, *Setsumon shingi*, 14B:2954; Wilhelm, *Heaven, Earth, and Man*, 35–36). One recent theory explains the transmitted *qian* as a synecdoche for heaven *(tian)* that originally denoted a particular constellation (Li, *Zhouyi tanyuan*, 281). Though tentative, this theory has the advantage of providing a reason stronger than random phonological coincidence for the adoption of the transmitted form of *qian*. A character already associated with Heaven would have allowed transmitted *qian/kun* forms to echo the Heaven/Earth dichotomy that was already a fixture of Han thought.

52. Scholars have associated the archaic *kun* with two quite different modern characters: "river" *(chuan)* and "obedient" *(shun)* (Shirakawa, *Setsumon shingi*, 2A:2324; Li, *Zhouyi tanyuan*, 232). The latter suggestion seems far-fetched; it probably arose from later, more detailed interpretations of the nature of *kun*. In contrast, *Guoyu* describes the river *(chuan)* as "director of *qi* (vital force, energy)." Wei, *Guoyu*, 3:35 (*Zhouyu xia*, Ling 22); Hu, *Xian Qin zhuzi yishuo tongkao*, 30. Perhaps this definition arose from an intermingling between *chuan* and *kun*.

53. Shirakawa, *Setsumon shingi*, 13B:2737.

54. Li, *Zhouyi tanyuan*, 281; Edward L. Shaughnessy, "The Composition of the 'Qian' and 'Kun' Hexagrams of the *Zhouyi*," in *Before Confucius: Studies in the Creation of the Chinese Classics* (Albany: State University of New York Press, 1997), 197–219.

55. Li, *Zhouyi tanyuan*, 281.

56. Chen, *Zhouyi*, 8:7a, 8a–8b, 14a, 15a, 18b; Wilhelm, *I Ching*, 267–68, 273–76; Li, *Zhouyi tanyuan*, 231, 233, 243, 247.

57. Chen, *Zhouyi*, 7:4a; Wilhelm, *I Ching*, 285.

58. Not everyone has accepted the hierarchy of *qian/kun*. Helmut Wilhelm dismisses the idea that *qian* and *kun* might be unequal. "This system of images linked to values lacked hierarchy, to be sure. No order of ranking the values is set up here, but rather a distribution of values is made to the various situations portrayed, which in themselves are equal to one another" (Wilhelm, *Heaven, Earth, and Man*, 32). A look beyond the actual text, to see how the pair was used in Han dynasty discourse, makes it obvious that many early readers began thinking of them as a hierarchy.

59. Guisso, "Thunder over the Lake," 49.

60. Chen, *Zhouyi*, 6:2b, 7:4b, 7:39a, 8:7a; Wilhelm, *I Ching*, 267, 285, 311, 332 (*Xici*); Li, *Wenxuan*, 1:16b–7a (*Dongdufu*); Knechtges, *Wen Xuan*, 1:163–65.

61. Chen, *Zhouyi*, 7:59b, 89a, 8:13a, 36a; Wilhelm, *I Ching*, 273, 327, 353.

62. Guisso, "Thunder over the Lake," 59–60.

63. Huang Gongzhu et al., *Liang Han jinshi wenxuan pingzhu* (Shanghai: Shanghai, 1935), 52.

64. Duan, *Shuowen jiezi zhu*, 14B:1b; Lin, *Zhouli*, 4:171 n. 2; [Sun Guangde] Sun Kuang-te, *Xian Qin liang Han yinyang wuxing shuo de zhengzhi sixiang* (Taipei: Jiaxin Shuini Gongsi Wenhua Jijinhui, 1969), 2–3. Sun's philological analysis of yin/yang is a comprehensive study of these two characters' developing meanings. Liang Qichao, "Yinyang wuxing shuo zhi laili," *Dongfang zazhi* 20, no. 10 (1923): 70–72, excerpts quotations from Zhou dynasty classics. On page 72 Liang discusses the use of *yang* to write an unrelated homonym.

65. *Laozi*, *Zuozhuan*, *Guoyu*, and Sunzi's *Bingfa* all use yin/yang according to this new view. See Sun, *Xian Qin liang Han yinyang wuxing shuo*, 7, 9–10 for excerpts and discussion. Also Fung, *Short History of Chinese Philosophy*, 1:32. Liang ("Yinyang," 72–73) attributes this shift in meaning to Laozi and Confucius. His reasoning regarding Confucius, however, is based on the flawed assumption that Confucius authored the *Ten Wings*, in which this new use of the words appears. *Lunyu* uses yin/yang in a purely naturalistic sense.

66. Chan, *Source Book*, 244 n. 3.

67. *Shiji* (74) gives Zou Yan's biography. This is translated in Chan, *Source Book*, 246–48. Zou's main contribution came from linking the cosmological duality of yin/yang to Confucian-style moral philosophy.

68. For the relation of yin/yang to gender, see Raphals, *Sharing the Light*, 158–62. Modern scholars have detected yin and yang in almost every iconographic pairing in Han art: east/west, beast/bird, dragon/tiger, red dragon/gray dragon, sky/earth, sun/moon, two bands crossing a central ring, and so on. Käte Finsterbusch, "Han-zeitliche Symbole," in *Studia Sino-Mongolica: Festschrift für Herbert Franke*, ed. Wolfgang Bauer (Weisbaden: Steiner, 1979), 231–44; Schuyler Cammann, "Symbolic Expressions of Yin-Yang Philosophy," in *Chinese Ideas about Nature and Society: Studies in Honour of Derk Bodde*, ed. Charles LeBlanc and Susan Blader (Hong Kong: Hong Kong University Press, 1987), 104–9; Wu, *Wu Liang Shrine*, 116–17; Akatsuka Kiyoshi, *Chūgoku kodai no shūkyō to bunka* (Tokyo: Kakugawa, 1977), 452. Some pairs involve gender: animals of the same species, Fuxi/Nüwa, Ji Star/Xiwangmmu, and Dongwanggong/Xiwangmu. Finsterbusch, "Han-zeitliche Symbole"; Martin J. Powers, "Hybrid Omens and Public Issues in Early Imperial China," *Bulletin of the Museum of Far Eastern Antiquities* 55 (1983): 1–55; Karlgren, "Legends and Cults," 232; Cheng, "Yin-Yang Wu-Hsing and Han Art," 182; Wu, *Wu Liang Shrine*, 111–17. But are these visual pairs symbols of yin and yang? At times artists explicitly intended to depict yin/yang symbols. Inscriptions on two Han bronze mirrors interpret their own iconography unambiguously as using "the Red Bird and Black Warrior to regulate *yin* and *yang* forces" and "the Red Bird and Black Warrior to conform

to the yin and yang forces." Cheng, "Yin-Yang Wu-Hsing and Han Art," 174–75, trans-
lating inscriptions on the Juxu and Shangfang mirrors. In most cases, though, attributions
of yin/yang intent to Han symbolic pairs are conjectural interpretations. Given the
breadth of correlative cosmology during the Han, it might be more accurate to see most
of these pairs as symbols of the general dichotomy underlying our world rather than limit
them to just yin and yang.

69. Huang, *Lunheng jiaoshi*, 3:132–33; Forke, *Lun-Heng*, 1:389. Calendrical, meteoro-
logical, and seasonal phenomena: Fung, *Short History of Chinese Philosophy*, 2:25–30;
Bodde, *Festivals in Classical China*, 45, 50–52, 80–81, 85, 170–71, 290, 342; Dull, "Apocryphal (Ch'an-wei) Texts of the Han Dynasty," 72; Lai, *Chunqiu fanlu jinzhu*, 11:287, 296,
305; Huang, *Lunheng jiaoshi*, 11:488, 506; 14:628, 633; 18:783; 22:942–43; Forke, *Lun-
Heng*, 1:99, 246, 258–59, 269, 279, 284. Astronomical phenomena: Han, *Hanshi waizhuan*, 8:11a; Hightower, *Han Shih Wai Chuan*, 274; Bodde, *Festivals in Classical China*,
174; David R. Knechtges, *The Han Shu Biography of Yang Xiong (53 B.C.–A.D. 18)* (Tempe,
Ariz.: Center for Asian Studies, Arizona State University, 1982), 79–81 n. 87. Links with
qi: Fung, *Short History of Chinese Philosophy*, 2:7–30; Nylan, "First Neo-Confucian," 56.
Medicine: Paul U. Unschuld, *Medicine in China: A History of Ideas* (Berkeley: University
of California Press, 1985), 71, 74, 77, 88, 115, 270, 283–84; Liang Yuntong, *Huangdi
neijing leixi* (Huhehaote: Neimenggu Renmin, 1986), 35, 399, 410–11; Harper, "Wu Shih
Erh Ping Fang," 103–4, 553. Natural world: Huang, *Lunheng jiaoshi*, 5:212, 22:941,
23:949, 23:954; Forke, *Lun-Heng*, 1:246, 299, 301; 2:1667; Dull, "Apocryphal (Ch'an-
wei) Texts of the Han Dynasty," 37; Lin, *Zhouli*, 6:253.

70. Emotions: Lai, *Chunqiu fanlu jinzhu*, 17:436; Hafo Yanjing Xueshe, *Zhuangzi yinde*,
4:9, 4:10; Graham, *Chuang Tzu*, 67, 71; Li, *Wenxuan*, 2:1b (*Xijingfu*); Knechtges, *Wen
Xuan*, 1:181. Ritual: Han, *Hanshi waizhuan*, 5:12a; Hightower, *Han Shih Wai Chuan*, 181.

71. [Bao Jialin] Pao Chia-lin, "Yinyangxue shuo yu funü diwei," in *Zhongguo funüshi
lunji xuji*, ed. [Bao Jialin] (Taipei: Daoxiang, 1991), 37–42, provides a general summary of
passages relating yin/yang to gender in Zhou and Han thought.

72. Bodde, *Festivals in Classical China*, 245–46. A similar analogy between the interaction of yin/yang and human sexual intercourse appears in Seng You, *Hongmingji* (Shanghai: Sibu Congkan, n.d.), 5:5b; Pokora, *Hsin-Lun*, 79.

73. Gender confusion embodies a radical otherness associated with foreign lands. Hao,
Shanhaijing qianshu, 7:1b–2a. Interestingly, *Zuozhuan* defines gu magical poison as a
"female yang thing," implying that its dreaded efficacy arises from perversion of the usual
gender associations of yin/yang. Legge, *Tso Chuen*, 581.

74. Lai, *Chunqiu fanlu jinzhu*, 17:415, 445; 446 n. 4. The wording of this passage does
not imply that yin is analogous to male and yang to female. Instead, by speaking of the
two concepts in conjunction Dong Zhongshu simply abides by the standard convention
of referring to the concepts in the usual order "yin/yang" and "male/female."

75. Yamazaki, *Chūgoku joseigaku*, 3:90 (*Nüjie*); Swann, *Pan Chao*, 85. Van Gulik (*Sexual
Life*, 42) asserts that even in early China the yin/yang dichotomy implied that man has a
feminine element in him and woman a masculine element. However, as with many of his
provocative assertions, Van Gulik provides no convincing proof.

76. Hafo Yanjing Xueshe, *Zhuangzi yinde*, 6:17; Graham, *Chuang Tzu*, 88.
77. Yamazaki, *Chūgoku joseigaku*, 2:87 *(Nüjie)*; Swann, *Pan Chao*, 84.
78. Lin, *Zhouli*, 2:71; 2:72 n. 3.
79. Ouyang, *Yiwen leiju*, 15:282.
80. Elisabeth Croll, *Feminism and Socialism in China* (London: Routledge & Kegan Paul, 1978), 12.
81. Hafo Yanjing Xueshe, *Zhuangzi yinde*, 24:69; Graham, *Chuang Tzu*, 62.
82. Ames, "Taoism and the Androgynous Ideal," 21–45.
83. Qian, *Lienüzhuan jiaozhu*, 3:3a; O'Hara, *Position of Woman*, 81. Here yin seems to have reverted to one of its ancient meanings: "to conceal." This refers to the concealed moral virtues proper to the modest and humble woman.
84. Lai, *Chunqiu fanlu jinzhu*, 12:315.
85. Lai, *Chunqiu fanlu jinzhu*, 10:290, 11:289, 11:291.
86. Lai, *Chunqiu fanlu jinzhu*, 11:303, 12:315.
87. Lai, *Chunqiu fanlu jinzhu*, 12:314, 317.
88. Lai, *Chunqiu fanlu jinzhu*, 12:317. He also calls it the "regulator of heaven."
89. Chen, *Zhouyi*, 8:3a *(Shuogua)*; Wilhelm, *I Ching*, 264; Yamazaki, *Chūgoku joseigaku*, 3:90 *(Nüjie)*; Swann, *Pan Chao*, 85.
90. Lai, *Chunqiu fanlu jinzhu*, 11:290–91, 12:314.
91. For example, the section in Wang, *Taipingjing hejiao*, 93:386–89 deals with the theme "yang is exalted, yin is base."
92. Ozawa, *Kandai ekigaku*, 42. Nylan ("First Neo-Confucianism," 42) explains the relationship of yin/yang to inauspicious/auspicious in another work, Yang Xiong's *Taixuanjing*. Nylan notes that in Yang's system, although yang is in principle auspicious, the overall situational and moral contexts must be considered before this conclusion is drawn.
93. Han, *Hanshi waizhuan*, 10:7b; Hightower, *Han Shih Wai Chuan*, 331; Li, *Wenxuan*, 2:11a *(Xijingfu)*; Knechtges, *Wen Xuan*, 1:213.
94. Lai, *Chunqiu fanlu jinzhu*, 11:290, 12:320.
95. Lai, *Chunqiu fanlu jinzhu*, 12:320.
96. Ban, *Hanshu*, 85:3475.
97. Zheng, *Liji*, 20:4a–4b; Legge, *Li Ki*, 28:433 *(Hunyi 12)*.
98. Lai, *Chunqiu fanlu jinzhu*, 12:320; Zheng, *Liji*, 10:19a; Legge, *Li Ki*, 27:411 *(Liqi 2:13)*.
99. Tjan, *Po Hu T'ung*, 1:244; Ban, *Baihutong*, 4A:9b.
100. Liu, *Handai hunyin zhidu*, 22, 39 n. 109; Fujikawa, *Kandai ni okeru reigaku*, 339, 343.
101. Ban, *Hanshu*, 72:3064.
102. Fan, *Houhanshu*, 62:2053. For some other diatribes by officials using cosmology to argue against the influence of women in government and society, see Ban, *Hanshu*, 85:3456–65, 97B:3977–81; Fan, *Houhanshu*, 62:2051–57; Ōzora, *Chūgoku no kokyu*, 42.
103. Hightower, *Han Shih Wai Chuan*, 243 (not italicizing "yin" and "yang"); Han, *Hanshi waizhuan*, 7:12a.
104. Dong Zhongshu believed that yin/yang embodied the relations of subject/ruler. Lai,

Chunqiu fanlu jinzhu, 12:320. In a memorial of 56 c.e., Lang Yi explained that unusual astronomical occurrences resulted from a shift in power away from the yang ruler and toward the yin officialdom. Fan, *Houhanshu*, 30B:1059.

105. Ban, *Hanshu*, 97B:3977–78.

106. Fan, *Houhanshu*, 62:2051–57.

107. Hu (*Lanse de yinying*, 5–6) sees the trend identifying yin/yang with female/male as an outgrowth of factionalism in government. Scholar officials used cosmology to fight the influence of women at court.

108. Croll (*Feminism and Socialism*, 12) sees this type of cosmology as a major factor leading to the general oppression of women by men in China. Paul Steven Sangren, *History and Magical Power in a Chinese Community* (Stanford: Stanford University Press, 1987), presents some contemporary Chinese views of yin/yang in relation to gender.

109. Guo Huaruo, *Sunzi yizhu* (Shanghai: Guji, 1984), 1:78.

110. Fung, *Short History of Chinese Philosophy*, 1:383. For some examples, see Hafo Yanjing Xueshe, *Zhuangzi yinde*, 21:55, 22:59; Graham, *Chuang Tzu*, 130, 133; Lin, *Zhouli*, 5:193, 6:258; Huang, *Lunheng jiaoshi*, 7:332, 16:730; Forke, *Lun-Heng*, 1:349, 368; Han, *Hanshi waizhuan*, 2:4a, 3:10a; Hightower, *Han Shih Wai Chuan*, 27, 44, 97; Wang, *Taipingjing hejiao*, 728.

111. *Tian*: Lai, *Chunqiu fanlu jinzhu*, 11:291, 303; 12:307, 309. *Tian* and *di*: Lai, 13:334; 15:384; 17:415, 429, 439. Fung, *Short History of Chinese Philosophy*, 2:30, 56–58.

112. Ban, *Baihutong*, 3A:2a; Tjan, *Po Hu T'ung*, 1:241.

113. Yamazaki, *Chūgoku joseigaku*, 2:87 (*Nüjie*); Swann, *Pan Chao*, 84.

114. Chen, *Zhouyi*, 7:75a; Wilhelm, *I Ching*, 343. The point is made more generally in the *Shuogua* (Chen, *Zhouyi*, 8:2a; Wilhelm, *I Ching*, 262). This concept from the *Shuogua* is echoed in Huang, *Lunheng jiaoshi*, 14:632; Forke, *Lun-Heng*, 1:283. For discussions of this between yin/yang and *qian/kun*, see Fung, *Short History of Chinese Philosophy*, 1:384, 2:103; Liang, "Yinyang wuxing," 72–73; Li, *Zhouyi tanyuan*, 252.

115. Chen, *Zhouyi*, 7:1b, 8:16b; Wilhelm, *I Ching*, 2:97; Gu, "Wude zhongshi shuoxia," 73–75.

116. Chen, *Zhouyi*, 8:9b; Wilhelm, *I Ching*, 269. For a discussion of the links between yin/yang and Heaven/Earth, see Raphals, *Sharing the Light*, 151–53.

Glossary of Chinese Terms

bao	報	jia	家
bei	卑	jian	鍵
ben	奔	jiao	交
budao	不道	jiupin	九嬪
chong	崇	jun	君
chuan	川	kun	坤
dani	大逆	li	禮, 里
dao	道	mu	母
di	地, 帝	nacai	納采
fu	婦, 夫	nazheng	納徵
fugong	婦工	nü	女
fushi	婦事	nüwu	女巫
gu	蠱	nüyu	女御
hejian	和姦	nüzhu	女祝
huai	懷	pang	旁
huangdi	皇帝	po	魄
huanghou	皇后	qi	氣
huangtaihou	皇太后	qian	乾
hun	魂	qiangjian	強姦

shang	尚	wuzhu	巫祝
sheng	聖	xia	下
shi	士, 始	xiao	小
shifu	世婦	xian	先
shiyi	食邑	xiannü	賢女
shun	順	yang	陽
su	俗	yin	陰
tangmuyi	湯沐邑	yinli	陰禮
tian	天	zhao	詔
tu	土	zhi	制
wu	巫	zhuzu	祝詛
wufu	巫婦	zongfa	宗法
wugu	巫蠱		

Bibliography

Ahern, Emily. *Chinese Ritual and Politics.* Cambridge: Cambridge University Press, 1981.

Akatsuka Kiyoshi 赤塚忠. *Chūgoku kodai no shūkyō to bunka* 中國古代の宗教と文化. Tokyo: Kakugawa, 1977.

Ames, Roger T. "Taoism and the Androgynous Ideal." In *Women in China: Current Directions in Historical Scholarship*, edited by Richard W. Guisso and Stanley Johannesen. 21—45. Youngstown, N.Y.: Philo, 1981, pp. 21-45.

Ayscough, Florence. *Chinese Women Yesterday & Today.* Shanghai: Modern BookCompany, n.d.

Bamberger, Joan. "The Myth of Matriarchy: Why Men Rule in Primitive Society."In *Women, Culture, and Society.* Edited by Michelle Zimbalist Rosaldo and Louise Lamphere. Stanford: Stanford University Press, 1974.

Ban Gu 班固. *Baihutong* 白虎通. In *Baojingtang congshu* 寶經堂叢書. Edited by Lu Wenchao 盧文弨. N.p.: Baojingtang, 1784; reprint, Beijing: Zhili, 1923.

———. *Hanshu* 漢書. Annotated by Yan Shigu 顏師古. Beijing: Zhonghua, 1962.

Ban Gu 班固 et al. *Dongguan Hanji* 東觀漢記. Fujian: Buzheng, 1895.

[Bao Jialin] Pao Chia-lin 鮑家麟. "Yinyangxue shuo yu funü diwei" 陰陽學說與婦女地位. In *Zhongguo funüshi lunji xuji* 中國婦女史論集續集, edited by [Bao]. 37—54. Taipei: Daoxiang, 1991.

Barber, Elizabeth Wayland. *Women's Work, The First 20,000 Years: Women, Cloth, and Society in Early Times.* New York: W.W. North, 1994.

Barnes, R. H. Introduction to Josef Kohler, *On the Prehistory of Marriage: Totemism, Group Marriage, Mother Right*, trans. R. H. Barnes and Ruth Barnes. Chicago: University of Chicago Press, 1975.

Beijing Daxue Xunzi Zhushi Zu 北京大學荀子注釋組. *Xunzi xinzhu* 荀子新注.Beijing: Zhonghua, 1979; reprint, Taipei: Liren, 1983.

Bielenstein, Hans. "Lo-yang in Later Han Times." *Bulletin of the Museum of Far Eastern Antiquities* 48 (1976): 1—142.

Birrell, Anne. *New Songs from a Jade Terrace: An Anthology of Early Chinese Love Poetry.* Harmondsworth, U.K.: Penguin, 1986.

Black, Alison H. "Gender and Cosmology in Chinese Correlative Thinking." In *Gender and Religion: On the Complexity of Symbols*, edited by C. W. Bynum et al., 166-95. Boston: Beacon, 1989.

Bodde, Derk. *Festivals in Classical China: New Year and Other Annual Observances During the Han Dynasty, 206 B.C. — A.D. 220.* Princeton: Princeton University Press, 1975.

Brown, Judith K. "A Note on the Division of Labor by Sex." *American Anthropologist* 72, no. 5 (1970): 1073—78.

Bui Quang Tung. *Le soulèvement des soeurs Tru'ng à travers les textes et le folklore viêtnamien.* Saigon: Imprimerie Nouvelle d'Extrême-Orient, 1961.

Cammann, Schuyler. "Symbolic Expressions of Yin-Yang Philosophy." In *Chinese Ideas about Nature and Society: Studies in Honour of Derk Bodde,* edited by Charles LeBlanc and Susan Blader, 101-16. Hong Kong: Hong Kong University Press, 1987.

Carlitz, Katherine. "Desire, Danger, and the Body: Stories of Women's Virtue in Late Ming China." In *Engendering China: Women, Culture, and the State*, edited by Christine K. Gilmartin et al., 101-24. Cambridge: Harvard University Press, 1994.

Chan, Wing-tsit. *A Source Book in Chinese Philosophy*. Princeton: Princeton University Press, 1963.

Chang Qu 常璩. *Huayang guozhi* 華陽國志. Taipei: Hongye, 1972.

Chavannes, Édouard. *Mission archéologique dans la Chine septentrionale*. Vol. 2. Paris: Ernest Leroux, 1913—1915.

———. *La Sculpture sur pierre en Chine au temps des deux dynasties Han*. Paris: Ernest Leroux, 1893.

Chen, Kenneth. *Buddhism in China: A Historical Survey*. Princeton: Princeton University Press, 1964.

Chen Mengjia 陳夢家. "Wuxing zhi qiyuan" 五行之起源. *Yanjiu xuebao* 研究學報 24 (1938): 35—38.

Chen Menglei 陳夢雷. *Zhouyi qianshu* 周易淺述. 4 vols. Shanghai: Guji, 1983.

Chen Ping 陳平 and Wang Quanjin 王勸金. "Yizheng Xupu 101 hao Xihanmu 'xianling quanshu' chukao" 儀征胥浦 101 號 西漢墓 '先令券書' 初考. *Wenwu* 文物 368, no. 1 (1987): 20—25, 36.

Chen Yu-shih. "The Historical Template of Pan Chao's *Nü Chieh*." *T'oung Pao* 82 (1996): 229—57.

Cheng Shude 程樹德. *Jiuchao lükao* 九朝律考. Beijing: Zhonghua, 1963.

Cheng Te-k'un. "Yin-Yang Wu-Hsing and Han Art." *Harvard Journal of Asiatic Studies* 20, no. 1—2 (1957): 169—71.

Ching-Chung, Priscilla. "Palace Women in the Northern Sung: Their Social Organization." *Bulletin of Sung-Yuan Studies* 15 (1979): 79—97.

Chou, Hung-hsiang. "Fu-X Ladies of the Shang Dynasty." *Monumenta Serica* 29 (1970—1971): 346—90.

Ch'ü, T'ung-tsu. *Han Social Structure*. Edited by Jack L. Dull. Seattle: University of Washington Press, 1972.

Creel, Herrlee Glessner. *The Origins of Statecraft in China.* Chicago: University of Chicago Press, 1970.

Croll, Elizabeth. *Feminism and Socialism in China.* London: Routledge & K. Paul, 1978.

————. *Changing Identities of Chinese Women: Rhetoric, Experience and Self-Perception in Twentieth-Century China.* Hong Kong: Hong Kong University Press/Zed, 1995.

Crump, J. I., Jr. *Chan-Kuo Ts'e.* Oxford: Clarendon, 1970.

Dai Sheng 戴聖. *Shiqu lilun* 石渠禮論. In *Yuhanshan fangji yishu* 玉函山房輯佚書. Edited by Ma Guohan 馬國翰. Jinan: Xinghuaguan, 1872; reprint, Taipei: Wenhua, 1967.

Davin, Anna. "'Mind That You Do as You Are Told': Reading Books for Board School Girls, 1870—1902." *Feminist Review* 3 (1979): 89—92.

De Crespigny, Rafe. "The Harem of Emperor Huan: A Study of Court Politics in Later Han." *Papers on Far Eastern History* 12 (1975): 1—42.

DeWoskin, Kenneth J. *Doctors, Diviners, and Magicians of Ancient China: Biographies of Fang-shih.* New York: Columbia University Press, 1983.

Doi, Takeo. *The Anatomy of Dependence.* Translated by John Bester. Tokyo: Kodansha, 1973.

[Dong Jiazun] Tung Chia-tsun 董家遵. "Cong Han dao Song guafu zaijia xisu kao" 從漢到宋寡婦再嫁習俗考. In *Zhongguo funüshi lunwenji* 中國婦女史論文集, edited by [Li Youning] Li Yu-ning 李又寧 and [Zhang Yufa] Chang Yü-fa 張玉法, 39—63. 2d ed. Taipei: Taiwan Shangwu, 1988.

————. "Lidai jiefu lienü de tongji" 歷代節婦烈女的統計. In *Zhongguo funüshi lunwenji* 中國婦女史論文集, edited by [Bao Jialin] Pao Chia-lin 鮑家麟, 111—17.Taipei: Daoxiang, 1978.

Dong Yue 董說. *Qiguokao* 七國考. Beijing: Zhonghua, 1956.

Drake, F. S. "Sculptured Stones of the Han Dynasty." *Monumenta Serica* 8 (1943): 230-318.

Du Guichi 杜貴墀. *Hanlü jizheng* 漢律輯證. N.p.: Falüguan, n.d.

Du You 杜佑. *Tongdian* 通典. Shanghai: Tushu Jicheng, 1902.

Duan Yucai 段玉裁. *Shuowen jiezi zhu* 說文解字注. Shanghai: Guji, 1981.

Dubs, Homer H. et al. *The History of the Former Han Dynasty: By Pan Ku*. Baltimore: Waverly, 1938—1955.

Dull, Jack L. "A Historical Introduction to the Apocryphal (Ch'an-wei) Texts of the Han Dynasty." Ph.D. diss., University of Washington, 1966.

————. "Marriage and Divorce in Han China: A Glimpse at 'Pre-Confucian' Society." In *Chinese Family Law and Social Change in Historical and Comparative Perspective*, edited by David C. Buxbaum, 23-74. Seattle: University of Washington Press, 1978.

Duyvendak, J. J. L. *The Book of Lord Shang: A Classic of the Chinese School of Law*. London: Arthur Probsthain, 1928.

Ebrey, Patricia Buckley. *Family and Property in Sung China: Yuan Ts'ai's Precepts for Social Life*. Princeton: Princeton University Press, 1984.

————. *The Inner Quarters: Marriage and the Lives of Chinese Women in the Sung Period*. Berkeley: University of California Press, 1993.

————. "Women, Marriage, and the Family." In *Heritage of China: Contemporary Perspectives on Chinese Civilization*, edited by Paul S. Ropp, 197—223.. Berkeley: University of California Press, 1990.

Eliade, Mircea. *Shamanism: Archaic Techniques of Ecstasy*. Translated by Willard R. Trask. New York: Bollingen Foundation/Pantheon, 1964.

Elias, Norbert. *The History of Manners*. Translated by Edmund Jephcott. Vol. 1. 1978. Reprint, New York: Pantheon, 1978.

Elvin, Mark. "Female Virtue and the State in China." *Past and Present* 104 (1984): 111—52

Engels, Frederick. *The Origin of the Family, Private Property and the State*. Edited by Eleanor Burke Leacock. New York: International Publishers, 1972.

Fan Ye 范曄. *Houhanshu* 後漢書. Annotated by Li Xian 李賢. Beijing: Zhonghua, 1962.

Feng, Han-yi [Feng Han-chi]. *The Chinese Kinship System.* Cambridge: Harvard University Press, 1967.

Feng, H. Y. and J. K. Shryock. "The Black Magic in China Known as *Ku.*" *Journal of The American Oriental Society* 55 (1935): 1—30.

Feng Yunpeng 馮雲鵬. *Jinshisuo* 金石索. Taipei: Dezhi, 1963.

Finsterbusch, Käte. "Han-zeitliche Symbole." In *Studia Sino-Mongolica: Festschrift für Herbert Franke,* edited by Wolfgang Bauer, 231-44. Weisbaden: Steiner, 1979.

Fontein, Jan, and Tung Wu. *Unearthing China's Past.* Boston: Museum of Fine Arts, Boston, 1973.

Forke, Alfred. *Lun-Heng. Pt 1. Philosophical Essays of Wang Ch'ung.* Berlin: Georg Reimer, 1911; reprint, New York: Paragon, 1962.

Frankel, Hans H. "The Chinese Ballad 'Southeast Fly the Peacocks.'" *Harvard Journal of Asiatic Studies* 34 (1974): 248—271.

Fujikawa Masakazu 藤川正數. *Kandai ni okeru reigaku no kenkyū* 漢代における禮學の研究. Tokyo: Kazama, 1968.

Fujino Iwatomo 藤野岩友. *Fukei bungaku ron: So Ji o chūshin to shite* 巫系文學論: 楚辭を中心として. Tokyo: Daigaku, 1951.

Fung Yu-lan. *A Short History of Chinese Philosophy.* New York: Macmillan, 1948.

Fyzee, Asaf Ali Asghar. *Outlines of Muhammadan Law.* Oxford: Oxford University Press, 1955.

Gan Bao 干寶. *Soushenji* 搜神記. Beijing: Zhonghua, 1969.

Gan Shu 干叔. "Lingnan Handai wenhua baoku: Guangzhou Xianggang Nan Yuewangmu" 嶺南漢代文化寶庫－廣州象崗南越王墓. *Lingnan wenshi* 嶺南文史 10 (n.d.): 15—17.

Gansu Sheng Wenwudui 甘肅省文物隊, ed. *Jiayuguan bihuamu fajue baogao* 嘉峪關壁畫墓發掘報告. Beijing: Wenwu, 1985.

[Gao Huaimin] Kao Huai-min 高懷民. *Xian Qin yixueshi* 先秦易學史. Taipei:Dongwu Daxue, 1975.

[Gao Mai] Kao Mai 高邁. "Zhongguo changji zhidu zhi lishi de soujiu" 中國娼妓制度之歷史的搜究. In *Zhongguo funüshi lunji* 中國婦女論集, edited by [Bao Jialin] Pao Chialin 鮑家麟, 118—27. Taipei: Daoxiang, 1978.

Goffman, Erving. *The Presentation of Self in Everyday Life.* Garden City, N.Y.: Doubleday, 1959.

Goody, Jack. "Religion and Ritual: The Definitional Problem." *British Journal of Sociology* 12 (1961): 142—64.

Gotō Kinpei 後藤均平. "Chō shimai no hanran" 徵姊妹の反亂. *Chūgoku kodaishi kenkyū* 中國古代史研究 3 (1969): 211—48.

Gough, Kathleen. "An Anthropologist Looks at Engels." In *Woman in a Man-Made World.* Edited by Nona Glazer-Malbin and Helen Youngelson Waehrer, 156-168. Chicago: RandMcNally, 1972.

Graham, A. C. *Chuang Tzu: The Inner Chapters.* London: George Allen &Unwin, 1981.

Gu Jiegang 顧頡剛. "Wude zhongshi shuoxia de zhengzhi he lishi" 五德終始說下地政治和歷史. *Qinghua xuebao* 清華學報 6 (1930): 71—268.

Guisso, Richard W. "Thunder over the Lake: The Five Classics and the Perception of Women in Early China." In *Women in China: Current Directions in Historical Scholarship*, edited by Richard W. Guisso and Stanley Johannesen, 47-61. Youngstown, N.Y.: Philo, 1981.

Guo Huaruo 郭化若. *Sunzi yizhu* 孫子譯注. Shanghai: Guji, 1984.

[Guo Licheng] Kuo Li-ch'eng 郭立誠. *Zhongguo funü shenghuo shihua* 中國婦女生活史話. Taipei: Hanguang Wenhua, 1983.

Guo Moruo 郭沫若. "Youguan Yijing de xin" 有關易經的信. *Zhongguoshi yanjiu* 中國史研究 1 (1979): 5—6.

Guo Moruo 郭沫若, Wen Yiduo 聞一多, and Xu Weiyu 許維遹. *Guanzi jijiao* 管子集校. 2 vols. Beijing: Kexue, 1956.

Gushihou Gudui Yihao Mu Fajue Zu 固始侯古堆一號墓發掘組. "Henan Gushihou Gudui yihao mu fajue jianbao" 河南固始侯古堆一號墓發掘簡報. *Wenwu* 文物 296, no. 1 (1981): 1—8.

Hafo Yanjing Xueshe Yinde Bianzuanchu 哈佛燕京學社引得編纂處. *Zhuangzi yinde* 莊子引得. Beiping: Hafo Yanjing Xueshe, 1947.

Hajnal, J. "Two Kinds of Pre-Industrial Household Formation Systems." In *Family Forms in Historic Europe*, edited by Richard Wall et al., 65-104. Cambridge: Cambridge University Press.

Hall, David L., and Roger T. Ames. *Thinking from the Han: Self, Truth, and Transcendence in Chinese and Western Culture*. Albany: State University of New York Press, 1998.

Han Ying 韓嬰. *Hanshi waizhuan* 韓詩外傳. In *Yingyin Wenyuange siku quanshu* 影印文淵閣四庫全書. Vol. 83. Taipei: Taiwan Shangwu, 1983.

Handlin, Joanna. "'Lü K'un's New Audience: The Influence of Women's Literacy on Sixteenth Century Thought." In *Women in Chinese Society*, edited by Margery Wolf and Roxane Witke, 13—38. Stanford: Stanford University Press, 1979.

Hao Yixing 郝懿行. *Shanhaijing jianshu* 山海經箋疏. Shanghai: Sibu Beiyao, n.d.

Harper, Donald. "The 'Wu Shih Erh Ping Fang': Translation and Prolegomena." Ph.D. diss, University of California, 1982.

Harrison, Jane E. *Ancient Art and Ritual*. Oxford: Oxford University Press, 1951.

[He Rongyi] Ho Jung-I 賀榮一. *Daodejing zhuyi yu xijie* 道德經註譯與析解. Taipei: Wuna, 1985.

[He Zhihao] Ho Chih-hao 何志浩. *Zhongguo wudaoshi* 中國舞蹈史. Taipei: Zhonghua Dadian, 1970.

Henricks, Robert G. *Lao-Tzu Te-Tao Ching: A New Translation Based on the Recently Discovered Ma-Wang-Tui Texts*. New York: Ballantine, 1989.

Hightower, James Robert. *Han Shih Wai Chuan: Han Ying's*

Illustrations of the Didactic Applications of the Classic of Songs. Cambridge: Harvard University Press, 1952.

Hinsch, Bret. "Women, Kinship, and Property as Seen in a Han Dynasty Will." *T'oung Pao* 84 (1998): 1—20.

Holmgren, J. "Observations on Marriage and Inheritance Practices in Early Mongol and Yuan Society: With Particular Reference to the Levirate." *Journal of Asian History* 20 (1986): 127—92.

Honigmann, John J. "Ceremony." In *A Dictionary of the Social Sciences*, edited by Julius Gould and William L. Kolb, 82—83. New York: Free Press, 1964.

Hong Gua 洪适. *Lishi* 隸史. Shanghai: Sibu Congkan, 1935.

Hsü, Cho-yun. *Ancient China in Transition: An Analysis of Social Mobility, 722—222 B.C.* Stanford: Stanford, 1965.

———. *Han Agriculture: The Formation of the Early Chinese Agrarian Economy (206 B.C. — A.D. 220).* Edited by Jack L. Dull. Seattle: University of Washington Press, 1980.

Hsü, Cho-yun, and Katheryn M. Linduff. *Western Chou Civilization.* New Haven: Yale University Press, 1988.

Hu Kun 胡坤. *Lanse de yinying: Zhongguo funü wenhua guanzhao* 藍色的陰影: 中國婦女文化觀照. Xian: Shaanxi Renmin Jiaoyu, 1989.

Hu Wenkai 胡文楷. *Lidai funü zhuzuo kao* 歷代婦女著作考. Shanghai: Shangwu, 1957.

[Hu Zifeng] Hu Tzu-feng 胡自逢. *Xian Qin zhuzi yishuo tongkao* 先秦諸子易說通考. Taipei: Wenshizhe, 1974.

Huang Gongzhu 黃公渚 et al. *Liang Han jinshi wenxuan pingzhu* 兩漢金石文選評注. Shanghai: Shanghai, 1935.

Huang Hui 黃暉. *Lunheng jiaoshi* 論衡校釋. Taipei: Taiwan Shangwu, 1983.

Huang Jinshan 黃金山. "Handai jiating chengyuan de diwei he yiwu" 漢代家庭成員的地位和義務. *Lishi yanjiu* 歷史研究 192, no. 2 (1988): 33—49.

Huang Yanli 黃嫣梨. *Handai funü wenxue wujia yanjiu* 漢代婦女

文學五家研究. Kaifeng: Henan Daxue, 1993.

Hulsewé, A. F. P. "'Contracts' of the Han Period." In *Il Diritto in Cina, Teoria e applicazione durante le dinastie imperiali e problematica del diritto Cinese contemporareo,* edited by Lionello Lanciotti, 11—38. Florence: L. S. Olschki, 1978.

————. "A Lawsuit of A.D. 28." In *Studia Sino-Mongolica, Festschrift für Herbert Franke,* ed. Wolfgang Bauer, 23—34. Wiesbaden: Steiner, 1979.

————. *Remnants of Ch'in Law: An Annotated Translation of the Ch'in Legal and Administrative Rules of the 3rd Century B.C. Discovered in Yün-meng Prefecture, Hu-pei Province, in 1975.* Leiden: Brill, 1985.

————. *Remnants of Han Law. Vol. I, Introductory Studies and an Annotated Translation of Chapters 22 and 23 of the History of the Former Han Dynasty.* Leiden: Brill, 1955.

Jay, Nancy. "Gender and Dichotomy." *Feminist Studies* 7, no. 1 (1981): 38—56.

Jia Gongyan 賈公顏. *Yili zhushu ji buzheng* 儀禮注疏及補正. Taipei: Shijie, 1970.

[Jin Fagen] Chin Fa-ken 金發根. "Dong Han danggu renwu de fenxi" 東漢黨錮人物的分析. In *Gu yuanzhang Hu Shi xiansheng jinian lunwenji* 故院長胡適先生紀念論文集, 505—558. Taipei: Zhongyang Yanjiuyuan, Lishi Yuyan Yanjiusuo,1962.

Judd, Ellen R. "*Niangjia*: Chinese Women and Their Natal Families." *Journal of Asian Studies* 48, no. 3 (1989): 525—44.

Kaltenmark, Max. *Lao Tzu and Taoism.* Translated by Roger Greaves. Stanford: Stanford University Press, 1969.

Kamata Shigeo 鎌田重雄. *Shin Kan seiji seido no kenkyū* 前漢政治制度の研究. Tokyo: Nihon Gakujutsu, 1962.

Kang Zhengguo 康正果. *Fengsao yu yanqing: Zhongguo gudian shici de nüxing yanjiu* 風騷與艷情: 中國古典詩詞的女性研究. Zhengzhou: Henan Renmin, 1988.

Karlgren, Bernhard. *The Book of Odes: Chinese Text, Transcription and Translation.* Stockholm: Museum of Far

Eastern Antiquities, 1950.

———. *Grammata Serica Recensa*. Stockholm: Museum of Far Eastern Antiquities,1972.

———. "Legends and Cults in Ancient China." *Bulletin of the Museum of Far Eastern Antiquities* 18 (1946): 199—365.

Katō, Shigeru. "A Study on the *Suan-fu*, the Poll Tax of the Han Dynasty." *Memoirs of the Research Department of the Tōyō Bunko* 1 (1926): 51—68.

Kinney, Anne Behnke. "Infant Abandonment in Early China." *Early China* 18 (1993): 107—138.

Knechtges, David R. *The Han Shu Biography of Yang Xiong (53 B.C. — A.D. 18)*. Tempe, Ariz.: Center for Asian Studies, Arizona State University, 1982.

———. *Xiao Tong: Wen Xuan, or Selections of Refined Literature.* 2 vols. Princeton: Princeton University Press, 1982.

Ko, Dorothy. *Teachers of the Inner Chambers: Women and Culture in Seventeenth-Century China.* Stanford: Stanford University Press, 1994.

Kuhn, Dieter. "Tracing a Chinese Legend: In Search of the Identity of the 'First Sericulturalist.'" *T'oung Pao* 70, no. 4—5 (1984): 213—45.

Lai Yanyuan 賴炎元. *Chunqiu fanlu jinzhu jinyi* 春秋繁露今註今譯.Taipei: Taiwan Shangwu, 1984.

Lang, Olga. *Chinese Family and Society*. New Haven: Yale University Press, 1946.

Lau, D. C. *Confucius: The Analects (Lun Yü)*. Harmondsworth, U.K.: Penguin, 1979.

———. *Lao-tsu: Tao Te Ching.* Harmondsworth, U.K.: Penguin, 1963.

———. *Mencius.* Harmondsworth, U.K.: Penguin, 1970.

Leach, E. R. "Ritual." In *A Dictionary of the Social Sciences,* edited by Julius Gould and William L. Kolb, 607—8. New York: Free Press, 1964.

Lee, Bernice J. "Female Infanticide in China." In *Women in China*, edited by Richard W. Guisso and Stanley Johannesen, 163—77. Youngstown, N.Y.: Philo, 1981.

Lee, Lily Xiao Hong. "Ban Zhao (c. 48 — c. 120): Her Role in the Formulation of Controls Imposed upon Women in Traditional China." In *The Virtue of Yin: Studies on Chinese Women*, 11—24. Broadway, N.S.W.: Wild Peony; Honolulu: University of Hawaii Press, 1994.

Legge, James, trans. *The Chinese Classics. Vol 5, pts. 1—2. The Ch'un Ts'ew, with the Tso Chuen.* Hong Kong: Legge, 1872.

———. *The Sacred Books of China: The Texts of Confucianism. Pts. 3—4, The Li Ki, in The Sacred Books of the East.* Edited by F. Max Muller. Vols. 27—28. Oxford: Oxford University Press, 1885.

[Li Changnian] Li Chang-nien 李長年. "Nüying shahai yu Zhongguo liangxing bujun wenti" 女嬰殺害與中國兩性不均問題. In *Zhongguo funüshi lunji* 中國婦女史論集, edited by [Bao Jialin] Pao Chia-lin 鮑家麟, 212—20. Taipei: Daoxiang, 1978.

Li Fang 李昉. *Taiping yulan* 太平御覽. 4 vols. Beijing: Zhonghua, 1960.

Li Genpan 李根蟠, Huang Chongyue 黃崇岳, and Lu Xun 盧勛. *Zhongguoshi shehui jingji yanjiu* 中國史社會經濟研究. Beijing: Zhongguo Shehui Kexue,1987.

Li Hengmei 李衡梅. "Woguo yuanshi shehui hunyin xingtai yaniu" 我國原始社會婚姻型態研究. *Lishi yanjiu* 歷史研究 180, no. 2 (1986): 95—109.

Li Jing 李勁. *Qinlü tonglun* 秦律通論. Jinan: Shandong Renmin, 1985.

Li Jingchi 李鏡池. *Zhouyi tanyuan* 周易探源. Beijing: Zhonghua, 1978.

Li Shan 李善. *Wenxuan Li Shan zhu* 文選李善注. Shanghai: Sibu Beiyao, n.d.

[Li Zefen] Li Tse-fen 李則芬. "Han dai funü de diwei" 漢代婦女的地位. In *Xian Qin ji liang Han lishi lunwenji* 先秦及兩漢歷史論文集, 153-173. Taipei: Taiwan Shangwu, 1981.

Liang Qichao 梁啓超. "Yinyang wuxing shuo zhi laili" 陰陽五行

說之來歷. *Dongfang zazhi* 東方雜誌 20, no. 10 (1923): 70—79.

Liang Yuntong 梁運通. *Huangdi neijing leixi* 皇帝內經類析. Huhehaote: Neimenggu Renmin, 1986.

Lim, Lucy. *Stories from China's Past: Han Dynasty Pictorial Tomb Reliefs and Archeological Objects from Sichuan Province, People's Republic of China.* San Francisco: Chinese Culture Foundation of San Francisco, 1987.

Lin Yin 林尹. *Zhouli jinzhu jinyi* 周禮今注今譯. Taipei: Taiwan Shangwu, 1972.

Liu Jingshan. "An Exploration of the Mode of Thinking in Ancient China." *Philosophy East and West* 35, no. 4 (1985): 387—396.

Liu Xiang 劉向. *Gulienüzhuan* 古列女傳. Shanghai: Shangwu, 1936.

[Liu Zenggui] Liu Tseng-kui 劉增貴. *Handai hunyin zhidu* 漢代婚姻制度. Taipei: Huashi, 1980.

———. "Shilun Handai hunyin guanxi zhong de lifa guannian" 試論漢代婚姻關係中的禮法觀念. In *Zhongguo funüshi lunji xuji* 中國婦女史論文集續集, edited by [Bao Jialin] Pao Chia-lin 寶家麟, 1-36. Taipei: Daoxiang, 1991.

Liu Zhiyuan 劉志遠 et al. *Sichuan Handai huaxiangzhuan yu Handai shehui* 四川漢代畫像傳與漢代社會. Beijing: Wenwu, 1983.

Loewe, Michael. "The Case of Witchcraft in 91 B.C.: Its Historical Setting and Effect on Han Dynasty History." *Asia Major*, n.s. 15 (1970): 159—96.

———. *Chinese Ideas of Life and Death: Faith, Myth, and Reason in the Han Period (202 B.C.— A.D. 220).* London: George Allen & Unwin, 1982.

———. "The Concept of Sovereignty." In *The Cambridge History of China, vol. 1, The Ch'in and Han Empires 221 B.C. — A.D. 220*, edited by Denis Twitchett and Michael Loewe, 726—46. Cambridge: Cambridge University Press, 1986.

———. *Crisis and Conflict in Han China, 104 B.C. to A.D. 9.* London: George Allen & Unwin, 1974.

————. "The Cult of the Dragon and the Invocation for Rain." In *Chinese Ideas about Nature and Society: Studies in Honour of Derk Bodde,* edited by Charles LeBlanc and Susan Blader, 195—213. Hong Kong: Hong Kong University Press, 1987.

————. "The Orders of Aristocratic Rank of Han China." *T'oung Pao* 48, no. 1—3 (1960): 97—174.

————. *Records of Han Administration.* 2 vols. Cambridge: Cambridge University Press, 1967.

Lowie, Robert H. *Primitive Society.* New York: Boni & Liverright, 1920.

Lü Kun 呂坤. *Lü Xinwu xiansheng guifan tushuo sijuan* 呂新吾先生閨範圖說四卷. In *Siku quanshu cunmu congshu* 四庫全書存目叢書, 3:129: 479—653. Tainan: Zhuangyan Wenhua, 1995.

Ma Daying 馬大英. *Handai caizhengshi* 漢代財政史. Beijing: Caizheng Jingji, 1983.

Ma Yong 馬擁. "Lun Changsha Mawangdui yihao Han mu chutu bohua de mingcheng he zuoyong" 論長沙馬王堆一號漢墓出土帛書的名稱和作用. *Kaogu* 考古 125, no. 2 (1973): 118—25.

Ma Zong 馬總. *Yilin* 意林. Shanghai: Sibu Beiyao, n.d.

Makino Tatsumi 牧野. "Kandai ni okeru kazuku no ōkisa" 漢代における家族の大きさ. In *Shina kazoku kenkyū* 支那家族研究. Tokyo: Seikatsu, 1944.

Manheim, Ralph, trans. *Myth, Religion, and Mother Right: Selected Writings of J. J. Bachofen.* Princeton: Princeton University Press, 1967.

Mann, Susan. "Learned Women in the Eighteenth Century." In *Engendering China: Women, Culture, and the State,* edited by Christina K. Gilmartin et al., 27—46. Cambridge: Harvard University Press, 1994.

Mawangdui Hanmu Boshu Zhengli Xiaozu 馬王堆漢墓帛書整理小組. "Mawangdui boshu 'Liushisi gua' shiwen" 馬王堆帛書六十四卦釋文. *Wenwu* 文物 334, no. 3 (1984): 1—8.

McLeod, Katrina C. D. and Robin D. S. Yates. "Forms of Ch'in Law: An Annotated Translation of the *Feng-chen shih.*" *Harvard Journal of Asiatic Studies* 41, no. 1 (1981): 111—63.

Morgan, Lewis Henry. *Ancient Society; or, Researches in the Lines of Human Progress from Savagery, through Barbarism to Civilization.* New York: H. Holt, 1877.

Muramatsu Ei 村松暎. *Chūgoku Retsujoden: Senzennen no rekishi no naka de* 中國列女傳: 三千年の歴史のなかで. Tokyo: Chūō, 1968.

Museum of Fine Arts, Boston. *Asiatic Art in the Museum of Fine Arts, Boston.* Boston: Museum of Fine Arts, Boston, 1982.

Nie Chongyi 聶崇義. *Sanlitu* 三禮圖. Edo: Sūmon Dō, 1761.

Nishijima Sadao 西島定生. *Chūgoku keizaishi kenkyū* 中國經濟史研究. Tokyo: Tokyo Daigaku Bungakubu, 1966.

Niu Zhiping 牛志平. "Gudai funü zhenjieguan" 古代婦女貞節觀. *Lishi yuekan* 歷史月刊 26, no. 3 (1990): 19—24.

Nylan, Michael, and Nathan Sivin. "The First Neo-Confucianism: An Introduction to Yang Hsiung's 'Canon of Supreme Mystery' (*T'ai hsuan ching*, c. 4 B.C.)." In *Chinese Ideas about Nature and Society: Studies in Honour of Derk Bodde*, edited by Charles LeBlanc and Susan Blader, 41—100. Hong Kong: Hong Kong University Press,1987.

Ochi Shigeaki. "Thoughts on the Understanding of the Han and the Six Dynasties." *Memoirs of the Research Department of the Tōyō Bunko* 35 (1977): 1—73.

O'Hara, Albert Richard. *The Position of Woman in Early China: According to the Lieh Nü Chuan, "The Biographies of Chinese Women."* Taipei: Mei Ya, 1971.

Okusaki Yūji 奥崎裕司. "Aka mayu no seikai" 赤眉の世界. *Chūgoku kodaishi kenkyū* 中國古代史研究 (1982): 141—167.

Ortner, Sherry. "Is Female to Male as Nature Is to Culture?" In *Women, Culture, and Society,* edited by Michelle Zimbalist Rosaldo and Louise Lamphere, 67—87. Stanford: Stanford University Press, 1974.

Ouyang Xun 歐陽詢. *Yiwen leiju* 藝文類聚. 2 vols. Taipei: Zhongwen, 1980.

Ozawa Bunshirō 小沢文四郎. *Kandai ekigaku no kenkyū* 漢代易學の研究. Tokyo: Meitoku, 1970.

Ōzora Fujino 大空不二男. *Chūgoku no kokyu* 中國の後宮. Tokyo: Tatsukei, 1977.

Pahl, Jan. *Money and Marriage*. New York: Macmillan, 1989.

Pickering, W. S. F. *Durkheim on Religion: A Selection of Readings and Bibliographies*. London: Routledge & K. Paul, 1975.

Pokora, Timoteus. *Hsin-Lun (New Treatise) and Other Writings by Huan T'an (43 B.C. — 28 A.D.)*. Ann Arbor: University of Michigan Press, 1975.

Powers, Martin. "Hybrid Omens and Public Issues in Early Imperial China." *Bulletin of the Museum of Far Eastern Antiquities* 55 (1983): 1—55.

Qian Tang 錢唐. *Lienüzhuan jiaozhu* 列女傳校注. Shanghai: Zhonghua, n.d.

Qin Bo 秦波. "Xi Han huanghou yuxi he ganlu ernian tongfanglu de faxian" 西漢皇后玉爾和甘露二年銅方爐的發現. *Wenwu* 文物 204, no. 5 (1975): 26—29.

Qin Huitian 秦蕙田. *Wuli tongkao* 五禮通考. 20 vols. Jiangsu: Jiangsu Shuju, 1880; reprint, Taipei: Xixing, 1970.

Qiu Jun 丘濬. Daxue yanyi bu 大學衍義補. Taipei: Taiwan Shangwu, 1971.

Queen, Stuart A., and John B. Adams. *The Family in Various Cultures*. Philadelphia: Lippincott, 1952.

Rankin, Mary Backus. "The Emergence of Women at the End of the Ch'ing." In *Women in Chinese Society*, edited by Margery Wolf and Roxane Witke, 39—66. Stanford: Stanford University Press, 1979.

Raphals, Lisa Ann. *Sharing the Light: Representations of Women and Virtue in Early China*. Albany: State University of New York, 1998.

Redclift, Nanneke. "Rights in Women: Kinship, Culture, and Materialism." In *Engels Revisited: New Feminist Essays*, edited by Janet Sayers, Mary Evans, and Nanneke Redclift, 133—44. London: Tavistock, 1987.

Rickett, W. Allyn. *Guanzi: Political, Economic, and Philosophical Essays from Early China.* Vol. 1. Princeton: Princeton University Press, 1985.

Rosaldo, Michelle. "The Use and Abuse of Anthropology: Reflections on Feminism and Cross-Cultural Understanding." *Signs* 5, no.3 (1980): 389—417.

Rowbotham, Sheila. *Hidden from History: 300 Years of Women's Oppression and the Fight Against It.* London: Pluto, 1973.

Russell, J. C. "Population in Europe 500—1500." In *Fontana Economic History of Europe*, edited by Carlo M. Cipolla, 1:1—70. Glasgow: Collins, Fontana, 1972.

Sangren, Paul Steven. *History and Magical Power in a Chinese Community.* Stanford: Stanford University Press, 1987.

Schafer, Edward. "The Development of Bathing Customs in Ancient and Medieval China and the History of the Foliate Clear Palace." *Journal of the American Oriental Society* 76, no. 2 (1956): 56—81.

―――. *The Divine Woman: Dragon Ladies and Rain Maidens in T'ang Literature.* San Francisco: North Point, 1980.

Seng You 僧祐. *Hongmingji* 弘明集. Shanghai: Sibu Congkan, n.d.

Shaughnessy, Edward L. "Composition of the 'Qian' and 'Kun' Hexagrams of the *Zhouyi*", in *Before Confucius: Studies in the Creation of the Chinese Classics,* 197-219. Albany: State University of New York Press, 1997.

―――. "The Composition of the *Zhouyi*." Ph.D. diss., Stanford University, 1983.

Shen Zhongchang 沈仲常. *Sichuan Handai taoyong* 四川漢代陶俑. Beijing: Chaohua Meishu, 1963.

Shi Shenghan 石聲漢. *Simin yueling jiaozhu* 四民月令校注. Beijing:Zhonghua, 1965.

Shirakawa Shizuka 白川靜. *Setsumon shingi* 說文新義. 16 vols. Kobe: Hakukaku Bijutsukan, 1969—1974.

Shuihudi Qinmu Zhujian Zhengli Xiaozu 睡虎地秦墓竹簡整理小

組. *Shuihudi Qinmu zhujian* 睡虎地秦墓竹簡. Beijing: Wenwu, 1978.

Song Boyin 宋伯胤 and Li Zhongyi 李忠義. "Cong Han huaxiangshi tansuo Handai zhiji gouzao" 從漢畫像石探索漢代織機構造. *Wenwu* 文物 137, no. 3 (1962): 23—24.

[Song Dexi] Sung Te-hsi 宋德熹. "Tangdai de jinü" 唐代的妓女. In *Zhongguo funü shi lunji xuji* 中國婦女史論集續集, edited by [Bao Jialin] Pao Chia-lin 鮑家麟, 67—122. Taipei: Daoxiang, 1991.

Soper, A. "King Wu Ting's Victory over the 'Realm of Demons.'" *Artibus Asiae* 17, no. 1 (1954): 55—60.

———. "The Purpose and Date of the Hsiao-t'ang-shan Offering Shrine: A Modest Proposal." *Artibus Asiae* 36, no. 4 (1974): 249—66.

Steele, John. *The I-li or Book of Etiquette and Ceremonial.* 2 vols. London: Probsthain, 1917.

[Sun Guangde] Sun Kuang-te 孫廣德. *Xian Qin liang Han yinyang wuxing shuo de zhengzhi sixiang* 先秦兩漢陰陽五行說的政治思想. Taipei: Jiaxin Shuini Gongsi Wenhua Jijinhui, 1969.

Sun Ji 孫機. *Handai wuzhi wenhua ziliao tushuo* 漢代物質文化資料圖說. Beijing:Wenwu, 1991.

Sung, Marina H. "The Chinese Lieh-nü Tradition." In *Women in China: Current Directions in Historical Scholarship*, edited by Richard W. Guisso and Stanley Johannesen, 63-74. Youngstown, N.Y.: Philo, 1981.

Swann, Nancy Lee. *Food and Money in Ancient China: The Earliest Economic History of China to A.D. 25, Han Shu 24, with related texts, Han Shu 91 and Shih-chi 129.* Princeton: Princeton University Press, 1950.

———. *Pan Chao: Foremost Woman Scholar of China.* New York: Century, 1932.

Takigawa Kametarō 瀧川龜太郎. *Shiki kaichū kōshō* 史記會注考證.Tokyo: Tōhō Bunka Gakuin Tōkyō Kenkyūju, 1932

—1934; reprint, Taipei: Zhongxin, 1977.

Tambiah, Stanley Jeyaraja. *Culture, Thought, and Social Action: An Anthropological Perspective*. Cambridge: Harvard University Press, 1985.

Tjan, Tjoe Som. *Po Hu T'ung: The Comprehensive Discussions in the White Tiger Hall:, A Contribution to the History of Classical Studies in the Han Period.* 2 vols. Leiden: Brill, 1949—1952.

Tomiya Itaru 富谷至 and Yoshikawa Tadao 吉川忠夫, eds. *Kansho gogyōshi* 漢書五行志. Tokyo: Heibon, 1986.

Turner, Victor. *The Forest of Symbols.* Cornell: Cornell University Press, 1967.

Twitchett, Denis, and Michael Loewe, eds. *The Cambridge History of China. Vol. 1. The Ch'in and Han Empires, 221 B.C. —A.D. 220.* Cambridge: Cambridge University Press, 1986.

Unschuld, Paul U. *Medicine in China: A History of Ideas.* Berkeley: University of California Press, 1985.

Van Gulik, R. H. *Sexual Life in Ancient China: A Preliminary Survey of Chinese Sex and Society from ca. 1500 B.C. till 1644 A.D.* Leiden: Brill, 1961.

Wang Fu 王符. *Qianfulun* 潛夫論. N.p.: Congshu Jiqing, 1937.

[Wang Jianwen] Wang Chien-wen 王健文. "Xi Han lüling yu guojia zhengdangxing: Yi lülingzhong de 'budao' wei zhongxin" 西漢律令與國家正當性: 以律令中的 '不道' 爲中心. *Xinshixue* 新史學 3, no. 3 (1992): 1—36.

Wang Ming 王明. *Taipingjing hejiao* 太平經合校. Beijing: Zhonghua, 1960.

Wang Ningsheng. "Yangshao Burial Customs and Social Organization: A Comment on the Theory of Yangshao Matrilineal Society and Its Methodology." *Early China* 11 —12 (1985—1987): 6—32.

Wang Shaoxi 王紹璽. *Xiaoqieshi* 小妾史. Shanghai: Shanghai Wenyi, 1995.

Wang Shunu 王書奴. *Zhongguo changjishi* 中國娼妓史. Shanghai: Shenghuo,1934.

Wang Tingqia 王廷洽. "Runiang, baomu ji qita" 乳娘, 保母, 及 其他. *Lishi yuekan* 歷史月刊 26, no. 3 (1990): 25—26.

Watson, James L. "Anthropological Overview: The Development of Chinese Descent Groups." In *Kinship Organization in Late Imperial China 1000-1940,* edited by Patricia Buckley Ebrey and James L. Watson, 274—92. Berkeley: University of California Press, 1986.

Wechsler, Howard J. *Offerings of Jade and Silk: Ritual and Symbol in the Legitimation of the T'ang Dynasty.* New Haven: Yale University Press, 1985.

Wei Hong 衛宏. *Hanjiuyi* 漢舊儀. In *Pingjinguan congshu* 平津館 叢書, edited by Sun Xingyan 孫星衍. N.p.: Huailu, 1885, *ce* 4, B:4b.

Wei Zhao 韋昭, ed. *Guoyu* 國語. Shanghai: Guoxue Jiben Congshu, 1935.

Whyte, Martin King. *The Status of Women in Preindustrial Societies.* Princeton: Princeton University Press, 1978.

Wilbur, C. Martin. *Slavery in China during the Former Han Dynasty, 206 B.C.— A.D. 25.* Chicago: Field Museum, 1943.

Wilhelm, Helmut. *Heaven, Earth, and Man in the Book of Changes: Seven Eranos Lectures.* Seattle: University of Washington Press, 1977.

Wilhelm, Richard, and Cary F. Baynes. *The I Ching or Book of Changes.* Princeton: Princeton University Press, 1977.

Wittfogel, Karl. "The Society of Prehistoric China." *Zeitschrift für Sozialwissenschaften* 8 (1939): 138—86.

Wolf, Margery. "Women and Suicide in China." In *Women in Chinese Society,* edited by Margery Wolf and Roxane Witke, 111—41. Stanford: Stanford University Press, 1979.

Wong Sun-ming. "Confucian Ideal and Reality: Transformation of the Institution of Marriage in T'ang China (A.D. 618—907)." Ph.D. diss., University of Washington, 1979.

Wu Hong [Wu Hung]. *The Wu Liang Shrine: The Ideology of Early Chinese Pictorial Art.* Stanford: Stanford University Press, 1989.

Wu Ronghui.吳榮會. "Qin de guanfu shougongye" 秦的官府手工業.In *Yunmeng Qinjian yanjiu* 雲夢秦簡研究, edited by Zhonghua Shuju Bianjibu 中華書局編輯部, 38—52. Beijing: Zhonghua, 1981.

Wu Zengde 吳曾德. *Handai huaxiangshi* 漢代畫象石. Beijing: Wenwu, 1984.

Wu Zhaoyi 吳兆宜. *Yutai xinyong jianzhu* 玉臺新詠箋注. In *Wenxue congshu* 文學叢書. Edited by Yang Jialuo 楊家駱. Pt. 1. vol. 2. Taipei: Shijie, 1956.

Xia Zhiqian. "Was There Ever a Matriarchy?" *Chinese Sociology and Anthropology* 25, no. 4 (1993): 8—13.

[Xing Yitian] Hsing I-tien 刑義田. "Muquan, waiqi, rusheng: Wang Mang cuan Han de jidian jieshi" 母權, 外戚, 儒生: 王莽篡先漢的幾點解釋. *Lishi yuekan* 歷史月刊 14, no. 3 (1989): 36—44.

[Xu Zhuoyun] Hsü Cho-yun 許倬雲. "Cong Zhouli zhong tuice yuangu de funü_gongzuo" 從周禮中推測遠古的婦女工作. In *Zhongguo funüshi lunji* 中國婦女史論集, edited by [Bao Jialin] Pao Chia-lin 鮑家麟, 51—62. Taipei: Daoxiang, 1978.

Xun Bing 迅冰. *Sichuan Handai diaosu yishu* 四川漢代雕塑藝術. Beijing: Zhongguo Gudian Meishu, 1959.

Yamazaki Makoto 山口真 and Yamato Shigeru 山手茂. *Chūgoku joseigaku gairon* 中國女性學概論. Tokyo: Aki, 1987.

Yan Wanli 嚴萬里. *Shangjunshu xin jianzheng* 商君書新箋正. Shanghai: Sibu Beiyao, n.d.

Yang, C. K. *Religion in Chinese Society: A Study of Contemporary Social Functions of Religion and Some of Their Historical Factors.* Berkeley: University of California Press, 1961.

Yang Kuan 楊寬. "Qinshihuang lingyuan buju jiegou de tantao" 秦始皇陵園佈局結構的探討. *Qinyongguan kaiguan sannian wenji* 秦俑館開館三年文集 10 (1982): 7—14.

Yang, Lien-sheng. "The Concept of *Pao* as a Basis for Social Relations in China." In *Chinese Thought and Institutions*, edited by John Fairbank, 291—309, 395—97. Chicago:

University of Chicago Press, 1957.

⸺. "Female Rulers in Imperial China". *Harvard Journal of Asiatic Studies* 23 (1960—1961): 47—61.

Yang Shuda 楊書達. *Handai hunsang lisu kao* 漢代婚喪禮俗考. Shanghai: Shangwu, 1933.

[Yang Yunru] Yang Yun-ju 楊筠如. "Chunqiu shidai zhi nannü fengji" 春秋時代之男女風紀. In *Zhongguo funüshi lunwenji* 中國婦女史論文集, edited by [Li You-ning] Li Yu-ning 李又寧 and [Zhang Yufa] Chang Yu-fa 張玉法, 20—38. 2d ed. Taipei: Taiwan Shangwu, 1988.

Yang Zongrong 楊宗榮. *Zhanguo huihua ziliao* 戰國繪畫資料. Beijing: Zhongguo Gudian Yishu, 1957.

Yokota Kenzan 橫田惟孝. *Sengoku saku seikai* 戰國策正解. Tokyo: Fujisan, 1915.

Yu Haoliang 于豪亮. "Boshu 'Zhouyi'" 帛書周易. *Wenwu* 文物 334, no. 3 (1984):15—24.

Yu Shinan 虞世南. *Beitang shuchao* 北堂書鈔. Taipei: Hongye, 1974.

Yü Ying-shih. *Trade and Expansion in Han China: A Study in the Structure of Sino-Barbarian Economic Relations.* Berkeley: University of California Press, 1967.

Yuen-Tsang, Angelina W.K. *Towards a Chinese Conception of Social Support: A Study on the Social Support Networks of Chinese Working Mothers.* London: Ashgate, 1997.

Yunmeng Qinmu Zhujian Zhengli Xiaozu 雲夢秦墓竹簡整理小組. "Yunmeng Qinjian shiwen (2)" 雲夢秦簡釋文 (二). *Wenwu* 文物 242, no. 7 (1976): 1—10.

⸺. "Yunmeng Qinjian shiwen (3)" 雲夢秦簡釋文 (三). *Wenwu* 文物 342, no. 8 (1976): 27—37.

Zhang Xincheng 張心澂. *Weishu tongkao* 僞書通考. Shanghai: Shangwu, 1954.

[Zhang Xiurong] Chang Hsiu-jung 張修榮. *Han Tang guizu yu cainü shige yanjiu* 漢唐貴族與才女詩歌研究. Taipei: Wenshizhe, 1985.

Zhang Zhenglang 張政烺. "Boshu 'Liushisi gua' ba" 帛書六十四
卦跋. *Wenwu* 文物 334, no. 3 (1984): 9—14.

———. "Zuotan Changsha Mawangdui Hanmu boshu" 坐談長沙
馬王堆漢墓帛書. *Wenwu* 文物 220, no. 9 (1974): 48—49.

Zhao Fengjie 趙鳳喈. *Zhongguo funü zai falüshang zhi diwei* 中國
婦女在法律上之地位. Shanghai: Shangwu, 1929; reprint,
Taipei: Shihuo, 1973.

Zhao Yi 趙翼. *Ershier shi zhaji* 二十二劄記. Shanghai: Shangwu,
1957.

———. *Gaiyu congkao* 陔餘叢考. Shanghai: Shangwu, 1957.

Zheng Xuan 鄭玄. *Liji Zheng zhu* 禮記鄭注. N.p.: Laiqingge,
1937.

[Zhou Cecong] Chow Tse-tsung 周策縱. *Guwuyi yu 'liushi' kao:
Zhongguo langman wenxue tanyuan* 古巫醫與 '六詩' 考 – 中
國浪漫文學探源. Taipei: Lianjing, 1986.

[Zhou Lin'gen] Chou Lin-ken 周林根. *Zhongguo zhonggu lijiaoshi*
中國中古禮教史. Taipei: Haiyang Xueyuan, 1969.

Zhou Shirong 周世榮. "Zuotan Changsha Mawangdui Hanmu
boshu" 坐談長沙馬王堆漢墓帛書. *Wenwu* 文物 220, no. 9
(1974): 49.

Zhou Xibao 周錫保. *Zhongguo gudai fushishi* 中國古代服飾史.
Beijing: Zhongguo Xiju, 1984.

[Zhu Tan] Chu T'an 朱倓. *Ban Zhao* 班昭. Taipei: Taiwan
Shangwu, 1977.

Index

231

About the Author

Bret Hinsch studied Chinese language and history at Yale and Nanjing Universities. He received a Ph.D. in history and East Asian languages from Harvard University and is currently associate professor of history at National Chung Cheng University in Taiwan, where he teaches early Chinese history.